THE FLOWERS
OF THE FOREST

DAVID GARNETT, 1923

DAVID GARNETT

THE FLOWERS
OF THE FOREST

Being Volume Two of
THE GOLDEN ECHO

HARCOURT, BRACE AND COMPANY
NEW YORK

© 1955 BY DAVID GARNETT

First American edition 1956

LIBRARY OF CONGRESS CATALOG CARD NUMBER: 54-6388

PRINTED IN THE UNITED STATES OF AMERICA

TO
Amaryllis Virginia Garnett

Le temps jamais ne change
Ses linges dégoûtants.
Quel horrible mélange
Font l'espace et le temps.

Ce qui nous quitte reste
Contre toute raison
Et notre moindre geste
Encombre la maison.

Haut et bas gauche et droite
Avenirs et passés
Sont dans la meme boîte
L'un sur l'autre entassés.

COCTEAU

Illustrations

Preface

At e'en in the gloaming, nae swankies are roaming
'Bout stacks wi' the lasses at bogle to play:
But ilk ane sits drearie, lamenting her dearie—
The Flowers of the Forest are a' wede away.

We'll hear nae mair lilting at our ewe-milking
Women and bairns are heartless and wae;
Sighing and moaning on ilka green loaning
The Flowers of the Forest are a' wede away.

MY second volume owes its title to its covering the years of the First World War and those while we were still living in its shadow. Any picture of that period must be dominated by a sense of bitterness and bereavement.

My next volume, which will be called *The Familiar Faces*, will deal with the years of freedom when we believed that war would not come again. It was a period of flowering, of emancipation. That the gains made in those years were not held was partly, I think, because the best and bravest of my generation had been killed and that the survivors had lost the confidence and courage of youth.

These are men whose minds the Dead have ravished.
Memory fingers in their hair of murders,
Multitudinous murders they once witnessed.
Wading sloughs of flesh these helpless wander,
Treading blood from lungs that loved laughter.
Always they must see these things and hear them,
Batter of guns and shatter of flying muscles,
Carnage incomparable and human squander
Rucked too thick for these men's extrication.

I have not dwelt much on the bitterness and hatred that the First World War inspired in me, for such feelings are difficult to remember and reproduce. Their finest expression is to be found in the poems of Wilfrid Owen, Robert Graves and Siegfried Sassoon who fought in it.

While they were risking their lives and living in hell, I, by extraordinary good fortune, was living in close intimacy with a group of brilliant artists and writers some of whom became my closest friends and all of whom moulded my ideas and took a kindly interest in my development. I did not suffer; I was not in danger and for me the years of bitterness and horror were years of spiritual and aesthetic growth. Thus my story is in the highest degree exceptional.

In conclusion I would like to acknowledge my debt of gratitude to Mina Curtiss and to Frances Partridge for reading and advising me on my manuscript, to Duncan Grant and Vanessa Bell for permission to reproduce their paintings as illustrations, to Reginald Hecks for permission to reproduce the painting of New House Farm by Duncan Grant, to Ralph Partridge for permission to reproduce a painting by D. Carrington, to Sir Arthur Bliss for permission to reproduce the bronze head of Betty May by Sir Jacob Epstein, to Mrs Armitage and Mrs Bagenal for permission to reproduce photographs and to James Strachey for permission to publish a letter from Lytton Strachey.

March 1955   D. G.

THE FLOWERS
OF THE FOREST

I

WAR is the worst of the epidemic diseases which afflict
mankind and the great genetrix of many of the others.
While it lasts it impairs the power of rational judgment;
millions are crippled and die and the accumulated riches of
empires are destroyed by fanaticism and fear; cruelty and
callousness are infectious and these toxins of the spirit make the
unconscionable claim that all personal life, happiness, art and
human expression must be subordinated to war, or serve it.
That exorbitant demand is constantly proclaimed and has to
be violently contradicted. Life, love and happiness go on
under almost any conditions. Indeed they are quickened by
war as the beauty of a face may be increased by fever. Certainly
they seemed to be in the years I am about to describe. In 1914
I was twenty-two and the four years of war which followed
were the flowering of my youth—years in which I overcame
the shyness and diffidence of adolescence and gained the courage and self-confidence of a man. During the last two of those
years I was regarded with contempt and aversion by many
people, including a few of my oldest friends. But I was also
loved and the loves and friendships of those years developed
my intelligence and sowed the seed which enabled me, later
on, to become a creative artist.

The record of love and friendship which follows is drawn
against the background of the bloodiest and most terrible war
that England has ever fought. I did not fight in it. Yet the views
and claims of the majority could not be ignored. So long as
rows of wounded, maimed and convalescent soldiers in light
blue jackets and trousers and scarlet ties sat along the streets
of every town, so long as the South-east wind brought the
sound of the guns in Flanders over the hill, so long as the
newspapers contained the names of friends concealed in the

I

endless Roll of Honour, so long heart and head were divided and the spirit ached.

At the beginning my opinions about the war were many and contradictory. The Germans nauseated me. I knew their complacent selfishness and vulgarity in peace and could well understand their brutality in war. Yet I saw that many of the stories of German atrocities were lies. It was an atrocity that they should have invaded Belgium at all. Yet, given the necessity, might not England have shown an equal political ruthlessness? Surely, war is founded upon the assumption that the end justifies the means? The invasion of Belgium was one instance of that and so were the stories of German Uhlans chopping off the right hands of Belgian babies. For the lie was thought justified because it made Belgian soldiers fight harder. I loved France, yet was not the war to save France also being fought to bolster up the Tsarist regime and postpone the Russian revolution? The war that Boris Sokolov* had longed for had come to pass a year later than he predicted. If I were to enlist I should be fighting (among other things) for a resurgent Russian Despotism holding Constantinople; Sokolov would be working like a beaver to corrupt the Russian Army and bring about its defeat.

Not all Russian Revolutionaries were as clear-headed as he was. Dear old Kropotkin, who had been preaching anarchism for half a century, was carried away by a burst of patriotic enthusiasm and predicted victory for the gallant Russian Army over the hated Prussian foe. But Kropotkin did at least see the war as one and indivisible. My parents and many of their friends were pro-Ally in the West, but by no means broken-hearted if they read of a Russian defeat in the Carpathians. Yet it was obvious that if the Germans defeated the Russians, they could greatly reinforce the Western front.

Rupert Brooke, I soon heard, had abandoned his original intention of going to help the French women gather in the harvest and the vintage, and had enlisted in the newly established Naval Division in which, thanks to his friendship with

* See *The Golden Echo*, p. 250.

2

Eddie Marsh, Winston Churchill's private secretary, he had been given a commission. Readers of *The Golden Echo* will remember that I had been camping out at Helston in Cornwall with the Oliviers, Frankie Birrell and Bertie Farjeon and his wife during the first week after war was declared.

Bertie wrote to me soon after the Helston camp to say that he had decided to enlist and would like to have me as a companion in arms. I was very fond of Bertie. His wit and astonishing gifts of parody later made him a brilliant writer of "intimate revues"—but his work in the theatre was only an extension of what he was constantly improvising for his friends. His wit would have made him an ideal companion in the army. I met Bertie and discovered that he proposed that we should enter the first recruiting office we came to and enlist at once. We walked, deep in argument, along Kensington High Street and came to where the 13th Battalion of the Middlesex Regiment had a recruiting office. I refused to go in and, taking Bertie by the arm, dragged him away. Maynard Keynes had told me that the war would be over in eighteen months at most, and I had no desire to spend them being drilled on a barrack square. If I enlisted I wanted to distinguish myself. I wanted a commission. Bertie promised to wait, but two days later he enlisted alone. A few weeks afterwards he was discharged, as not up to the required medical standard. The 13th Battalion of the Middlesex was wiped out two years later.

I was eager to start work at College and went back before the beginning of term. My father Edward was away. I was alone at 19 Pond Place and was delighted to discover that D. H. Lawrence and Frieda were in town, staying at a little house off the Fulham Road. I asked them to come to supper to meet H. G. Newth, a demonstrator in Zoology and my closest College friend. I cooked the meal myself and felt justified in opening a bottle of Edward's wine. Our flat, or more properly maisonette, at 19 Pond Place was in the top half of the building and was reached by a dark staircase shared with the lower tenant, on which a strong smell of a mixture of hot vinegar, herrings and lapdog was always noticeable.

3

My cooking was appreciated; Lawrence liked Newth: Frieda was warm and expansive, and, as we finished our bottle of Civil Service Stores Beaune, she began to talk about the war and her divided sympathies. As a young girl she had lived at the Prussian Court and had always taken pains to keep out of the way of the Kaiser, whom she much disliked. His vanity and stupidity, she believed, had played a large part in producing the atmosphere which had made war probable. Yet she had loved and admired her young cousins the two von Richthofens, who had just joined the German Air Force, and who became its greatest tactical leaders. Frieda also adored her younger sister, who was married to the Crown Prince's aide-de-camp. And now, with English children and committed by all ties of love to England, she found herself already being cold-shouldered and disliked because of her German origin. We all listened in sympathy, for Lawrence was in his sweetest and gentlest mood and, before they left, Frieda turned the conversation to more cheerful subjects. Finally, about midnight, when they said goodbye, Newth, who stayed to discuss them and help me wash up, called down the odoriferous staircase in his most gutteral accents:

"Auf Wiedersehen, Gnädige Baronin!" and Frieda called back gaily to us in German.

Some days later there was a knock at the door and, when I opened it, two men pushed their way in and told me they had come from the police to make enquiries. They looked more like bookmaker's touts than policemen, so I asked them for their cards. This precaution seemed to annoy them and I noticed that the cards had only been issued a few days before. They wanted to know how many Germans were living in our flat and who and what were its inhabitants. Although their manners were truculent, I remained polite, gave them truthful answers and finally got rid of them. Two days later another pair arrived on the same errand. A week later there was a third visit. This time it was an older man. I shall never forget his face: he had yellow green tigerish eyes and very even perfect teeth and I guessed that had I been a criminal he would have known it at once.

"Do you know that you are the fifth detective to come here to enquire about the same dinner party?" I asked him. He said it was news to him. I then told him about the evening with the Lawrences and explained how I thought the suspicions of our neighbours downstairs had been aroused. Lawrence had married a woman of German origin who had, however, been a British subject for twelve years or more before that, and he could easily discover that neither Newth nor I had any German affiliations. Then I asked him to strike my name and address off the list of suspected German spies. He laughed, showing his even strong teeth, and told me that Scotland Yard was getting hundreds of letters every day from people denouncing their neighbours and that they all had to be investigated.

"I'll do my best to stop your being worried again." I think before he left the building my visitor told our downstairs neighbours that they were to stop their denunciations, for there were no more police visits. These inquiries in London were, however, only the beginning of the persecution to which Lawrence and Frieda were subjected. They were, indeed, expelled from Cornwall lest Frieda should be signalling from the cliffs to German submarines.

Early in October, 1914, we held the first of the weekly play-readings which Frankie Birrell had planned at our Cornish camp. We called ourselves the Caroline Club as, at first, we met in a little house in Caroline Place to which Hugh Popham and Brynhild Olivier had moved a year after their marriage. The Club was regarded as a rival of the play-readings organised by Clive Bell and Virginia Woolf which were attended by Vanessa Bell, Duncan Grant, Lytton Strachey, Leonard Woolf and Desmond and Molly MacCarthy. Play-reading was only one of that group's activities—for they had also a Novel Club originally invented to bring Desmond MacCarthy to the point of writing a novel, but which failed in its object. Later this became the Memoir Club which, many years afterwards, I was invited to join, and which has played a part in bringing this book into existence.

But when I first went to read Dryden at the Caroline Club I was unaware of such activities among the older denizens of Bloomsbury. We greatly enjoyed our readings. The company consisted of Hugh Popham, who however soon joined the Royal Naval Air Service, Arthur Waley, Justin Brooke, James Strachey, Frankie and myself. The women were my oldest friends and childhood playmates, Hugh's wife Brynhild and her three sisters, Margery, Daphne and Noel Olivier. Much of the success of the readings was due to Frankie, who had a gift for allotting the parts.

Frankie's casting of Vanbrugh's *The Relapse* produced three magnificent impersonations: James Strachey was Sir Novelty Fashion, newly created Lord Foppington. Frankie, who always excelled in the bawdiest parts, was Coupler, whose indecencies made Daphne wrinkle her nose in disgust. Noel outshone the whole company as Miss Hoyden. " Sure, never nobody was used as I am. I know well enough what other girls do, for all they think to make a Fool of me: it's well I have a husband a-coming, or, icod, I'd marry the Baker, I would so. Nobody can knock at the Gate, but presently I must be lock't up; and here's the young Greyhound Bitch can run loose about the House all the day long."

In contrast to Adrian Stephen's poker parties in adjacent Brunswick Square, our meetings were abstemious. Often, after our readings, we refreshed ourselves with cocoa, though if friends such as Clive and Vanessa Bell or Adrian dropped in, cider or shandygaff might be produced.

At one of our very early meetings, Noel was late in appearing and, when she came, brought Rupert Brooke with her. He had just come out of hospital and was on leave, recovering from "pink-eye" contracted during the Antwerp expedition from which most of his battalion of the Naval Division had been lucky to get away. Would that he had been interned until the end of the war with those who accidentally crossed the frontier into Holland. Rupert was in uniform and his hair was

6

short. He was changed in other ways from the Rupert of Grant-chester and our camps. I was at once aware of the strained relationship between Rupert and James and Frankie. To dispel this, Brynhild got Rupert to tell us about his experiences at Antwerp. It was a story of untrained men hastily rushed to a place which they were not equipped to defend and from which they had to be withdrawn when they were seriously attacked. I listened with eager interest, feeling Rupert's hostility, and I was surprised when he crossed the room to where I was sitting and asked me whether I would join the Royal Naval Division as he would so much like to have me with him in his battalion. He added that he felt sure that he could get me a commission through Eddie Marsh, but that I should have to decide at once as the Division might shortly be sent abroad again. I thanked him and said I would think it over and let him know. If the suggestion had come six weeks earlier I should probably have accepted it and the subject of this volume would have been very different, if I had survived to write it. But the moment had passed and Rupert's marked hostility to James and Frankie antagonised me. Later the patriotism of his famous sonnets seemed to me to ring false and to be mixed up with an almost insane repudiation of many of his oldest friends. Nor was his attitude unmixed with a longing for social success and public esteem which came so easily to him that it was strange that he should value it so much.

I am glad that on the last occasion of our meeting, Rupert looked on me as a friend whom he wished to have beside him in the tedious months of training and afterwards in action.

I had got to know Gilbert Cannan when I was a schoolboy, just after his first novel *Peter Homunculus* was published. My father had brought him to our flat in Hampstead and I admired his work. I had met him again in 1914 and in October he invited me down for a weekend to his house near Chesham as Lawrence and Frieda were staying in a cottage near by. Cannan had first eloped with and later married J. M. Barrie's wife, Mary. It was her taste, rather than Gilbert's, which was reflected in the decoration of the millhouse in which they lived. The wooden windmill stood just behind it. I arrived in time for lunch on Saturday and was shown into the dining-room which was decorated with a dado of brightly coloured frescoes by Polunin, a Russian artist—very different in style from Duncan Grant's mural paintings at Adrian Stephen's house in Brunswick Square. When we sat down I noticed many artificial fruit piled up in a big majolica dish: semi-transparent glass grapes, alabaster peaches, and a pottery pineapple lent their stony support to the three little apples, two bananas and a gritty pear which were all that one could actually eat. Before I left on Monday it had occurred to me that the heaped profusion of inedible fruits was perhaps symbolic of Gilbert's marriage.

After luncheon Gilbert rewarded me, as an early admirer of his work, by taking me off into the windmill—still fitted with sails—in which he ground out the long series of windy novels which had followed his first, and which have served to make him a forgotten writer today.

I was a bit of a connoisseur of literary workshops but the windmill was of a type new to me. The special high desk, the lofty perch in monkish seclusion, with its view over the surrounding woods and fields—all struck me as affected. Compared with Hudson's musty room in St Luke's Road or the foreign exercise books and penny bottle of ink which had served D. H. Lawrence in the Tyrol, it was all wrong,— though obviously it had not checked the flow of words. Gilbert wrote a thousand of them every morning. But Sunday was a holiday and Lawrence and Frieda turned up, so winding scarves about our necks, calling the dog and taking Mary with us, we set off for a country walk. The dog, by the way, was the greatest literary celebrity of the whole party, far more widely known and beloved than Lawrence or Gilbert could ever hope to be, for it was said to be the actual original Nana of *Peter Pan*. When Mary had left J. M. Barrie it had been a double piece of treachery: she had taken Nana with her.

The object of our walk was to visit, on the way, another cottage inhabited by humbler literary fry. The cottage was so

8

small that conversation with its inmates, Middleton Murry and Katherine Mansfield, was almost impossible. Lawrence and Murry were to collaborate in writing *The Signature*, which ran to three numbers, a few months later. Lawrence was friendly, Frieda gay and Katherine mysterious and attractive and I felt I belonged with them and not with the stone fruit, the windmill and the world-famous sheepdog.

One Sunday in November, Frankie and I went down to visit Lawrence and Frieda. After a walk during which Frankie talked without stopping, we reached a horrid little cottage called The Triangle. Lawrence had warmly invited me to pay him a visit, but when we arrived he seemed in a bad mood. Frankie and Frieda got on much too well and carried on a noisy and, as Lawrence and I thought, snobbish conversation about the Lichnovskys and other titled Germans whom Frankie had met in London, or Berlin, and whom Frieda had known all her life.

Lawrence was dangerously silent and I foresaw an explosion in which he would turn his wrath on Frieda. Fortunately before it came, the door opened and two other visitors entered—a dark handsome young Jewish painter, called Mark Gertler, and a girl to whom I was at once powerfully attracted. Her thick hair, the colour of a new wheat straw thatch, was cut pudding-basin fashion round her neck and below her ears. Her complexion was delicate, like a white-heart cherry; a curious crooked nose gave character to her face and pure blue eyes made her appear simple and childish when she was in fact the very opposite. Her clothes labelled her an art-student and she was in fact, like Gertler, at the Slade. She concealed her Christian name, which was Dora, and was always called by her surname, Carrington, even after her marriage. My interest in her was returned, though I did not know it, and later we became warm friends until her death.

On this occasion, she scarcely spoke but sat down on the floor to listen, at intervals stealing critical looks at each of the company in turn out of her forget-me-not-blue eyes. The reason why she sat on the floor was because there were only two chairs. Frankie sat in the most comfortable and Gertler in the other. Frieda sat on the table swinging her legs and I sat on a trunk, or box, in a corner of the room. Lawrence was engaged in cooking spaghetti on an oil stove in the scullery and kept putting his head round the corner of the door. Gertler was as entertaining a talker as Frankie and held forth amusingly about himself. Frankie and Frieda joined in and Lawrence, who liked Gertler, cheered up considerably. I did not listen to much of the conversation: my attention was focused on Carrington. I longed to carry her off from Gertler whom I at once disliked, not so much because he was somewhat aggressive, as because he was Carrington's chosen companion. I knew that there was no way in which a humble science student could cut out a painter and I feared that she might be in love with him.

We ate the meal which Lawrence had been cooking for us and then Frankie and I set off to walk back to Chesham station. Before we left, Gertler told us that if we were challenged by a sentry guarding the water-works we need feel no alarm: it was only Gilbert armed with nothing but a walking stick and a brassard. For Gertler and Carrington were staying the weekend with the Cannans. Gilbert had perhaps already begun to plan his novel, *Mendel*, about them and Gertler's friend and fellow-student, Curry, who murdered a model and committed suicide. It was a most tragic story and Gilbert turned it into a novel.

Gertler's intuition was right: we were challenged and recognising the voice which demanded: "Who goes there?" I replied: "David Garnett and Francis Birrell." Gilbert was surprised; we talked for a little, described our visit to The Triangle and ran on down the hill to catch our train to London.

Frankie was, as Lawrence and I had both felt that day, rather a snob. He had been educated at Eton and was the son of a Cabinet Minister who was holding an impossibly difficult job as Chief Secretary for Ireland. I must have exasperated him very often by holding violent political opinions on subjects about which I knew very little. He retaliated by talking about the great ones with whom he was familiar, and though I accused him, with some justice, of snobbery, I soon became far more snobbish myself. Snobbery was something that Frankie grew out of and that I grew into.

As his father was in the Cabinet, Frankie had some interesting information, much of it about Lord Kitchener who was violently opposed to the passage of the bill putting Home Rule for Ireland on the Statute Book. For several years Augustine Birrell's chief work had been to get Home Rule accepted. Kitchener had been most active in intrigues designed to wreck the passage of the Home Rule Bill ever since his declaration on joining the Cabinet as Secretary for War: "As a soldier I have no politics."

Kitchener was in an almost unassailable position owing to his recent appointment and public faith in his military capacity. In addition Asquith was very loth to estrange his new-found supporters, the Conservatives. Sir Edward Grey was opposed to Home Rule.

But Birrell, after saying he would resign unless the Bill were passed, found unexpected allies. Winston Churchill, though in Birrell's opinion fundamentally a Conservative, had a clear enough head to assess the question on its military merits, and he agreed with Birrell that if the Home Rule Bill were not passed it would mean immobilising two Army Corps in Ireland.

Lloyd George, in Birrell's opinion, cared for nothing except himself and Wales. But he realised that if Home Rule was dropped and Birrell led a secession group, Asquith would have to form a Coalition and depend on the Conservative vote. In that case they would demand places in the Cabinet and Lloyd George would at that time have inevitably been sacrificed.

At the last minute Grey was brought round by the return of his private secretary from the United States, who told him that American opinion would be more influenced by Redmond, the Leader of the Irish Nationalist Party, than by any number of White papers—and that we might easily lose America's support if Home Rule was dropped. Grey therefore came out in support of Birrell. It was a very near thing. Asquith had already made tentative proposals to the Conservatives on paper and Bonar

Law waved them in the Prime Minister's face before the Unionists walked out of the Commons. They were not, however, divulged.

Birrell was also furious with Kitchener for having an article published in Ireland saying: "Lord Kitchener is disgusted at the poor response in Ireland to his appeal for recruits; unless you enlist, Territorials will be sent to Ireland which will be a humiliation—etc."

In point of fact 18,000 Irishmen had by then enlisted of whom 14,000 were Nationalists. Birrell and Kitchener were by then not on speaking terms, and were soon fighting over another matter.

Birrell asked that a large proportion of "Kitchener's Army" should be trained in Ireland. He pointed out that the presence of half a million soldiers in training in Ireland would make all thought of rebellion impossible. He also believed that the presence of the British Army would be very popular—there was nothing the Irish liked better than the fox-hunting, steeple-chasing British officer—and the money spent in Ireland by the Army would be a very powerful influence against Sinn Fein.

Kitchener refused absolutely to agree to this proposal and urged that there was still the likelihood of a German attempt to invade East Anglia and that the transport of a great body of men to and fro across the Irish Sea was almost impossible in view of German submarines.

Birrell would have done well to resign on that issue. Had he done so, he would have been proved right eighteen months later and his political reputation would have been immensely enhanced, and not ruined, by the Easter week rebellion.

One other piece of secret information which Francis told me in the autumn of 1914 turned out to be important. He had been to stay with his friends the Cromptons and told me that Colonel Crompton was busy inventing an immense bullet-proof armoured vehicle carrying a gun which could crawl over any country—in and out of trenches and over them, and that Winston Churchill had urged that it should be amphibious—

so that it could crawl out of the sea on to the enemy coast. Such a weapon would revolutionise warfare.

I had won a prize and had been given a scholarship at the end of my fourth year at the Imperial College which enabled me to do a year's research, and I had elected to work under Clifford Dobell in the Zoology Department though I was really a botanist. The piece of research work which he had given me turned out to be extremely boring. An Italian zoologist called Zweibaum had published a paper stating that he could produce conjugation at will in *Paramecium caudatum*, by immersion in dilute solutions of various salts. He gave the optimum strength for each salt, in a whole series of quite elaborate tables. Dobell was doubtful of these results and wanted me to repeat the experiments in order to confirm or to disprove them.

I accordingly spent hours in making up salt solutions of various strengths, put them in watch-glasses and introduced a few paramecia in a drop or two of water.

I had a long empty laboratory to myself and set out on the table about fifteen covered watch-glasses. Paramecium remains conjugated for about twelve hours; it was clear therefore that if I looked at the watch-glasses in the morning and again late at night, I should be able to observe any conjugations which took place. It was easy to observe them with a low-powered binocular dissecting microscope.

No conjugations took place. After a month I was certain that there was no truth in Zweibaum's theory. But Dobell wanted me to go on, so I continued for several months. It took no skill and very little time—and the result was a foregone conclusion. After about three months during which the paramecia multiplied solely by fission, I observed about a dozen conjugations most of which were in my control glasses containing no salt solution.

One result of this research was that it kept me in London over the week-ends, except when my friend Newth was willing to look through my watch-glasses for me; the second was that once I had disproved Zweibaum's claims, I only did a bare minimum of work.

However the war turned out, it was impossible not to think about it. The insistence by Mr Asquith and Sir Edward Grey that we had drawn the sword because of the German attack on Belgium seemed extremely suspect. For if the Germans had not violated Belgian neutrality, should we not have gone to the help of France? Could anyone honestly say that we should have allowed Paris to be occupied and France defeated without lifting a finger?

Why was France fighting? In the first place to support Russia. The origin of the war was a Slav conspiracy to dismember the Austro-Hungarian Empire. The war was in fact that which Sokolov had so confidently predicted two years before, and which he looked forward to with joy because he was confident Russia would be defeated and her defeat result in a revolution. I thought he was probably right in believing Russia would be defeated. But if she had been left unaided to receive the punishment she deserved for her schemes for a Russian hegemony of the Balkans, and a Russian occupation of Constantinople, her defeat would be more certain and more rapid.

Looked at in that way, we were being asked to prevent an Austrian and German pacification of Serbia—and to keep the Czar on his throne. Were those objects for which the whole of the young manhood of France and England should be sacrificed?

Sir Edward Grey, according to this view, was the villain of the piece:—a charming Northumbrian flyfisher and bird-watcher who had allowed himself to be entangled by Slavs plotting against Austria and Frenchmen who were terrified that, if there were a revolution, Russia would default upon the vast loans she had borrowed from France, and were taking advantage of the gamble in the hope of recovering Alsace and Lorraine.

I do not say that in December 1914 I already believed this view of the war; or had thought it out for myself. But it seemed to me to make sense—and I partly believed it. But my belief was greatly coloured by my love for France and my growing hatred for Germany.

All the arguments I have put forward left a practical question unanswered: we were at war and it was essential to fight for our preservation. Yet that argument was also fallacious. The Battle of the Marne had supplied the answer. The war had already reached a stalemate in the West and it seemed an admirable time for those who had made war to make peace.

I still, however, sometimes hankered after the excitements and glory of being a soldier. The idea that if I enlisted I might be killed scarcely entered my head and did not weigh with me at all.

In December Frankie and I were invited by Lytton Strachey to a Christmas party he was giving at The Lacket at Lockeridge near Marlborough, a cottage belonging to Hilton Young, now Lord Kennet. It had been previously occupied by Desmond and Molly MacCarthy and, long afterwards, was the abode of Mrs Lawrence, the mother of T. E. Lawrence. The other guests were to be Daphne and Noel Olivier, James Strachey, and Duncan Grant. There would not be room in the cottage for the whole party, but Lytton took a room in the local inn for Frankie and me.

We decided to go for a few days walking tour, timed to end at The Lacket on Christmas Eve. Starting at Yatton in the Mendip hills, we walked to Cheddar. Here I involved Frankie in telling a lie which turned out to be as much nuisance as any lie I have ever been concerned in.

Augustine Birrell had once been to Cheddar and had visited the famous Cheddar Gorge and seen the stalactite. This apparently had made an impression on him only comparable to that which Chartres made on Henry Adams, or the Colosseum on Gibbon. Thus when Frankie told his father he was going to Cheddar, he was instructed to visit the Gorge and see the stalactite.

We spent the night in Cheddar. "That is the more sensible cheese," said the old cheesemonger next morning as I chose the larger of two to send home. But after sending off this present to my parents, I had no patience with Frankie's less materialistic form of filial piety as he announced in a slightly halfhearted manner: "Now we must see the stalactite."

"We can't waste time like that," I said. "We have got to be on the road. I want to spend some time looking at Wells Cathedral and then get on to Glastonbury by nightfall."

"I *promised* my father I would go to see the stalactite," said Frankie irresolutely.

"Oh, that's all bosh," I replied and firmly over-ruled him. "You can always tell him you've seen it."

"How can I, when I don't know what it looks like?" replied Frankie.

"Oh it's only a stone icicle with a drop of water on the end which enables it to grow half an inch every five thousand years," I replied.

Frankie unluckily was over-ruled and took my advice. On his return to Elm Park Gardens he was greeted with: "Had a good holiday me boy? And what did ye think of the stalactite?"

Frankie committed the unpardonable fault in a liar of being luke-warm. If he had praised it to the skies or damned it, or even told the truth, not much harm would have been done. As it was, Augustine Birrell was quite ruffled. When I met him a month or so later, he started on me. "How did ye like that walk with Francis when ye visited the Cheddar Gorge?" I knew what was coming and had the wit to be enthusiastic and I think I convinced him, if he had entertained suspicions, that I at all events had been to the Gorge and had appreciated the stalactite.* But Frankie was never forgiven and the Cheddar Gorge was always brought up if Augustine wished to accuse his son of caring nothing for natural beauty, and his indifference to the stalactite adduced as proof that he had no curiosity about the wonders of the world. In fact Frankie became so worried that I told him that he had better make a special journey to Cheddar to see it—but pointed out that if he felt a hereditary enthusiasm for it he would be involved in the even more difficult lie of maintaining his earlier indifference.

* I have since learned that there are hundreds of stalactites in the Cheddar caves, Augustine Birrell may have thought it odd that Frankie and I believed there was only one.

16

Though we missed the Gorge, we saw Wells Cathedral, Glastonbury Abbey and also a display of illuminated meat in the Glastonbury butchers' shops. The town band marched from butcher's shop to butcher's shop and played a rousing tune in front of each. Frankie was delighted when the pretty serving girl at the inn asked us if we had been to see the meat and said it was the most beautiful sight she had ever seen in her life. It was a remark that Samuel Butler would have recorded in his *Notebooks*.

Next day we pushed on through Frome, but did not reach the Lacket until after dark. It was a small, thatched house sheltering behind a huge box hedge, with a boulder-strewn hillside rising behind it. Noel, Daphne, James and Duncan arrived directly after us and we were all welcomed with gentle cries of delight by Lytton whom I met then for the first time.

Lytton was tall and rather emaciated, with a reddish beard and lank dark hair which hung in a long lock over his forehead and was cut off squarely, in pudding-basin fashion, at the back of his head. His nose was large with a high bridge; he wore gold-rimmed spectacles and was obviously rather short-sighted. I was struck first of all by his gentleness and his hospitality. Then I could see that he was very much alive and very responsive. That evening the response may sometimes have concealed boredom, for Lytton was easily bored and the prospect of Christmas with two young women in the house—one of whom often spoke in tones of indignant emotional idealism—may have seemed rather appalling. James had let him in for them, and his curiosity and affection for Frankie had let him in for the shy, but good-looking hobbledehoy he had brought with him.

The next day was Christmas and, after breakfast, the animal spirits of the low-brow members of the party got out of hand.

Daphne and I exchanged a wild glance after we had stood on the road above the cottage admiring the great box hedge below us encircling the little garden—and then she spread out her

17

arms and took a running dive on top of the soft, round, springy mass. I followed like a flash. The sensation was wonderful and Noel, Frankie and even Duncan followed our example. It was almost as exciting as taking running dives into water. If one leaped high and far one could reach the top of the hedge and once I slid slowly over into the garden beyond.

But our sport was soon interrupted. Lytton came out and in despairing tones forbade it. Frankie tactfully remembered Peter the Great's exploits in smashing John Evelyn's hedge in Hampstead. We realised that Lytton was really a little upset and, sorrowfully, we desisted and for the rest of the day accepted Strachey canons of behaviour, though some of us passed up our plates for second helpings of turkey and plum pudding.

Once again I was struck by the rigidity of the Strachey outlook. We had to conform to Strachey views and Strachey habits: the Stracheys would not even try to pretend to adapt themselves to manners or customs which were not their own.

That evening, when we gathered round the fire after tea, Lytton said he would read us a story he had written.

It was a correspondence between two young ladies, written somewhat in the manner of *Les Liaisons Dangereuses*, describing their first sexual adventures and their awakening to physical love.

On Boxing Day, the Oliviers and I decided to go for a walk on which James, Frankie and Duncan accompanied us over the high Downs and Lytton was left for an hour or two to rest from the labour of entertaining us.

Noel and James paired off, Frankie and Daphne were deep in conversation, and I found myself walking beside the proud figure who, as I was aware, had disliked me at Adrian Stephen's parties. I must have been unlike what Duncan Grant had supposed, for he was a most entertaining companion and that walk on the Marlborough downs was the beginning of a lifelong friendship. For that reason alone, Lytton's Christmas party marked an epoch in my life. It was also the beginning of my friendship with Lytton.

But it was important also, for me, in another way. I had been brought up to share my parents' free views on the relations of the sexes, but I had, up till then, been, in my love-affairs, an unrepentant sentimentalist and, like most sentimentalists, an unconscious hypocrite. Lytton's little tract made it clear that sincerity was a chief virtue in love, or lust. I realised this was true and adopted for ever afterwards a more honest attitude to my amours. I became and for the rest of my life have remained, in what I take to be the true meaning of the word, a *libertine*: that is a man whose sexual life is free of the restraints imposed by religion and conventional morality. But I am not, and had little impulse ever to become, a *rake*: that is a man whose loose life is the result of a reaction against the restraints imposed by his upbringing, or one who has a psychological craving for self-destruction and seeks it in the brothel, or the gutter.

In my experience, most men are, or would be, rakes if they followed their impulses. Libertines among men are rare, and the rakes are often greatly shocked by them. On the other hand there are more women libertines than women rakes. Contrary to the general belief, libertines have warmer hearts as well as clearer heads.

I have been the lover of very many women, but, by nature, I have only been attracted by certain types among them. I have been sensual but never cold. The things I have always sought in the women whom I loved have been, in Blake's words: "the lineaments of satisfied desire." It was only when they have been lacking that I have felt ashamed.

I have never had reason to share Donne's regret:

> "Ah cannot we
> As well as cocks and lions jocund be
> After such pleasures?"

For it is at those moments that I have most felt my kinship with the lion and have least felt either a sense of sin, or shame.

Sir Charles Darwin has recently published the comforting discovery that man is a wild animal. I have always known it as regards myself and I have seldom wished to mate with a woman who was not one also. I shall not write much about physical love in these pages. Donne, Wyatt, and Carew have said nearly all that I should have liked to say. The passionate physical love which I have felt for many women has been the most important part of my life for forty years. But it could only be written about freely in poetry: in prose there is the chance that it would seem dead, and for that reason obscene. Moreover love is in its very nature private, and several of the women I have loved are living.

Among some of my friends, I got, at one time, the reputation of being something of a Casanova. But that was only because such a large proportion of the love-affairs of the younger people in Bloomsbury were unhappy:—A eating his heart out vainly for B; B breaking hers in vain for C, and so on in interminable interlocking circles of frustration. Maynard Keynes once called me "earthy" and I took it as a compliment, for I have always had deep within me the knowledge that:

> Whoever loves, if he do not propose
> The right true end of love, he's One that goes
> To sea for nothing but to make him sick.

Perhaps it was my single-mindedness that led to its reward. For most women like a man who has no doubts or scruples in taking what he wants of them and, in so doing, giving them what they want in return.

That I was not so well-endowed, or so catholic in my tastes, as Casanova is proved by the fact that I have always had many young and attractive women friends as well as older ones with whom I never thought of trying to have a love affair. I have very seldom ever felt jealousy and have only once let that terrible emotion get the better of me and influence my conduct. I have also been freer than most men of *amour de vanité*; my one experience of it led to great unhappiness and shame.

II

SHORTLY after New Year's Day 1915, I received an invitation: "Mr Keynes requests the pleasure of Mr Bunny's company at dinner at the Café Royal, before Mrs Bell's party."

Seventeen of us sat down to dinner. Maynard, Clive and Vanessa, J. T. Sheppard, then a classical don at King's College, Cambridge, Gerald Shove, Cecil Taylor, who had recently left King's to become a schoolmaster at Clifton, Frankie, Duncan, Leonard and Virginia, Desmond and Molly MacCarthy are the ones I remember. Maynard put me between Vanessa and Duncan. I was a little shy of Vanessa, whose beauty and strong character had always attracted me. However, Maynard had ordered plenty of champagne and confidence soon returned. Vanessa left early to greet the first arrivals at her party, and Sheppard, who had been sitting on her right, turned and entered into conversation with me. I had heard much of his comic gift, his passion for Greek, his brilliance as a lecturer and the warmth and kindness of his character from Frankie, so that presently I said to him:

"My friends tell me that you are responsible for so much of what I like best in them."

Had I tried for a hundred years I could not have hit on anything to please Sheppard more. Yet there was truth in my compliment: Sheppard had greatly influenced Frankie and other friends of mine from King's and it was for that reason that it pleased him.

46 Gordon Square, where the Bells lived, is a large house in the middle of the East side of one of the most pleasant squares in Bloomsbury. There was already a large party when we arrived and were ushered into the dining-room on the ground floor. I immediately noticed a cubist painting by Picasso,

which I had seen reproduced in Clive's book *Art*. I also
noticed a Vlaminck which I liked better. The pictures gave
dignity to a room which was beautiful, although already
crowded with people, among whom I recognised many old
friends. James, Lytton and several other Stracheys were there.
So were Karin and Ray Costello, who soon afterwards married
Adrian Stephen and Oliver Strachey. Brynhild had brought
Harold Hobson's sister Mabel Scott. There was also the
strikingly handsome figure of Lady Ottoline Morrell, whom I
had admired from a distance two or three years before at a
political dinner, given at the Savoy Hotel, to Mr Morgan
Shuster, the American financial adviser of the Persian Government who had been driven out of his job by Russian intrigue
backed by the policy of Sir Edward Grey. My parents felt
passionately about the division of Persia into Anglo-Russian
spheres of influence, and had taken me with them to attend the
dinner. Here was Lady Ottoline again and soon I was introduced and she was purring out in a cajoling drawl: "Do come
to a party I am giving after dinner, next Thursday, Mr Garnett.
Why do they call you Bunny?" Her words and instant invitation turned my head.

We sat down to listen to Mozart played by the three
D'Aranyi sisters. Jelly, the youngest, was then in the first
flower of her beauty. After the music we went upstairs to see a
performance of the last scene of Racine's *Bérénice*, acted by
three gigantic puppets, eight feet high, which had been made
by Duncan. They were cut out of thick cardboard and were
flat, but could move their jointed arms and legs.

At a crisis in the play, Bérénice, who had been seated up till
then, rose to her feet, and the puppet in the centre moved
his eyes to look at his companions as they spoke in turn.
The scene acted was the tragic ending when Antiochus confesses his love for Bérénice to Titus and all three part for
ever.

The words were spoken by members of the Strachey family
whose excellent French accents and elocution were almost as
impressive as the puppets. The size and artificiality of the

figures made them perfect mouthpieces for Racine's heroic poetry.

The evening ended with Gerald Shove enthroned in the centre of the room, crowned with roses, which must have been taken from a vase of hot-house flowers. His charming good humour was the best possible tribute to Clive's hospitality and the excellent quality of the whisky. But I do not remember which lady saw that it was appropriate for Gerald to be wearing a wreath of roses, or set it round his Roman brow.

Soon after that party I found myself on terms of warm friendship not only with Duncan and Maynard, but with Clive and Vanessa. 46 Gordon Square became for me a house where I felt sure of being welcome and Blanche, the thin tall housemaid who opened the door, and the children, Julian and Quentin aged six and four, soon began to greet me as a friend.

I do not think such a rapid friendship would have been possible but for Clive, whose character was in many ways complementary to Vanessa's, just as that of Jack Sprat was complementary to that of his lady who could eat no lean. Clive created the atmosphere of Number Forty-six more than Vanessa and I shall therefore attempt a superficial sketch of his character.

In one of Hans Andersen's fairy tales there is a Princess who is so sensitive that she cannot sleep if there is so much as a crumpled rose petal beneath the mattress of her bed. Clive is like the princess, he cannot be happy if he is aware of anyone feeling unhappy in the vicinity. Thus, perhaps for selfish reasons, he does everything to create happiness about him. He is an almost perfect example of James Mill's Utilitarian theory that a man cannot become rich without enriching his neighbours. If everyone were like Clive, the theory might be generally true.

At this time Clive was not in the slightest degree interested in me and would not have cared if he had never seen me again. But if I was going to haunt Gordon Square, it was essential for his comfort that I should be feeling happy when I did. He was

23

therefore far kinder to me than an altruistic man would have been. When the door was opened, a warm stream of Clive's hospitality and love of the good things of life poured out, as ravishing as the smell of roasting coffee on a cold morning. Heaviness, dullness, coldness, the besetting sins of English people and of the English climate, were impossible in Clive's house and Clive's company. Such jolly hearty good-fellowship is traditionally associated with fox-hunters and shooting parties and it was, in fact, from that milieu that Clive inherited his temperament. His tastes had led him into the chillier world of philosophers, mathematicians, critics and artists where the spiritual virtues of the hunt breakfast were unknown. Clive therefore provided an essential element in the formation of Bloomsbury. He brought to what might otherwise have been a bleak intellectual world

> a beaker full of the warm South
> Full of the true, the blushful Hippocrene
> With beaded bubbles winking at the brim.

He saved Bloomsbury from being another Clapham Sect, devoted, in the same cold unworldly way, to aesthetics and the pursuit of abstract truth instead of to evangelical religion. This was by no means all of Clive's contribution, for though he gives the impression of an airy quick-witted talker, he has the habits of a scholar. He always spends a good many hours a day reading. Clive's wide reading, quick wit and common sense was an essential ingredient in the brilliant talk to be heard in Bloomsbury. The other most important elements in it were the talk of Lytton, Virginia, Maynard, Desmond MacCarthy and Harry Norton. Clive cannot endure illness and he is often an absentee at the sick-beds of his nearest and dearest. Yet in other ways he is not squeamish. A secret horror of 46 Gordon Square was that the basement kitchen was infested with cock-roaches. When the pest became bad, Clive would put on his shooting boots and go down in the middle of the night to stamp on them. No one else in Bloomsbury (except myself) would have done that.

During the week after Vanessa's party the paramecia lived as chastely as ever in the watch-glasses of dilute salt-solutions, but I spied upon them for the very minimum of time.

The next day, Friday, I lunched with Sheppard and Cecil Taylor and went to a matinée with them. The following Monday I dined with Duncan, Adrian, Clive, Vanessa, Oliver Strachey and Karin Costello at the Café Royal. On Tuesday Frankie and I had dinner together before going to the Caroline Club play-reading. On Thursday I went to Lady Ottoline's party after dinner, where I danced with a young French actress, Valentine Tessier, since famous, and talked to Gilbert Cannan. Next day I gave a little dinner-party myself to a zoologist friend, now Professor Fox, who was just going off to the war, and his sister, who is now the well-known journalist Alison Settle. Afterwards we went to the Omega workshops to see a performance of marionettes made by a mysterious figure called De Bergen, the husband of Nina Hamnett, the painter.

In the intervals, and after the performance, I met and talked to Professor Bateson, the great geneticist, Lady Ottoline Morrell and Clive and Vanessa. That week-end I stayed in London and, on Saturday, Duncan started a portrait of me which he continued next day. On Monday Vanessa came and had tea with me at Pond Place. We sat in my dingy little back room, drinking China tea and eating chocolate éclairs which I had bought in her honour—or at least I ate them. She must have come to see me out of curiosity—to see for herself whether I was a purely silly creature, or intelligent, a frivolous and snobbish climber, or disinterested and sincere. Though I may not have got very high marks for intelligence, I did not, I think, get bad ones for character. That afternoon Vanessa decided that she liked me, and thereafter I felt as sure of her affectionate friendship as I did of her brother Adrian's.

When she rose to go she gave me a kiss and that kiss sealed a friendship on which I could rely. Two or three years later, Vanessa told me that my character was not nearly as good as I believed, but my intelligence was far better. She was right in so far as my intelligence was certainly sharpened by my life in Old Bloomsbury, but I don't think my character changed at all. It is more probable that it took her some time to discover my bad qualities.

Vanessa was a very beautiful woman, tall and striking in appearance. She had a very lovely, sensitive mouth, strangely innocent grey-blue eyes, with hooded lids, and straight brown hair, parted in the middle, which swept over her ears and was worn in a bun on the nape of her neck. Her face was a perfect oval and recalled that of a gothic madonna sculptured at Chartres, or Reims.

She was extremely alive and gay; almost always critical, but full of humour, and she possessed, when among her friends, the great attraction of complete unselfconsciousness and spontaneity. Vanessa's intelligence and her freedom from the vanity and self-obsession which poisoned Virginia, made her occupy a unique position in Bloomsbury. Roger Fry, Maynard Keynes, Duncan Grant, Oliver Strachey, Harry Norton and I all felt that she was unique among women. Her mind and manners were not in the least masculine, yet she was the only woman that any of us knew who could join in the talk of a group of men and allow them to forget that she was a woman, forgetting it herself. Her brain was original and logical and she was a quick reasoner, never hesitating to put forward her views. She never produced the same impression of being a brilliant conversationalist as Virginia, but she was witty and very fond of making bawdy jokes. Like Virginia, she often showed her teasing affection by jokes at the expense of those she loved.

But already she had developed an aristocratic characteristic which grew with the years: that of dividing the human race into two groups, those within the charmed circle of her intimates and those outside it.

I have given a list of my social engagements during about ten days early in 1915 in order to show that my life had suddenly become a very full one. There were two causes for this, though I did not at the time separate them. One was an

DUNCAN GRANT AND MAYNARD KEYNES
AT ASHEHAM

ephemeral social success, represented by Lady Ottoline's weekly invitations to dinner, to tea and to after-dinner parties; the other was my being accepted as an intimate friend by Duncan, Vanessa, Lytton and Maynard.

Duncan James Corrowr Grant is five years older than I am. He is a first cousin of the Stracheys—Lady Strachey having been a daughter of Sir John Peter Grant, 11th Laird of Rothiemurchus. Duncan's father, Major Bartle Grant, was a younger son who, after enlisting in an expensive and fashionable regiment to gratify the vanity of his father, improvidently married the most beautiful young woman, a portionless Scottish girl called Ethel McNeill, whom he met in India. Duncan was the only child of this love-match. His father, who was by gifts and inclination a musician, a botanist and a cook learned in the history of gastronomy, was left a poor man after his father's death. He exchanged into a line regiment, but the army bored him; he could not earn a living by writing accompaniments to Victorian drawing-room songs, or by his knowledge of Burmese orchids.

Mrs Grant was about forty-five when I first met her and one of the most lovely women I have ever known. There was not a grey hair among her thick dark tresses; she had rather pale grey eyes, a magnificent carriage, and about her was that indescribable quality which women only have who have been greatly loved all their lives, and who have always known that they were beautiful. She was not in the least intellectual, but had that rich warmth which comes to women who have created the world they wanted around them, in face of all sorts of difficulties. She was very straightforward, not subtle, but with humour. My last charming memory is of her playing duets with Angelica Bell, then a girl of sixteen. Mrs Grant's back was as straight and as elastic as the child's.

Duncan inherited his mother's beauty and more than his father's intelligence and aesthetic tastes. He was sent to the same prep. school as James Strachey, and went, with him, afterwards to St Paul's School. But, as a young man, he was nevertheless almost uneducated. Just as I had escaped from

University College School by a stupidity and incapacity to learn which alarmed my mother, Duncan played the dunce to such purpose that Lady Strachey, who was temporarily in charge of him, took him away from St Paul's and sent him to the Westminster School of Art. Some few years later he was given a hundred pounds by one of his aunts and went to Paris where he studied under Jacques Emile Blanche.

Duncan used to be teased by Clive and Maynard because they said he had never learned the multiplication table. That I believe was true. But he could add and subtract so fast in his head that he would diffidently suggest that seven eights were fifty-six after a pause of only five or six seconds. To stupid people this may suggest that he is slightly half-witted, but the intelligent soon discover that Duncan is a genius who can only do things in his own way, or not at all. He was and is the most original man I have ever known. If one appreciates originality, he is a continual source of delight. His friendship was a great piece of good luck for me, particularly as it came at a time when I might have succeeded in my ambition of becoming a purely conventional person. He effectively prevented that. Duncan is a pure artist and nothing else. The artist in me had been over-laid and almost smothered. In Duncan's company I learned how an artist approaches his work and, when I came to write, I approached my subject as a conscious artist. This gave me, or so I think, an enormous advantage over the writer who comes to story-telling from the practice of journalism or essay-writing. If, as I believe, my slender talent has expressed itself with originality and success, I owe it to a great extent to the formative years spent in Duncan's company. Very early in our friendship he recognised that I was a writer, and greatly surprised and encouraged me by his good opinion of something that I had written. Though so talented that any scribble he makes on a bit of paper looks like the work of a master, Duncan used to start any big picture with sweat and anguish and there was almost always a big strain when it was about two-thirds finished. In my experience no work of art is really any good unless there is a period of strain about that time. Duncan

28

is an intensely serious painter who is never content to repeat a formula which he has hit upon. It was some time before I found out how Duncan approached his work and to what extent he was keyed up before starting a big picture and when he was about two-thirds of the way through it, for that was a side which he kept hidden.

Like his father and several of his Strachey cousins, particularly Oliver, Duncan is extremely musical, and I learned to appreciate music from him. Duncan was always buying and playing gramophone records—especially Mozart. Being untaught and unable to read a note of music, Duncan was shy of playing in front of other people, but if there was a piano in the house he was always attracted by it. He soon came to regard my presence as no more important than that of the cat, and I was able to enjoy his playing when he thought nobody was listening.

His love of music expresses itself also in his dancing. He is an excellent dancer of Scotch reels and of the sword dance. Once after giving a performance of the latter in his stockinged feet over sharp swords at a party of Adrian's, he ended by nearly cutting off his toe. He was carried off to University College Hospital where it was stitched up. But his false step on that occasion may have been due to too much whisky.

Duncan is even better as an improviser of character, or ballet dancing, and I have seen him perform admirably at parties as a partner to Lopokhova. My own efforts as a character dancer always gave *me* much pleasure but showed more physical stamina than talent.

Duncan was the most entertaining companion I have ever known. He had a liveliness of mind which never struck upon the obvious; he was intensely observant and amused and interested in everything he saw: and the things he saw were especially those to which the majority of people are blind. One had only to walk down the street with him to find this out. Duncan's eye was always roving; he would notice a woman brushing her hair in front of a second-floor window, or a cat stealing fish on a basement table while the cook's back was turned: all the little dramas which were going on were instantly perceived and they delighted him. If his visual sense was exceptionally acute, a similar sensibility made him respond instantly to the mood of his companion. I have often known Duncan cross or surly, but I have never known him guilty of bad manners. Though he has the national failing of the Highland Scot of being too proud, he is entirely without arrogance and is in many ways as modest and unworldly as Dostoevsky's hero, Prince Myshkin. He was sometimes, as a young man before he became famous—for fame prevents such mistakes—like Myshkin, taken for an idiot by narrowly conventional people. This, when it occurred, was one of the ironical jokes which amused some of his intimate friends and infuriated others.

Duncan had a most charming way of affectionately teasing the people he was fond of, in which he resembled my father. I came in for a lot of it, although Vanessa, I believe, got the largest share (she laid herself open to teasing). Lytton, Clive and Maynard were by no means immune. Duncan, himself, was teased a good deal in return, particularly by Clive, who excelled at it. Often some little eccentricity or personal way of doing things, confessed by him perhaps at dinner, would set us all in a roar of laughter at his expense. When this happened, Duncan might laugh himself but would always defend himself vigorously and sometimes even turn the tables effectively upon the teasers.

Duncan sometimes played jokes upon his friends, which, though on a smaller scale, were as successful as the famous hoaxes perpetrated by Adrian Stephen and his accomplice Horace Cole. On one occasion, when he was living in the house of his aunt Lady Strachey, he dressed up as an old lady and called upon her on the afternoon when she was at home. He gave a German name and was ushered into the drawing-room and announced by the housemaid. The name he had given meant nothing to Lady Strachey, but he explained in guttural accents that he was the friend of a certain Fraulein Grüner, a formidable and highbrow schoolmistress acquaintance of Lady Strachey's. He then entered into a lively conversation with the visitors round the tea-table and eventually got up and took his departure without his aunt having the slightest suspicion that her visitor was not what she had appeared.

One day I went to tea with Lytton at his mother's house in Belsize Park Gardens and, after tea, he confessed that he was somewhat agitated. He had received that morning a poem in French in rhymed couplets, which hinted that the writer had seen Lytton one night in some extremely compromising and possibly comic situation. Unfortunately I can remember nothing of the poem but the last lines:

> "C'est toujours plus discret de monter en fiacre
> Tel est le conseil de votre ami Delacre."

Delacre was a sober and taciturn French actor who was frequently to be met with, accompanied by Valentine Tessier, at Lady Ottoline's parties. Lytton had once engaged him in conversation about the intellectual drama in Paris and this teasing *jeu d'esprit* had come as a bombshell, particularly as Lytton was not quite sure what indiscretion of his had been observed. Lytton assured me that it was all a complete mistake —but what really distressed him was that Delacre would probably show his poem to Ottoline, tell her his version of the affair and she, of course, would immensely enjoy maliciously spreading a story at his expense.

Lytton then told me that he had gone that morning to see Delacre at his hotel, had thanked him for his witty poem but had asked him, as a man of honour, not to show it to Ottoline. Delacre had then behaved in a most extraordinary and alarming manner. He had listened to Lytton's little speech without making any comment whatever. He had then excused himself and left the room. After waiting three quarters of an hour Lytton had asked a waiter to find Delacre and had been told that he had left the hotel. Lytton was completely baffled by this behaviour and felt that he had not improved matters by his *démarche*.

I listened with great amusement to this ridiculous imbroglio and read the lines again. It struck me that it was highly improbable that M. Delacre, who was presumably a vain, as well as a serious actor, should choose the word *fiacre* as a rhyme to his own name. "You don't think that Duncan wrote it by any chance?" I asked. Lytton stared in dismay. "What, that monster! Of course! But it never occurred to me that it might be him!"

Duncan was in the very seventh heaven of delight when I told him about Lytton's interview with Delacre and the poor Frenchman's precipitate flight. He laughed and laughed until the tears came, and after the tears, a slight twinge of remorse. The result of this practical joke was that whenever Lytton chanced to meet Delacre, either at Ottoline's, or in the foyer at the theatre or the ballet, the actor would glance at him apprehensively and seize the first opportunity to escape from the society of a dangerous lunatic.

One evening, after leaving 46, as Duncan reached the corner of Gordon Square, he saw in front of him an unmistakable street-walker in full warpaint, with her features somewhat muffled by a huge fox fur. She was swinging her bag provocatively and puffing a cigarette. In those days respectable women rarely smoked in public. As Duncan came abreast of her, she sidled up to him and accosted him with the formula:

"Hullo darling, I'll give you a good time. I know you're a naughty boy."

Duncan stepped quickly aside and hurried past her but was horrified to hear hoarse endearments and high heels tapping in pursuit. When he reached the corner of Woburn Place and Tavistock Square, he waited for a moment and boarded a bus. But his pursuer reached it just in time to climb on to it after him. Duncan bolted up the stairs and was almost on the point of ringing the bell for the conductor, as the painted Jezebel plopped down beside him.

"Testing your virtue!" cried a Miss Strachey and gave a shriek of high-pitched laughter. Duncan's cousins had taken their revenge.

On my first visit to her house in Bedford Square Lady Ottoline had asked me about D. H. Lawrence whom she wanted to meet and I promised to introduce him to her next time he was in London. But before I was able to arrange it they had met and, when I went in to dinner the following Thursday, I found that Ottoline had placed me next to Frieda. On the opposite side of the table Lawrence was talking to E. M. Forster. I had first met Morgan, as I afterwards learned to call him, when I was a boy of fifteen and he had come to tea with my parents in our workman's flat in Hampstead. He was then a young novelist whom my father had criticised favourably in the columns of *The Nation* and whom he encouraged in letters and by word of mouth. We were great admirers of his work, reading each book as it came out, but thinking *A Room With a View* the best. Morgan was extremely modest about his work.

After dinner we soon followed the ladies upstairs to the drawing-room and listened to a Mozart quintet, and after the music there was dancing. Duncan was one of those who had joined the party after dinner and both he and I met with misfortunes that evening. I was dancing with a lively little Slade student with dark blue eyes, bright red cheeks and a small round head covered with short dark curls, called Barbara Hiles. She had arrived after dinner with Gertler and Carrington. It was Barbara's pretty little head that was my undoing, for after improvising a violent pirouette, she leapt into the air like Nijinsky and struck me full in the eye with the top of it and also made me bite my tongue severely. That was the end of my dancing for the evening. As she whirled happily away with her next partner, I watched, out of the other eye, Duncan dancing with Ottoline who was wearing a Spanish dress with a high comb and a lace mantilla. They were improvising free steps when Duncan caught his toe in her train, clutched her, and both of them lost their balance and crashed to the floor. Ottoline, fortunately, was unhurt, but Duncan was shaken and bruised.

Ottoline, undeterred, then took Gertler as her partner and though my eye was rapidly swelling I went up to Carrington and got into conversation with her. She told me that she hoped to go on a visit to Sarawak and asked me if I knew anything about Malaya. I gave her a vivid description of it, founded on Schimpfer's *The Geography of Plants* and Trelawny's *The Adventures of a Younger Son* and next day I lent her a copy of the latter book.

Ottoline had talked to Lawrence about Duncan's pictures and, as Lawrence asked to see some of them, Duncan invited him and Frieda and E. M. Forster to tea in his studio the following afternoon. Morgan was the first to arrive. I came next, a woeful spectacle, as I had a very bad black eye. Then came the Lawrences. While we drank a cup of tea, Duncan brought out his pictures. On one very large canvas there was a green giant kneeling and overshadowing St Paul's Cathedral. The green giant was the spiritual form of Sir Christopher Wren. Then came an astonishingly good portrait of Ottoline—a three-quarter view of her head. Round the neck Duncan had pinned a string of Woolworth pearls. Lawrence had done a little painting himself and had his own ideas about the art. He was, indeed, to take up painting again and have his rather washy indefinite nudes seized by the police and destroyed by the order of a London magistrate. But Mr Mead, on the bench in Marlborough Street, was not much stupider than Lawrence himself that afternoon. We all sat in silence as Duncan brought out one picture after another. Then Lawrence rose to his feet —a bad sign—and walking up and down the studio, began to explain to Duncan what was wrong with his painting. It was not simply that the pictures themselves were bad—hopelessly bad—but they were worthless because Duncan was full of the wrong ideas. He was barking up the wrong tree and would have to learn to approach his subjects in a completely different frame of mind if he wanted ever to become an artist.

Soon after Lawrence's first words, Morgan made some gentle remark about catching the train to Weybridge and faded out of the studio. Lawrence warmed to his subject and went on speaking with absolute frankness, having decided that it was better to open Duncan's eyes and tell him the truth. But as he talked

34

he held his head on one side, as though in pain, and looked more at the floor than at the pictures. Frieda, unfortunately, was aware both of Duncan's feelings and of mine. Each time that Duncan rose in silence and brought out another picture, she exclaimed: "Ah, Lorenzo! I like this one so much better! It is beautiful!" Her interventions were ignored by both sides. Lawrence would give a wincing glance at the new picture and discover in it new material for his argument. Finally, in despair, Duncan brought out a long band of green cotton on two rollers. I stood and held one roller vertically and unwound while, standing a couple of yards away, Duncan wound up the other, and a series of supposedly related, abstract shapes was displayed before our disgusted visitors. That was the worst of all.

Before Lawrence had reached his peroration, there was a ring at the bell and the lecture was held up while Duncan went down and returned with an uninvited figure—a dark Russian Jew called Koteliansky—who had come to pick up Lawrence and Frieda with whom he had arranged to spend the evening. He sat down and the lecture was resumed. Lawrence paced uneasily up and down looking at the floor. Koteliansky sat black and silent; Frieda occasionally burst out: "But no, Lorenzo! We liked that portrait so much!"

Duncan himself appeared to have developed toothache and sat with his hands on his knees, rocking himself gently in his chair, not attempting a word in defence of his works. Everything, however, has an end, and at last Lawrence, feeling he had done his good deed for the day, said that they must be going. Frieda and Koteliansky rose and followed and Duncan showed them down the dimly lit stairs and ushered them politely out into the foggy night. I stayed in the studio. The blast of Lawrence's attack had been directed at Duncan, who no doubt felt that he had suffered an unexpected assault, but he had lost nothing. I knew that the hope I had nursed of happy hours with them both was vain. My two friends would never understand each other.

When Duncan came back, I did not make any attempt to

console him in the style of Frieda. We stacked the canvasses back against the walls and washed up the cups and saucers in silence. Next day Lawrence who was living in Sussex at a cottage lent him by Alice Meynell, wrote:

27 Jan. 1915, Greatham, Pulborough, Sussex.

Dear Lady Ottoline,

We liked Duncan Grant very much. I really liked him. Tell him not to make silly experiments in the futuristic line with bits of colour on moving paper. Other Johnnies can do that. Neither to bother making marionettes —even titanic ones. But to seek out the terms in which he shall state his whole. He is after stating the Absolute—like Fra Angelico in *The Last Judgment*—a whole conception of the existence of man—creation, good, evil, life, death, resurrection, the separating of the stream of good and evil and its return to the eternal source. It is an Absolute we are all after, a statement of the whole scheme—the issue the progress through Time —and the return, making unchangeable eternity. In a geometric figure one has the abstractions ready stated ◯ so, or △ so. But one cannot build a complete abstraction, or absolute, out of a number of small abstractions, or absolutes. Therefore one cannot make a picture out of geometric figures. One can only build a great abstraction out of concrete units. Painting is not architecture. It is puerile to try to achieve architecture— third dimension—on a flat surface, by means of "lines of force". The architecture comes in painting, only with the conception of some whole, some conception which conveys in its own manner, the whole universe. Most puerile is that clabbing geometric figures behind one another, just to prove that the artist is being abstract, that he is not attempting representation of the object. The way to express the abstract whole is to reduce the object to a unit, a term, and then out of these units and terms to make a whole statement. *Do* rub this in to Duncan Grant and save him his foolish waste. Rembrandt, Corot, Goya, Manet have been preparing us our instances—now for the great hand which can collect all the instances into an absolute statement of the whole. I hope you aren't bored, but do tell this to Duncan Grant.

From that spate of verbiage one might think that Lawrence was refuting ideas that Duncan had put forward. But I was a witness to the fact that Duncan had behaved like Tar-Baby while Lawrence had worked himself up into a passion like Brer Rabbit. In his letter, Lawrence was belabouring a figment of his imagination, as well as pouring out a lot of nonsense.

What would an abstract statement of the instances of Rembrandt, Corot, Goya and Manet look like?

It seems certain that a memory of the visit to Duncan's studio inspired the passage at the end of Chapter XVIII of *Lady Chatterley's Lover*. Mellors, the gamekeeper hero (Lawrence) is taken to the studio of Duncan Forbes, "a dark-skinned taciturn Hamlet of a fellow with straight black hair and weird Celtic conceit of himself." "His art was all tubes and valves and spirals and strange colours, ultra-modern, yet with a certain power, even a certain purity of form and tone: only Mellors thought it cruel and repellent."

Lawrence's letter did not influence Ottoline as regards Duncan's pictures: indeed, at that time, she bought several: a most lovely one of a vase of hot-house tulips, which she had given him, I remember particularly as it was painted while I was writing in the studio, and though I was glad that Duncan should get ten or fifteen pounds, I was sorry to see it go.

Lady Ottoline Morrell, born Cavendish-Bentinck, was a half-sister of the sixth Duke of Portland. Though in no way an artist, she was an original character who had managed by strength of will to escape from the conventionality of her up-bringing, without losing her position in Society. Physically she was extremely handsome: tall and lean, with a large head, masses of dark Venetian red hair, which, when I first knew her, she had not rashly begun to dye, glacier blue-green eyes, a long straight nose, a proud mouth and long jutting-out chin made up her lovely, haggard face. Spiritually her best quality was generosity: her worst, meanness and the love of power. The good and evil in her waged frequent warfare. Balanced between them was her strong schoolboy's sense of humour, which was, however, almost always malicious and never, as far as I can remember, at her own expense. If her love of power, or longing for love (often the same thing in her) were not aroused, her generosity would have it all its own way. Those whom she merely *liked* were indebted to her for a hundred acts of kindness, sympathy and help. When, however, her passions became more deeply involved, it was another matter. Love can be tigerish and those whom Ottoline loved were lucky if, sooner or later, a tiger's claws did not rend them in pieces.

I was only *liked* and no one could have been kinder to me than Ottoline, while the liking lasted. In the end I offended her by refusing to join with her in a malicious discussion of Vanessa's character, after which I received no more invitations. But there was no stormy scene. Only once did I realise that I might be torn limb from limb, but I was sufficiently adroit to escape her wrath by a lie. It occurred very early in our acquaintance. I had made an engagement to spend the evening with a girl, but was pressed by Ottoline to fill a last-minute place in her dinner party. When I explained to my female friend that I had accepted, I was told that I was thoroughly selfish. I was much agitated by her reproaches: what I had thought to be of no consequence, turned out to be unforgivable behaviour. So I rang up Ottoline and bluntly told her husband, Philip Morrell, that I was very sorry but that I could not come to dinner after all. He seemed a good deal surprised.

An hour later Frankie came unexpectedly to Pond Place with the terrible news that his mother was dying after a stroke. He adored her and was completely shattered. After telling me, he rushed back to her bedside. He had scarcely gone when a telegram arrived:

Do not quite understand your message, Ottoline Morrell.

I saw I had made a really dreadful mess and sent a note by special messenger in which I said that the mother of a friend of mine was dying and that after being with him I had felt that I could not bear to come to dine and dance. The rest of my evening was equally discreditable. When I went to keep my original engagement, the girl had found another companion for the evening, so I went to a cinema where I got into conversation with a Czech woman. I parted from her outside it after arranging to meet her the following Saturday and went home angry at the way in which I had spoilt my evening. To my surprise, I discovered next day that Ottoline had been greatly touched by my letter. She had learned that her old friend Mrs Birrell was dying and my refusal to come to dinner was interpreted as a sign of uncommon sensibility. My woman friend was delighted when she heard that I had played Lady Ottoline false because of her reproaches. Thus by a series of lies, I had gained good opinions all round. The odd thing was that it was not entirely hypocrisy and lies, for, after Frankie's visit, I had not felt at all inclined for Ottoline's dinner party. When Saturday came I did not keep my assignation with the Czech. No telegram could come, for she did not know my address, and I felt no qualms at playing her false.

A week later I went again to a dinner at the Morrells'. I had never seen Ottoline looking more beautiful. She was for some reason in wildly high spirits and was particularly charming to me. Augustus John, Josiah Wedgwood and Gerald Shove were there. Jelly D'Aranyi and her sisters played, and after the music Ottoline insisted that we should all dress up and act—I don't know what. She carried me off to her room; there was a flurry of seizing and sorting out the clothes we were to put on and a momentary sensation of great intimacy with Ottoline as she made up my face with greasepaint and powder and gurgled with delight at the results.

Then there came cries for help from some young soldier who needed assistance in putting on the robes he had been lent.

But the war was always there and we were awakening to its growing horror. It was to Ottoline that I gave the following account of a young soldier's experiences. She was so struck by it that she gave it to Bertrand Russell, as a result of which it was published some months later in *The Labour Leader*.

One day when I was in the Zoological Library, a student came in whom I had last seen the previous July when he was going off into camp with the London Scottish. He was a reticent young man, conventional in outlook and upbringing but I had liked him. To my surprise he was not in uniform and I was still more surprised when he told me that he was being discharged from the army as the result of a breakdown. The term "shell-shock" had not become current at that time. I asked him to give me an account of his experiences and he told me his story. Directly he had gone I wrote down what he had said, as nearly as possible in his own words. A year later, it would have sounded intolerably familiar—and today it reads like the epitome of any realistic novel about the 1914–1918 war. But in February 1915 it came as a shock. I will quote only the concluding sentences.

The earth of La Bassée is full of bits of dead bodies. Wherever you scratch, you find a hand or an arm. At one place there was a communication trench which led to the German trenches, only it had been stopped up with clay and stuff. We used to listen there every night, but they never came along it. One can stand the lice and the stench and standing on a dead body all the time, but one can't get used to seeing one's friends killed: their brains running over their faces and living beside their bodies while they rot. And one can't stand the shells coming nearer and nearer ... London seems so quiet.

I believe that I was one of those dining with the Morrells when Vanessa was put beside Mr Asquith, then Prime Minister and a man with many burdens, including the conduct of the war. Vanessa very rarely read a newspaper in those days, though she was always interested in picture papers, such as *The Daily Mirror*, which might suggest subjects for pictures. She had missed Mr Asquith's name, but his face was almost intolerably familiar to her: it was indeed to be seen, enormously enlarged, upon almost every hoarding, exhorting the British People to Save for Victory. Yet she could not place him. Giving him the smile of an innocent but daring child, she risked the remark:
"Are you interested in politics?"
Vanessa's best remarks were like that, experimental and haphazard shots in the dark. When she coined an epigram it was often because she had forgotten a cliché.
"In that house you meet a dark horse in every cupboard," she once exclaimed with some indignation. And of Maynard: "It runs off his back like duck's water." But of all her sayings the most withering was: "Ah, that will be canker to his worm."
Maynard went to the Treasury in January 1915 and not long afterwards thought it better to exchange the rooms he had taken

in Great Ormond Street, where the landlord was a drawback, for a house of his own in Gower Street. He let some of the rooms to Gerald Shove, who had just married the Stephens' cousin, Fredegond Maitland, and the attics to Middleton Murry and Katherine Mansfield. He engaged a housekeeper, a formidably ugly and genteel lady, whose father had been a Bank Manager. Her name was Miss Clapham, Clappers behind her back. With her assistance, Maynard gave a series of gay parties. One of them was attended by Clive, Vanessa and Lytton, the four Olivier sisters, Gerald and Fredegond Shove, Duncan, Frankie, James Strachey and Pauley Montagu, who had enlisted but was on leave. Pauley brought his gittern on which he accompanied himself as he played all our favourite ballads and Elizabethan songs. The younger members of the party sat around on the floor and Daphne and Noel may have joined in the singing. But I became aware of a faint restiveness among the older generation, who preferred conversations to communal heartiness and who did not, I think, recognise that Pauley was a remarkable artist. Suddenly, however, there was an interruption—a loud knock on the door. Duncan was nearest and opened it and there stood Clappers, erect in her best black dress, bedizened with jet bugles.

"Would you kindly give this to Mr Keynes?" she said, handing him a tiny slip of paper, and she shut the door upon herself.

Duncan handed it to Maynard who read it aloud.

"Mr Keynes, for God's sake give me a glass of brandy." Applause greeted it but Maynard was worried. Was she ill? He poured it out and Clive insisted on a generous measure. The door was opened, Clappers received it and we heard no more of her. Nor did she ever afterwards transgress the strict decorum which governed the relations between Victorian servants and their employers. Nevertheless we discovered that it was no illness, or fainting fit. Clappers, who was a Dickensian character, needed her glass of spirits, but that evening Maynard had brought all the bottles upstairs to the drawing-room and our merrymaking was more than her flesh and blood could stand.

41

Later in the evening, Pauley, who had spent the previous year as the zoologist attached to an anthropological expedition in New Caledonia, took off most of his clothes and danced some native war dances. Once more I got the impression that the older generation would have preferred intellectual and witty conversation. Duncan, however, was fascinated by both songs and native dances.

I was still at this time seeing a good deal of the Oliviers, who were rather puzzled that the ugly duckling they had known all their lives was being taken by so many people for a cygnet. They even seemed to think at moments that there must be something in the idea. We continued to read plays every week, though we had lost Justin Brooke, as well as Hugh Popham.

I do not know exactly how my changed relationship with the outside world, which continued to puzzle my old friends, had come about. So far as I knew and they could see, I was still the same individual as the student who had lived for four years off the Fulham Road exciting no particular interest in the people he met. But suddenly the attitude of most people changed to me. Men liked me and became confidential intimates after meeting me twice; women fell in love, or were charmed, at the first meeting. The odd thing is that this was so generally felt. In the six months that I was attractive, I made not a single enemy. Nobody had the originality to declare that I was an ill-conditioned puppy without sense, manners or morals.

One friendship I made then was with a very thin, tall fair girl whom I met at a party given by Clive and Vanessa. At our first meeting she said something, and catching my expression, asked me whether I agreed with her. I replied that I thought what she had said showed ignorance. She gave me an enchanting smile and a long look from tired blue eyes and talked to me for the rest of the evening. There followed a curious indeterminate relationship, half friendship, half love-affair. It was pursued on her side as much as on mine and marked by a stream of letters and telegrams, many of which, sent to the wrong addresses, reached me too late.

The influence of Swinburne's poetry and the spirit of the

42

nineties was strong in her and in one of her letters she wrote:

My nerves are on edge. . . . If I could go and live for a little while among real people who are doing real things and living real lives. However you know and I know that I shall go on existing among the accessories of life . . . so that's that. Meanwhile I shall continue to cry "Hurrah for sport!" (a sign I saw once in a shop where there were some toy cricket bats).

I am now going to bed. I wish I were going to a tiny gold room all gold, even the light, marvellously warm, and a glass table covered with the rarest things of the world and the reddest lips to kiss me with all the heat of summer in them till I should sink back among amber cushions and hear the hum of bees and the waving of palm trees and then tighter and tighter would I be held, and the height of mountains, the depths of green valleys, the dizzy whirl of cascades of falling water, would all be mine; tiny mosses and grasses would kiss my feet, the perfume of violets should hang over my hair and my body washed with golden wine, would tingle with pine needles. After it would hurt, hurt from the sharpest of white teeth. That I should not mind. I adore brutality. Goodnight. I won't forget about going to the country.

If our friendship did not develop into a love-affair, it appeared to be only because her social engagements left no time for one. When we met she was almost always an hour late for some other engagement—so most of my love-making was done while I was taking her in a taxi to meet some other man whom she had kept waiting. I found out afterwards, however, that on her first visit to Pond Place, the squalor of my room had distressed her so much that she could not bear to come there again.

One evening I dropped in at the Café Royal and found Anna Wickham, the poet,* talking to an artist's model called Lillian Shelley and John Flanaghan, a painter who had recently enlisted. I joined them and soon afterwards Betty May, whom I had frequently seen and heard singing love songs at The Crabtree night club, came in and sat down beside me. She was a very small creature with some of the qualities of a passionate, wilful child. Her face was like a tom-cat's: a broad, straight, powerful little nose, a large mouth with beautiful, even white teeth, broad cheek-bones, wild hazel-green eyes set wide apart.

* See *The Golden Echo*, pp. 235–237

Her hands and feet were very small. In every look and gesture she revealed the toughness and independence that one sees in the women who work in circuses and travelling shows.

Betty had married some months before, but her husband was in the army and had left her a neatly furnished little semi-detached house in a suburb. She had not, she told me, been near it for a fortnight—but she would have to go that evening, before the trains stopped running, as she had nowhere else to sleep. I was alone at Pond Place, so I offered to put her up and she agreed to come back with me. When we were in the taxi, she told me that she could not come until she had been to a chemist's. Would I go in, please, and buy her some cocaine? The sale of narcotics had not, at that time, been made illegal, but it was already frowned on, and the assistant at Heppell's looked at me with considerable surprise and refused to serve me. After two more refusals, I began to feel uncomfortable, but Betty was adamant. Finally I was successful and was sold a small packet of white powder. Betty took a sniff, put it away carefully and was very loving until we reached Pond Place. I had assumed that we should sleep together and, as my single bed was very narrow, began to make a bed up with two mattresses on the floor. Suddenly, to my astonishment, Betty struck an attitude of outraged virtue and began a melodramatic scene.

"In that case there's a bed upstairs," I said and led her up to the spare room. Five minutes later my door opened and Betty marched in. "I can't sleep in that cold room. It's freezing up there."

"Light the gas-fire then; here's a box of matches."

Betty struck the book I had been reading to soothe my ruffled feelings out of my hand. "I shall stay here as long as I like. You can go to that horrible cold room," she announced.

As I did not lose my temper, she struck me a hard blow on the cheek and, when I picked her up in order to dump her outside on the stairs, she dug her nails into my arm. But suddenly the pretence of anger turned to love and I was almost suffocated with fierce kisses. Then she insisted on my taking some cocaine. I took a pinch, sniffed the powder and felt my nostrils

44

turn ice-cold as the little crystals evaporated. My heart began to beat faster and faster with a terrifying acceleration. I lay flat on my back and listened. In a few seconds my heart-beats became almost indistinguishable, like the ripple of machine-gun fire. I was frightened but Betty was terrified.

"What an idiotic way of killing myself by mistake," I thought, and shut my eyes waiting for unconsciousness and death, and feeling very much alone. But at last the beats of my heart became separately identifiable: it was slowing down. A few minutes later the frantic thumping had died away and my pulse was almost normal.

"Promise me never, never to take cocaine again," cried Betty. Even at that moment the situation struck me as extremely comic. I gave the promise and have never had the least inclination to break it.

Next morning I woke early. The light from the uncurtained window filled the room with a radiance which illuminated the innocent and fragile beauty of the tough little dope-fiend who was my bedfellow. As she lay unconscious she seemed like a butterfly spreading its wings in the sun. Her face had the innocence, the tenderness, the freshness of a child's. I raised myself on my elbow and watched her for fully half an hour, wondering whether I could stop her from destroying herself. But I did not feel hopeful. Then she stirred, her eyelids fluttered, she looked about her and turned to kiss me.

For several months afterwards I was very much in love with Betty, but I soon realised that I could have no influence on her. Often the realisation that she was deliberately poisoning herself was so painful to me that I avoided looking for her in her haunts. I knew that she could only be cured by someone with a will stronger than her own and the authority to use force to keep her from the drug. I knew also that she was dangerous; if I bound myself to her she would ruin me, and I never seriously thought of doing so. And yet my vision of her that first morning, as she lay asleep, was not a piece of sentimentality, but a true one. She might drink and dope and behave with tigerish ferocity, but there was no vice in her and none of

45

what are called the vices had touched the innocence of her character. She was spontaneous and changeable, pursuing pleasure wherever she found it and caring nothing for money so long as she had a few shillings in her purse. And since she was without calculation, she was without corruption.

When my father Edward was at 19 Pond Place, Duncan suffered from my amours as I used to take my light o' loves to his studio with the promise that we should be gone by one a.m. In Betty's case this was not all—for failing to find me one evening at Pond Place, she called on Duncan and insisted on his buying some cocaine for her—which I had refused to do after the first experience. Duncan had an even more difficult time than I in obtaining it. Fortunately, not long afterwards, the sale of narcotics was made illegal. Betty amused Duncan and their liking was mutual. One day, when I came into the studio unexpectedly Betty came running out from behind a screen where she had hidden herself.

She had a great sense of humour as well as extraordinary vitality, but at that period in her life she was a terrific egotist and lived in a dream world in which she was an important figure. I might have soon fallen out of love with her if I had seen her all day long, or every day, but I never did. She would spend an evening with me and then disappear for a week or two, only to greet me with delight when we met again. Had she been more reliable, Duncan might have painted her and at that time she had a most striking savage beauty. The only portraits I have seen which are at all like her are the lovely bust and the head by Sir Jacob Epstein. Betty often sat to him and he and his wife were very good to her.

Duncan's studio was on the top floor of 22 Fitzroy Street, with windows looking out over the street. It was a large, oblong room, with a big skylight on the East, and incredibly dirty. Duncan had a most peculiar little folding bed which, when unoccupied, rose vertically in the air and concealed itself inside a piece of furniture not much larger than a very wide grandfather clock. He pulled it down and jumped into it when he was ready for bed but if he got out inadvertently in the

46

BETTY MAY.   A HEAD BY SIR JACOB EPSTEIN

LYTTON STRACHEY EXPLAINING GIBBON
TO CARRINGTON

middle of the night, it flew up with a whang. Some years later he acquired a bath, operating on the same principle, which was disguised, when not in use, as a deal cupboard.

An old charwoman came to clean out the studio, but she did practically nothing. Every week, however, she would steal Duncan's gold cuff-links, engraved with the Grant crest of a mailed arm brandishing a claymore. Every Friday, Duncan used to say to her: "I shall want my cuff-links for the week-end. Will you please find them." The charwoman was paid on Fridays and redeemed the cuff-links from the pawnbroker so she could always "find" them on Saturday morning. This went on until she fell ill and could not come to work any more, after which the cuff-links were lost for ever.

During the winter Duncan had been occasionally bitten and, as the spring brought warmer weather, a plague of bugs appeared. In the evenings the revolting insects would begin to crawl up the walls. Walking round the room one evening, I killed thirty-six. Soon it became impossible to stay in the studio. I consulted Professor Maxwell Lefroy, the greatest of British entomologists, who was on the staff of the Imperial College of Science. He advised washing the floors and furniture with a preparation of petroleum and soap and gassing the room with carbon tetrachloride which he had used against the death-watch beetles in the roof of Westminster Hall. As Duncan was going down to stay with the St John Hutchinsons for a fortnight, in their farmhouse at West Wittering, we determined to gas the bugs in his absence. He first packed his bag and put it with his paintbox and easel on the landing outside, then we pasted up the window joints, poured carbon tetrachloride into saucers spread about the floor, locked the door and pasted up the cracks all round it, not forgetting the key-hole.

"I hope the people downstairs will be all right," said Duncan as we left. In the room below the studio there lived an enormously large Jewish family. The father made his living by writing phylacteries and a small son of seven practised the violin incessantly.

Eleanors was a small farmhouse which stood about fifty

yards from the shore of Chichester Harbour and was perhaps a mile from the village of West Wittering, then practically unspoiled. Close to the house was a large, disused, corrugated-iron life-boat house with immense double doors and rails running down the middle of the floor and out over the mud-flat in front. It belonged to Professor Tonks, of the Slade School of Art, who was a friend of Jack and Mary Hutchinson. She is a cousin of the Stracheys, being a grand-daughter of Sir John Strachey, who was an uncle of Lytton's. Mary was very fair, with a beautiful forehead and eyes and a small mouth. She was obviously intelligent, but rather repressed: a young married woman who was only just beginning to order her own world. Tonks was away in Italy and Mary, rather unscrupulously, gave Duncan the key of the boat-house and allowed him to sleep and work in it, but warned him that he must be very careful not to disturb Tonks's possessions, as he was fussy and easily upset.

Left to himself Duncan would have followed her injunctions, but he invited me down to stay with him and I began to look around while Duncan was painting. Presently I unearthed a case of claret from Hedges and Butler which had been opened, but not unpacked. I soon persuaded Duncan that it would be the easiest thing in the world to replace the bottles that we borrowed and, that evening, we drank a Chateau-bottled wine of admirable vintage. Before Duncan left, the case was empty. Later he discovered that the claret in question was no longer on Hedges and Butler's list, and, though he replaced it, the vintage was not the same. There was nothing for it but to confess to the larceny which I had instigated. Duncan scarcely knew Tonks and it was Mary who got into trouble. I went down for several week-ends to Eleanors which Mary, shortly afterwards, let to Clive and Vanessa. In the meantime, Duncan came up and went to his studio. The street door was wide open and a coffin was being carried out to a waiting hearse. Duncan went up and unsealed his studio. The treatment prescribed by Lefroy had been effective. There were no more bugs that summer and the writer of phylacteries and his entire family had disappeared. Duncan thought it wiser to make no enquiries from his landlord as to their fate. I have always maintained that if they had all been found gassed, there would certainly have been an inquest and we should have heard of it. But Duncan's story of the coffin and the undoubted disappearance of the downstairs family made me hesitate to recommend Lefroy's method of gassing bugs in future.

I went down to Eleanors almost every week-end after Clive and Vanessa took it and, while I was there, I started painting myself, and finished a large canvas of Chichester Harbour with the tide out and the mudflats painted in streaks of green and burnt sienna. A few weeks later, Roger Fry came down and he found my picture.

"Who painted it?" he cried. "It's exactly like a Monet." And he looked at me with interest dawning, for the first time, in his eyes. Roger was right. My picture was extraordinarily like a Monet—though whether I should have continued to paint like Monet had I gone on, nobody can tell. I have always flattered myself that I should have done so, for Monet is a painter whose work I very much admire. A year or two later, I cut up my masterpiece for canvas shreds with which to nail up the fruit trees in the walled garden at Charleston. Vanessa invited a number of friends to stay at Eleanors. Maynard was there often, Lytton came, also Ka Cox, Margery Olivier, and Marjorie Strachey. There was an atmosphere of great gaiety. Duncan and Vanessa painted charming pictures on the panels of several of the doors as a surprise for Jack and Mary on their return. When we met for meals, there was a lot of high-spirited, rather bawdy conversation at which, in those days, Vanessa used to excel. It amused her greatly to shock, or at least to astonish, such young women as Ka Cox, or Margery Olivier. One evening Clive asked each of us what we thought was our most beautiful feature. The ladies were coy but made some truthful reply. When it came to Duncan's turn, he pretended great embarrassment and refused to answer.

"It's impossible for me to answer that question, Clive, with ladies present."

Duncan was very often in wild spirits. Maynard, Lytton and Clive complained to Vanessa that the water at Eleanors tasted of earth and the butter of turnips and were ready to settle down after breakfast to reading their books, but Duncan rushed into the field outside and made them all laugh by dancing round a cow which became sufficiently excited to prance and curvet in response. He called the others "the old gentlemen" making a partial exception for Maynard, and when they went for walks along the beach of Chichester estuary, which they called the lagoon and which reminded them of Venice, he suddenly pretended to be a bull and rushed at Lytton, butting him a few steps into the sea so that his big sombrero hat fell off. Then, to Lytton's indignation, Duncan pretended to make water into it. But in face of high spirits of that kind, indignation is impossible and Duncan's escapades raised the temperature and restored the circulation of the whole party. The "old gentlemen" groaned and made mock protests and grumbled that life was unbearable with such lunatics around, but the books were often laid aside and animated conversation took their place.

Talking to Vanessa about people's personal appearance, Duncan said that he disliked looking at himself in the glass. Vanessa replied that she on the contrary liked looking at herself.

"That *is* clever of you," said Duncan admiringly, thinking apparently that he had paid her a compliment. He was surprised to find the remark greeted with laughter.

It must have been a warm spring, for Duncan and I went for a short bathe in February and for a long swim in May when he got rather into difficulties as we struggled back against a swift tide off West Wittering point. I became rather worried that I might not be able to save him from drowning but luckily discovered that though we were about two hundred yards from land we were only just out of our depths. This news encouraged Duncan to continue swimming and five minutes later we were able to wade the rest of the way ashore.

In the middle of April, Frankie and I accepted an invitation to visit Lawrence and Frieda and spend a night in the cottage which the Meynells had lent them at Greatham in Sussex. We took a train packed with young soldiers. Their complexions, burned by sun and wind, were clear bright red; their uniforms new and they themselves as soft and amiable as young foxhounds, with the same good-tempered doggish interest in each other's movements. If one lifted his pack from the rack, or searched his tunic pocket for a packet of Woodbines, it caused a stir in the whole carriage. Frankie and I got out at Steyning, and walked up the Downs to Chanctonbury Ring, then down to the Washington Inn and, from there, by Storrington to Greatham which we reached in plenty of time for supper. Frankie, as usual on our walks, did not stop talking and had no idea of the direction in which we were going. I, alone, found the way, looked at the trees, the short turf, the stray flints, the view over the weald, and listened to the larks singing and Frankie talking as effortlessly as the birds sang. Once or twice I may have broken in to defend my views on literature. At that time Frankie dismissed all contemporary writers with contempt and had not embarked on either French or Russian literature. He thought I was uneducated because I had not read Gibbon and the names of Lord Acton and Goldwin Smith meant nothing to me. I thought him hidebound, but our bickerings were always blown away in gales of laughter.

After supper, Lawrence and Frieda took us round to pay our respects to the Meynells and Saleebies. They seemed as remote to me as so many dark-eyed, dark-skinned South Sea Islanders. Some aura, their mother's poetry, or their Catholicism, separated them from the world in which I lived. When we left the big room, with its Italian bric-à-brac and Morris patterns and the glowing hearth with the young people grouped about the Poetess and the Patriarch, we went to bed early for we were very tired.

We had been invited to breakfast by the Meynells. The Patriarch was rustling the pages of *The Observer*; the room was filled with dark madonna-like girls and women; the Poetess was stretched upon a couch, and there was the question, to which I instinctively felt that a painful answer was expected:

"Where is Francis?" No one could say, but, just before we had finished our eggs and bacon, a tall handsome young man with a rapt expression came eagerly into the room. It was Francis Meynell who had run three miles across the marsh to mass with the Holy Fathers (or maybe Brothers) at Amberley. With what benign and holy joy did his parents look upon him then! And how like to a Blake engraving was the whole family at that moment!

Lawrence had disappeared to work after breakfast and Frankie and I were joined by Bertie Farjeon, his wife Joan, and his sister Eleanor and Margaret Radford and we all sat happily gossiping and roasting in the sun. It was only the 17th of April but it was as hot as midsummer. We were happy and little suspected that trouble might be brewing as we first talked, and then played, with a gnome-like Saleeby child. Our high spirits lasted all day. After the Farjeons and Margaret had departed for London Frankie talked, and I talked and I think Frieda laughed a lot at supper and looked as though she would have kissed us for being so noisy. But slowly I became aware that Lawrence was silent and that something dreadful was going on inside him. He was in the throes of some dark religious crisis and seemed to shrink in size with the effort of summoning up all his powers, all his spiritual strength. The muscles knotted and he became smaller—but he said nothing. Frieda, however, had observed what was going on. I said we were tired and that I had a long day's walk in front of me. Then Frankie and I took our candles and retired to our little rooms.

I was, actually, rather tired but I was kept awake by angry and incessant whispering in the next room which sounded most sinister. At last, however, Lawrence stopped and I soon dropped off. Suddenly, in the middle of the night, I was woken by a series of bangs and tumbles and strangulated sounds. I sat up and realised that someone was blundering about outside the door of my room. I lit a candle and investigated. Frankie was standing, swathed in a pair of thick flannel pyjamas, in the passage, dumb and obviously in great distress. He pointed to his mouth and in the light of the candle I saw it was open and choked with a large object. His tongue had swollen to an enormous size. I shoved the handle of my tooth-brush into his mouth and he winced and gave nasal moans. Then Frieda, followed by Lawrence, came in and stared at us in astonishment. I explained matters and discussed doctors, poultices and fomentations with Frieda. There was a quiet, triumphant certainty in Lawrence's manner. He had prayed for deliverance to his Dark Gods and they had sent this mysterious sign, blasting his enemy in what had hitherto seemed his strongest organ. For a little while, Frieda and I tortured Frankie, one of us holding the candle, while the other tried to insert teaspoonfuls of almost boiling water into his mouth. Finally we pushed him off to bed and he was glad to escape from us. I had discovered by that time that his temperature was normal and went off to sleep encouraged to hope that he would last till next day, when I could take him to a doctor.

Morning came at last and, to the astonishment of us all, Frankie's tongue had resumed its normal size and functions. It was neither larger nor smaller than usual. Frieda and I con-tented ourselves with giving him a big dose of salts.

On the way to the station Frankie was more silent than usual. He went to London and I to Eleanors. After our visit Lawrence wrote to Ottoline:

We had David Garnett and Francis Birrell here for the week-end. When Birrell comes, tired and bit lost and wandering—I love him. But, my God, to hear him talk sends me mad. To hear these young people talk really fills me with black fury: they talk endlessly, but endlessly—and never, never a good thing said. They are cased each in a hard little shell of his own and out of this they talk words. There is never, for one second, any outgoing of feeling and no reverence, not a crumb or grain of rever-ence. I cannot stand it. I will not have people like this—I had rather be alone. They made me dream of a beetle that bites a scorpion. But I killed it—a very large beetle. I scotched it and it ran off—but I came on it again, and killed it. It is this horror of little swarming selves I can't stand.

On the same day, the 19th of April, 1915, Lawrence wrote to me:

Never bring Birrell to see me any more. There is something nasty about him like black beetles. He is horrible and unclean. I feel I should go mad when I think of your set, Duncan Grant and Keynes and Birrell. It makes me dream of beetles. In Cambridge I had a similar dream. I had felt it slightly before in the Stracheys.* But it came full upon me in Keynes and in Duncan Grant. And yesterday I knew it again in Birrell—you must leave these friends, these beetles. Birrell and Duncan Grant are done for forever. Keynes I am not sure—when I saw Keynes that morning in Cambridge it was one of the crises of my life. It sent me mad with misery and hostility and rage. The Oliviers and such girls are wrong. I could sit and howl in a corner like a child. I feel so bad about it all.

Enclosed was a letter from Frieda:

You always admire other people too much, you are really more than Birrell and the others. I *know*, but you daren't trust yourself, I think that Anna whom you loved, but there was something hopeless in it from the beginning, that has left such a lot of unbelief in you. But you do really want so much and much will come if you will only let it. Anyhow you are my dear friend. Frieda.

In a postscript after Frieda's letter, Lawrence had added:

You have always known the wrong people. Harolds and Olivier girls. Love. D. H. Lawrence.

Lawrence's letter made me angry. He seemed to me to be mad and determined to interfere in my life. I therefore decided not to see him again. It was a great loss, for I loved both Lawrence and Frieda—especially Frieda—and I took the greatest interest in his work. Already it had begun to seem to me that he had taken a wrong turning, for how could the author of *The White Peacock* and *Sons and Lovers* write such turgid nonsense as *The Lion and the Crown* in Murry's *The Signature*? At Edward's request I had been responsible, eighteen months before, for choosing the selection published in *Love Poems and Others*, Lawrence's first volume of poems. I knew that, at his best, Lawrence was a very fine and very original poet. *Snapdragon*, which was not among those from which I could choose in 1913, was, I was certain, a very great poem and *Red Moonrise*, which I thought the best of those in *Love*

---

* It would be interesting to know which members of the family had produced this quasi-coleopterous impression. Oliver was still in India and Lawrence had not met Lytton: see p. 96. It must have been one of the Miss Stracheys and James.

Poems and Others, an extraordinarily original and exciting one. Lawrence had really forced me to break with him because of his dislike, and perhaps jealousy, of my friends. He hated their respect for reason and contempt for intuition and instinct.* But angry as I was, I was deeply unhappy that Lawrence should have forced me to break with him. Frieda's letter made me love her more than ever. In retrospect the most astonishing thing was Lawrence's dislike of Frankie. Everyone else who ever knew him, of whatever age or sex, nationality or class, was charmed and delighted by him. The quality which made his friends love him was, above all, his innocence. Frankie had a sparkling though not a profound intelligence, an immense sense of humour, a quick wit and a ready tongue. He developed greatly and became a widely read man with a remarkable knowledge of European history, French and English literature and drama and a great gift for the exposition of ideas. But his innocence remained unaltered and showed itself constantly in his words and actions. It was the innocence of Mr Pickwick which revealed itself as an incapacity for selfish calculation. An *arrière pensée* was beyond him. He was constantly saying slightly malicious things and he could wound people without being aware of it—usually by being unaware of *them*—but he was as incapable of wishing to hurt or to wound, as he was of wishing to take advantage of anybody on earth.

Sometimes Frankie's stream of talk could become exhausting, his habit of exaggeration could become tiresome, his tendency to see everything in black or white could be exasperating, but in spite of these defects he was never a bore. How did he escape from the besetting vice of the brilliant talker? By his sympathy, his spontaneity, the warmth of his affections, his goodness, his sincerity. He had also the wonderful gift of increasing the vitality of others, of diffusing a rosy sense of well-being, of imparting a slight tipsiness in which all sorts of undertakings seemed less difficult while he was talking about them.

Under his gaiety and enthusiasm was a streak of stoicism.

* See J. M. Keynes, *My Early Beliefs* (Hart-Davis 1949).

55

He would declare, with the broadest of grins, that he was as careworn as Hamlet, or as jealous as Othello, but he never pitied himself and he bore physical pain with unconscious fortitude. Sometimes it seemed to me that in spite of his spate of psychological explanations which came with his later interest in Freud and Proust and Pirandello, he was really a Victorian, a creature of simpler outlook than most of his generation. I once told him so and he was naturally infuriated but half an hour later my accusation was forgotten and forgiven, for he had no vanity.

III

IT was obvious that Maynard Keynes's prediction of a short war brought to an end by economic causes was not going to be realised and that the war was likely to last until the supply of cannon-fodder ran out—which might not occur for several years. I realised, also, that there would be no more scientific research for me while the war lasted, if ever, and I was not altogether sorry. Research had so far proved to be the exploration of blind alleys carved into the rock of fact, which led nowhere. I had offended Dobell, the only first-class mind doing research with whom I had come in contact. Moreover he was by temperament a conservative, more concerned to debunk the generalisations of others than to put forward sweeping theories of his own. If I had gone to work under Bateson I might have gone on to achieve more and have known my life was being well-spent in pushing our knowledge of genetics a stage further, or have come across one of the epoch-making discoveries that stares everyone in the face unseen until someone can be bothered to notice it. Such for example was the discovery of penicillin.

But, from the practical point of view, it was necessary for me to know what I was going to do. Frankie's position was also difficult. Unlike me he was physically unsuitable for the army: too short and too blind—and he was temperamentally entirely unfitted for it. Both he and his father were too honourable and too far-sighted to try to obtain a sheltered position for him in one of the Government Departments. After discussions with Augustine and with Edward, Frankie decided to join the Friends War Victims Relief Mission and asked me to join it with him. I discussed the matter in several letters to my mother Constance, who was settled permanently at The Cearne, and, as late as June, listed the possibilities open to me as: joining the Quakers; getting a job as a bacteriologist;

joining the Officers' Training Corps; getting a job in a factory. I added that I preferred joining the Officers' Training Corps to the other possible courses of action. Though I did not say so, my preference was because it was the expected thing for a young man to do and because it might lead to adventures and distinction. Thus I was, in June 1915, very far from having a conscientious objection to military service. However, in the event, I agreed to join the Friends War Victims Relief Mission with Frankie, if they would accept us, and I did so owing to the combined persuasions of Frankie, Edward and Constance.

The leader of the Friends War Victims Relief Mission was Edmund Harvey, a Liberal M.P. who fully realised the usefulness of having a Cabinet Minister's son as a member of the Mission and thus acquiring a powerful friend in case of need. Moreover it would impress the French Authorities on whose good will the whole work of the Mission depended. Such considerations were, however, worldly and it was necessary for them to be concealed. Frankie and I, therefore, were interviewed by a number of leading Friends who did not seem to like us, but were not prepared to veto our joining. The only one of them who was at all favourable to us was Miss Ruth Fry, Roger's youngest sister. We were then accepted, provided with uniforms and a lot of kit we never used and sent out to France.

The day before our departure Edward invited me to have lunch with him at a Soho restaurant. We had a *carafe* of wine but there was a slight feeling of constraint about the meal. Towards its end Edward cleared his throat with what seemed a shade of embarrassment and said: "Dear Boy, you are going abroad alone, for the first time. . . ."* He paused and cocked a solemn eye at me and the thought flashed through my mind that he was going to touch on the moral dangers to which I might be exposed. It was incredible . . . but his manner was decidedly odd. The pause lengthened interminably while he searched through several of his pockets without success. I had time to wonder what he was trying to find. Could it conceiv-

* Untrue. I had been alone twice to Germany and once to Russia.

ably be some specific . . . against venereal disease? It would be very sweet of him—but I had studied the spirochaetes and knew their weak points and far more about them than he did. At length he discovered what he was looking for.

". . . You will be all alone . . . the Quakers probably won't have one. . . . I think you may find this useful in France," and his big, exquisitely shaped hand, with its tapered fingers, opened. On his palm was lying a pocket corkscrew.

I took with me also a little four-volume edition of Racine which Lytton gave me before my departure, a charcoal sketch of Betty May, and a writing case given me by Vanessa, with a joking inscription which I kept hidden at the bottom of my locked kit-bag. This was a sensible precaution as the older Quakers lacked an ordinary schoolboy sense of honour and, as we were to discover, employed spies to report on each other's morals—i.e. private affairs.

One of the unlucky features of the Quaker uniform was a large star on the cap, and embroidered on the sleeve, in the German colours of black, white and red. This had been allotted to the Friends by Prince Bismarck during the Franco-Prussian War, when they had worked on the German side. The uniform itself was grey—far nearer to the German grey-green, than to British khaki, or to French horizon blue. Wearing odd uniforms, decorated with a German Star, behind the French lines, often led to awkward questions being asked. Some of us were lucky enough to get hold of *Service de Santé* brassards, for we were, in the eyes of the French, technically a part of that branch of their army. I obtained such a brassard and sewed it round the arm of my British Warm, over the star. I also discarded the peaked cap and wore a French forage cap of horizon blue. During the greater part of the summer, while actually at work, I wore nothing but cotton trunks and a blue boiler-suit, belted round the waist. Thus attired I never excited comment among French troops, or military police.

Our route from Paris lay along the Marne. We went by train to Vitry-le-François where, to our astonishment, Frankie and I were given a pi-jaw by a young Scottish Quaker of our own age, about the temptations to which we should find ourselves exposed among the immoral French. I do not wish to be unfair, but I formed the opinion that he had no personal experience of what he was talking about.

From Vitry we were taken on by car, passing through several ruined villages on our way to Sermaize. The battle of the Marne had been fought ten months before and time had already changed the aspect of the battle-field. Weeds had grown up and were in flower beside the blocks of masonry split by flames which had turned the grey limestone pink. The road along which we drove had been the line on which the exhausted French Armies halted on their retreat from the Belgian frontier and where the German armies had run into them. Graves were thick, not only round every village, but all along the road, on the verges and under the shelter of the trees which bordered it. Thousands, possibly tens of thousands had died there. The battle had been fought at close quarters and French and German graves were intermingled, each man being buried where he fell, with his identity disc and sometimes his medals tacked to the wooden cross above him, which, if he were French, was bedizened with a shred of tricolor and an imitation cypress wreath. The graves ran in a ribband for kilometre after kilometre across the breadth of Eastern France. The ones we were passing were those of the soldiers who died in the very hard fighting of the French Fourth Army, under Langle de Cary, which held firm against a tremendous onslaught by the Saxons under Haussen. The long line of graves marked the turning point of the whole war and the battle which saved three-quarters of France for a quarter of a century from occupation by the Boches. The Frenchmen in those graves had not died in vain.

No road could have been more peaceful: the luxuriant happiness of early summer lay over the land. Birds flew up among the young poplar groves; the water-meadows were already high with hay, or dotted with sweetly smelling cocks and the soft air along the dykes was scented with meadowsweet and peppermint.

When we reached a village, we saw shattered houses, standing walls pitted with rifle bullets, and women and children who looked up from the ruins without much interest.

Neither Frankie nor I had the slightest idea of what we were really going to find and none of the Quakers could have begun to explain, for almost without exception they had come to France with preconceived ideas. Thanks to the Quaker Mission, we were to have the experience of being adopted into a French village. To understand our relationship with its people the reader should know what it had been in peace and what had befallen it since the previous August. For that reason I break off my narrative here and put in the story of the village.

On the southern fringes of the Argonne forest lay a beautiful village, the name of which was well suited to its aspect of repose. Sommeilles slumbered in peace, amid scenes of beauty which were afforded by its situation. It lay on the eastern shoulder of a low hill.

From the church one looked east to the Forest of Belval, and across the fertile plain to Laimont and to Noyer, whilst south-west the eye could not see much further than the Maison du Val. Over the hill to the north-west was the village of Charmont, on the road to Rheims. To the north one could not see more than a mile, because the wooded country stretches as unbroken forest beyond Givry, Le Chatelier and Ste Menehould to the Grurie wood in the extreme north; woods the mere names of which came to inspire the inhabitants of that district with melancholy and horror.

The houses of the village were of brick and stucco, or of limestone. Many of them were old, but they were not the worse for that, and the people they sheltered were prosperous and happy.

Opposite the church was the town hall, an imposing structure of limestone, that dated from 1836.

It had a Greek portico with slender columns, flanked by stone lions—the pride of many a mayor.

Under the portico was a telephone and a pillar box. Every service of the State was represented, for, besides a noticeboard where the edicts of the Republic were displayed, one side of the building was the schoolhouse. In another wing lived the schoolmaster with his family.

In the centre was a little enclosed garden with marigolds in the border.

There was a village shop where groceries were to be bought, kept by Georges Leglaye, who turned out, when the test came, to be the natural leader of the village. He was a thin, tall man who had been a pilot on the coast of Morocco, but had retired after losing his right arm. He was well read, dispassionate and calm. I never saw him angry or agitated. Under every stress he kept his head, and behaved with a natural dignity which inspired respect. He was the very finest type of Frenchman. Besides the village shop, there was a butcher and a baker, a cobbler and a *sabotier*, and everything usual in a village of a hundred and forty houses. Almost all the inhabitants were farmers, who tilled their own soil. They were industrious and thrifty.

Besides these there were, it is true, a few persons retired from business, who existed comfortably upon their savings. There was Choppet, the miser, who lived at the top of the hill and had an orchard and kept bees. At the other extreme were a few families who did not own the land they cultivated and having to pay rent were poorer than their neighbours.

If anyone was very poor, like the old drunkard Nicolas Grosjean, it was because he was unable to work, but these helpless creatures would never live in misery, for their richer neighbours would send their growing girls to tidy up the house, put a pot of soup on the fire, and a jug of cider on the table.

The routine of work did not absorb the whole time of the inhabitants. On market days and public holidays well-dressed farmers and their wives drove in dogcarts to Revigny or Bar-le-Duc; bought and sold, or listened, somewhat incredulously, to public orations on political events.

There were brilliant weddings and costly funerals, village fêtes and church festivals.

In winter the farmers met several times a month to hunt wild boars. Foxes were shot to protect the poultry. It was fifteen years since the cry of wolf had given anxiety to the shepherds of the district. Roedeer fell to the gun of the fortunate sportsman. Old Onesime Commenil had a buck's head: "Such as one does not see two in a lifetime." After the hunt the party would adjourn to Jules Adnot's farm, or would accept the hospitality of Brémont or De Fontaine; and there, whilst they drank glasses of cider and ate slices of apple-tart, the game was displayed. Men who had not gone that day to the hunt came to listen to the stories of the day's sport, to accept a glass of spirits, to crack walnuts in their horny palms. The greatest talker among them was Monsieur Thomas the postman, not to be confused with his brother the sawyer. He was also the worst shot. Little Michel Meunier, brother-in-law of the said sawyer, would pop in from his roadmending; peer through his steel spectacles at the tusky boars and make pedantic remarks which amused the company.

Such gatherings made life pleasant.

In summer the solitary sportsman found fishing in the lake over the hill and spent quiet evenings tempting carp to take the hook. Everything was fruitful, pleasant, remote. The village slumbered in profound peace.

It was exactly like a thousand villages, save it was rather richer, the women were more industrious, the men more good-tempered and atheistical, the children more intelligent.

In July nineteen hundred and fourteen there came rumours of an impending war. Monsieur Emil Adnot, the schoolmaster, took it very seriously and discussed the situation gravely with M. De Fontaine and Georges Leglaye. M. Thomassin explained the effect the murder of Sarajevo would have on the wheat market at Bar, and Paul Adnot advised his father to sell his wheat early.

Then all the men were called to the army, and Jules Adnot was so short-handed that he wondered if he would get his wheat in at all.

He managed it, however. The women went into the fields and

laughed courageously at the prospect of doing all that work.

Everyone was anxious: train-loads of troops were going north to Ste Menehould. News came of the German advance through Belgium, of the great French defeat in front of Metz, of England joining the war.

Then came the fighting at Longwy, the German advance, the fighting in the Argonne. No doubt wounded came back, no doubt troops went up, no doubt they heard that Ste Menehould was taken, and then the French troops came down the road in retreat.

Some of the younger women decided to fly from the Prussians. Aline Weber insisted on going to a cousin's at Bar-le-Duc, her sister Andrée remained. When the news came that the Germans were at Givry and might be expected the next morning, there was great excitement. Many people packed up a few belongings and drove off, leaving their houses locked up, and hoping they would not be interfered with. Old Lorcey told everyone for the ten thousandth time how he had taken part in a bayonet charge in 1870; how he had been sabred in the head, and shot in the heel. Thomassin said: "Well, we shall see the Germans again." As a boy in 1870 he had been commandeered to drive a forage wagon for the Germans, had slept out in the snow, and had been roughly treated. Yet on the whole the old people, who remembered the Germans, had nothing much against them. They were a well-behaved people and had respected life and property. In many cases they had behaved very humanely, with much consideration for the peasantry. The younger people expected all kinds of horrors; the old were confident that there was little to fear.

A few straggling French soldiers, too exhausted to march any further, entered the village before dawn, and, concealing themselves behind points of vantage, prepared to sell their lives dearly. Two men at least took shelter behind the wall of the fountain: there was another at the corner of the Givry road, others up near the cemetery. On their heels came the Germans. The pair behind the fountain must have delayed hundreds of men for half an hour or more. Drilled deeply into the limestone wall of the school, above their heads were the holes of hundreds of bullets aimed at them. French cartridge cases littered the ground.

Mademoiselle Leblanc, an old maid not perfectly right in her head, came down to the fountain with a couple of buckets. She found a miniature battle in progress. Eventually the French soldiers, having used all their cartridges, fled up the road, and were shot down as they ran.

Their graves are at the bottom of the hill below the church.

Meanwhile, everywhere, the German army was advancing. From the forest fringes it streamed across the fields, while the main body came down the Menehould road into the village. Wherever one looked German scouting parties could be seen, issuing from the forest in the clear light of dawn. But they did not come quietly; they did not respect life and property. They shot the mayor as he came out to meet them, as they shot the cattle grazing in the fields. Instantly they began to destroy the village. Soldiers with petrol sprays and boxes of celluloid tablets went systematically from house to house, setting each on fire. The inhabitants ran into the streets, and were ordered to march to the top of the hill.

Not only were the houses burnt, but the outhouses, the barns, the cattlesheds, everything. Every plough, every reaper and binder, every mowing machine was set on fire. Rabbits in their hutches, chickens in their coops, bees in the hive, each were separately consumed. Haystacks, wheatstacks, faggot-stacks, all were burnt. Two hours after the Germans entered the village, there were only six houses, the communal wash-houses, and the church standing. The town hall and school was a roaring mass of flame.

Meanwhile the bulk of the inhabitants was crowded together in a field at the top of the hill. The men were separated from the women and children, and were ordered to kneel down. German soldiers kept guard over them with rifles and bayonets. There was Georges Leglaye with his one arm, Maurice Grosjean the lame cobbler; the only two men of military age. There was old Thomassin, dignified with sixty years of honourable labour, there was Lorcey, silent now about his wounds of 1870, there were Raffner, Demanger, Nicole Humbert, Thomas, Colas, Zins, old Choppet and all the others.

They were a strange collection of kneeling men, before whose eyes the flames rose and fell, destroying everything that each of them had toiled to buy or build during so many years. They did not show much emotion as the damp struck through their trousers, but waited to see what the invaders would do next.

The sun had risen among the flames and smoke, and beat into their eyes. They knelt in silence. At length an officer came up and picked out a few hostages from among them, to be sent to Germany.

Old Michel Meunier, in his steel spectacles, was one of them. He was sent off to Ehrfurt and interned. The people were kept at the top of the hill for most of the morning, then, sending away the hostages under a guard, the officers went down to Nettancourt, a village they did not burn, and where the officers billeted themselves.

Not everyone, however, had gone to the top of the hill. Germaine Dommartin ran off with a number of other women to the woods, where they remained all day in hiding.

The German soldiers made their camp at the top of the hill near where they had assembled the inhabitants and then their officers left them to their own devices. They got drunk. Indeed many of them had got drunk directly they entered the village. It is very easy for a hungry man to get dead drunk on *prunèlle*, a spirit distilled from plums, and in many houses there were barrels of the raw spirit. It is said that four German soldiers got accidentally burnt in houses where they were lying intoxicated. It is also remarkable that, of the six houses that were spared, four were houses where drink was sold.

A badly wounded French soldier had concealed himself under some gooseberry bushes in De Fontaine's garden and was discovered by an officer. The German was furious. With his emergency dressing he bound up the man's wound and took him off at once to the ambulance. The fate of another wounded French soldier was different. He was dragged out into the street and then beaten with rifles. But "he could not die," as Madame Martin said, so the Germans threw him alive into a burning house.

Madame Martin Thierry and a number of women watched this being done.

Georges Raiwoit, a boy of thirteen, went next morning, entirely on his own initiative, and raked the ashes of this soldier out of the embers. He put them in a little pot, and took the palms of the hands which were not burnt, and, going to the cemetery alone, buried them. It was an action of great courage.

There was an old woman who took refuge in her cellar. Her husband found her body much carbonised: she had been killed by the heat of the burning house above.

Her husband was an old man, crippled by rheumatism and, forgotten by everyone, lived for the rest of the war in a room at Belval in the forest.

The daughter of the widow Leglaye with her four children were discovered by a German hiding in a cellar and murdered —bayoneted. The head of the youngest child was cut off and its body was in the dead woman's arms. The exact circumstances of the murder are unknown.

The murdered family were all afterwards buried in the cemetery. There is not the slightest doubt about these murders. Numbers of people saw the bodies—Madame Machinet, for example, the sister of the murdered woman.

The German general put up in a little cottage just outside Nettancourt, and the woman who lived there said that he was a humane man, who always addressed her imperiously as "*Française*." She always replied: "*Général*." She told him about the murder of a woman and four children at Sommeilles,

He pooh-poohed the story, but she insisted that it was true. so that finally he rode up to see. He returned very much upset, having seen the bodies. No more murders were committed at Sommeilles.

The German officers behaved in many cases with humanity, though no doubt they ordered the burning of the village. The outrages committed by the men seem to have been due to hysteria, drunkenness, the revulsion after the fear of being in action and the *furor teutonicus*, the beastliness to which Germans are prone when they get the upper hand.

During the occupation of the village there was scarcely anything to eat. When the German soldiers saw anyone with a loaf of bread they took it away at once. Many families ate all sorts of strange things during that week. One dog at least was eaten.

A week after the Germans entered Sommeilles they were forced to abandon it. Just before they left, a German officer drew up at the church on a foaming horse and, climbing up into the belfry, scattered incendiary tablets and set fire to it. The roof caught and blazed, the beams of the belfry burnt away and the bells came tumbling down to be broken in their fall. The steeple fell in. Till that day the Germans had respected the church and their priest had said mass in it to a crowd of German soldiers. Lucille Bourgeat had the keys of the vestry and helped the priest to get everything ready for mass. She was going then, but the priest asked her to stop. She sat in front near him, the only French person at the service, packed with German soldiers.

The burning of the church was a departure signal for the German army. As it burned, half a dozen 75 mm. shells were thrown into the village by French artillery. One went through the church roof, all the others fell in the presbytery garden, a plum-tree and an apple-tree were cut down and holes knocked in the garden walls. A few minutes later the French troops passed through the village in pursuit of the invaders.

The enemy had gone. Children stared to see the blue uniform of their country. Women smiled again, wept, and waved handkerchiefs. Old people climbed out of cellars and began to look about them. Tears were shed over rubbish heaps which ten days ago had been houses. Going into the fields, men found some things much as usual. The sugar beet stood in rows. It was almost the time to lift it. Beet could be sold, though the sugar refinery at Sermaize was partly burnt. Sermaize itself was in ruins. Nine hundred houses had been destroyed out of not quite a thousand which had stood there. Still sugar beet could be marketed somewhere further south. Looking at the shining leaves standing in well-ordered ranks, it was impossible to believe that what had happened was more than a bad dream. Everything was quiet and peaceful.

Autumn had nowhere come upon the woods. There were apples to pick on the trees beside the road. It was warm. Swallows still slid through the windless sky. They had not gathered yet for departure. Painted butterflies came bobbing along the ditch. Beyond the sugar beet was a strip of pasture-land. There a sickening odour hung in the air. In one corner the putrescent carcase of a cow lay blackening in the sun. The hindquarters had been taken. The rest was rotting. Other cattle and horses lay rotting in other fields. Looking back to the village it was seen to be different. Where there had been order and red roofs was indistinguishable confusion. Butter-flies could ramble along the ditches but man could not walk far without perceiving the spectacle of his own ruin. Soldiers went hurriedly up the road. Sometimes all night long they passed through the village. Their hurrying feet, all out of step, sounded like the falling of multitudes of leaves in the quietness of an immense forest. In the night, trains of motor lorries could be heard approaching from a long way off. They passed through the village with a shaking rattle like the chattering of infernal teeth. From the woods came the sound of the guns. Everyone listened anxiously, but the sound came no nearer.

People stayed on where there were buildings to shelter them. Old Choppet and his wife lived in their bee-house in the orchard until they moved into their new brick house in August 1915. They could have well afforded to go to an hotel in Paris; but misers are not subject to ordinary considerations. Everyone who had relatives at Nettancourt went and lived with them: everyone who could, hired rooms there. Several families went to the farms at Vieux Montier. Others found shelter in the saw-mill on the road to Nettancourt, and there it was that Hector Molyneux Colas built a little shed for himself and his wife. Their eight sons were in the army.

In Sommeilles there were six houses which had not been burnt: the Dommartins' in their farm, Madame Pierron L'Oste in the house opposite, the Thomas family in their house, the old Webers who put up their son and his family in their house.

There was a family in the smithy on the Givry Road. The Zins family clung to their half-burnt house until part of it was repaired.

Wherever a roof could be found, people crept under it to shelter from the rain. Georges Leglaye, his wife and Eglantine Brabant, his mother-in-law, and all his children, found shelter in a barn of the Dommartins. They spent the winter there, sleeping miserably on straw. Often it froze and they were too cold to sleep. Keeping the younger children clean was the great difficulty. All the winter they scarcely took their clothes off. They lived in a muckheap for six months, they went hungry; they were cold for want of firing. They were cold for want of blankets. They suffered every privation, and endured every degrading circumstance of squalor. They lived with dignity but with little hope. It appeared impossible to build up again all that they had lost. Georges Leglaye had only his one arm to work with and, every day, they heard the thudding of artillery not twenty miles away.

In the Grurie wood the enemy, under the Crown Prince, was attempting to break through and recapture the land he had already ravaged. Sometimes the light of exploding shells could be seen on the horizon. When the Germans captured St Mihiel their artillery could be heard a long way off, in the east. The inhabitants of the district south of the Argonne knew that they might expect to see again an army of greenish figures issue from the forest and men in spiked helmets snatch away their bread, letting them and their children starve. They were afraid of the Germans, but even the children concealed that they were afraid. When it was too cold to get to sleep they heard the long rumble of the German high explosives falling.

Somehow the winter went by.

Nothing was done in the fields where the wild pigs wallowed at their ease. It had been forbidden to fire a gun and there were few guns left. When spring approached, the Sommeilles people who had taken shelter in Nettancourt went home each day to dig their gardens among the ruins. Old women trudged along the road and worked all day with shovel and wheelbarrow to clear away the debris of their houses.

Old Thomassin went into his fields to plough before he knew where he could get the grain to sow.

Already the English Society of Friends were helping the refugees at Sermaize. The first thing that they brought to Sommeilles was seed. It was what was most wanted. The spring was come, and what did the people care if they were hungry or cold, or dressed in filthy rags, as long as they could be digging the earth, sowing haricots and planting potatoes. Their gardens and their fields were their hope.

Grasping her spade, Madame Paul Adnot silently affirmed her belief in the future. Her husband had disappeared. There was no news that he was dead, or that he was a prisoner in Germany. He had disappeared. But his wife went out, with her heavy brows shading her humorous eyes, and dug.

The women worked silently, turning the sodden spits of earth. They expressed in every movement a savage concentration of hope. By their sides orphaned children fumbled over the ruins of their birthplaces and dragged out twisted knives, contorted forks, fused glass bottles. It was spring. The women looked forward. Dibbling in potatoes they became momentarily unaware of the past.

Marie Raffner drove her brown ox up from Nettancourt and laughed when she found some shapeless thing among the calcined limestone that reminded her of the past.

Suffering had become habitual: their characters were unaltered. They made the same jokes, were interested in the same things and were the same people as before. The English came to live at Nettancourt and began to build wooden houses at Sommeilles. Everybody who had not yet got a house, put seeds into the earth, determined at all events to have a garden.

The worst was over.

Sommeilles was in that stage when Frankie and I arrived.

71

IV

THE *Mission Anglaise* had divided its work into housing, agricultural assistance, medical work and the distribution of clothing and other forms of relief to the destitute. Housing, which was at that time the most important activity, consisted in making sectional wooden huts in workshops and erecting them where they were most needed. When the houses were finished, the Mission distributed furniture which was provided by a French Society, called *Le Bon Gîte*. The cost of both huts and furniture was debited from the compensation claim eventually paid by the French Government for War Damage, which in turn was eventually paid by the German Government as part of Reparations. No charge was made for the labour provided by the Mission. Agricultural assistance consisted in the loan and maintenance of mowers, reapers and binders and threshing tackle, and the provision of some forms of livestock, chiefly day-old chicks and domestic rabbits. Most of the livestock in the region that had survived the German occupation had been eaten during the winter.

During the short time that Frankie and I were at the Mission Headquarters at Sermaize, we found the atmosphere rather uncongenial and, at the risk of seeming malicious and ill-natured about the Friends, who had accepted us to help in their work which was inspired by their practical Christianity and belief in the Brotherhood of Man, I shall try and explain why we were critical.

The ethos of the Mission was intensely British and almost ndistinguishable from that of a school holiday camp. But there were also undercurrents, due no doubt to the repressions of the older Quakers, and their obsession with sin. Watching for each other's sins was, for some of them, the only way in which they could allow their minds to dwell on sex.

There was also a conscious striving after saintliness and a story which became current during the summer affords an illustration of the forms this might take. One evening, one of the older men, whose wife was also working on the Mission, got back to Sermaize after a most exhausting day's work to find that all the supper had been eaten except for a large bowl of stewed plums. His wife helped him and after he had eaten a plateful, offered him a second helping. He hesitated, eyed the plums longingly, but refused. His wife pressed him again.

"For thy sake, dearest," he said, meekly passing up his plate. Young men, who believed with Blake, that:

> Abstinence sows sand all over
> The ruddy limbs and flaming hair,
> But Desire Gratified
> Plants fruits of life and beauty there

and who were intensely suspicious of all forms of religion, were unlikely to feel that Sermaize was their spiritual home.

Frankie and I were therefore much relieved when Edmund Harvey informed us that he proposed to send us north to a village called Nettancourt, from which base the Mission had just begun to rebuild Sommeilles.

Edmund Harvey was a tall man with a shiny red face and thin dark hair, with a lock falling over his forehead. He was eager and energetic and tried to hold the balance between the older strait-laced type of Quaker and the younger men who felt that adventures beckoned and that the war provided a release from home.

Nettancourt was a rambling little town on low ground; a stream meandered through the flat park-like meadows behind the Chateau where the Marquis and the Marquise lived and worked, for he was a busy farmer. It was altogether a delightful spot. Nevertheless Frankie and I found life irksome, as overt saintliness was *de rigueur* and frequent Quaker meetings were held. More over we were fed almost entirely on tinned foods The lack of salad, fresh vegetables and wine was exasperating as we were in the midst of plenty of them, though meat was very scarce. Every morning, we builders were driven off to

Sommeilles in a lorry which came out all the way from Révigny, and every afternoon we were fetched back again. So long as we were living at Nettancourt we should remain strangers to the people whom we had come to help. Time was wasted in waiting for the lorry which was seldom punctual.

Within a week, Frankie and I, employing Quaker technique, developed "a concern" that we ought to live at Sommeilles. We imparted this to the other young men, who agreed with us, and when Edmund Harvey paid us his next visit, we got them to present him with a cut-and-dried plan. The next house to be built should be in the Presbytery Garden and we should live in it until the work at Sommeilles was completed and hand it over to the village for communal use when we departed. Harvey agreed to the proposal. We set to work at once on our new house and a fortnight later we moved into it. It was built in a sheltered garden in the middle of the village and the entrance looked out upon the old water trough and fountain, which was the centre for the casual gossip among the women of the village. The really serious gossip, which lasted for hours on end and was safe from male intrusion, was done at the *lavoir* where the weekly wash was carried out, the dirty clothes being beaten and rinsed again and again in the slowly flowing water. But the *lavoir* was necessarily on the outskirts of the village, where a little brook meandered.

We named our new home *La Fontaine* and made stone benches on either side of the doorway, where we could sit in the shade on a summer's evening.

The temporary houses which we built were supposed to last for ten years. A number of them were still standing in 1952 though by that time they were only used as toolsheds. We began by putting up the floor joists, supported on short stone or brick pillars. Then the frames of the walls, which arrived in sections, were bolted to the floor joists and to each other. Then the triangular gables were swung up into position and held by the purlins of the roof. The rafters followed and were roughly boarded over. The outer walls were put on—vertical poplar boards with the joints between them covered with battens. In

74

some villages the roofs were covered with bitumenised felt, but we made great efforts to obtain *tuiles méchaniques* and all but one or two of the earliest huts at Sommeilles were pantiled and had good over-hanging eaves under which the peasants could hang their harvest of haricots to dry. It is thanks to those roofs that so many of the Sommeilles huts have now lasted nearly forty years.

When the roofs had been put on and the hut was safe from the weather, the floors were cut and laid from thick tongue and groove deal boards and the walls lined with light deal match-boarding. Lastly our two French territorial soldiers Messieurs Heriot and—was it Mouflon?—professional carpenters in civil life, put in the windows and hung the doors, fitted locks and stoves. The huts were of one, two, three or four rooms according to the number of persons in the family to be housed. They were thus square, or multiples of a square. For ourselves, we built a treble square but divided it with only one internal wall. Thus we had a big dormitory furnished with our eight camp beds and a small kitchen with a cooking stove, a table and chairs which would just hold all of us at mealtimes.

We were lucky in our first *Chef d'Équipe*, Gill, the only middle-aged, married man among us. Sparely built, grey-faced, grey-haired and wearing pince-nez, he was a convinced vegetarian and an apostle of Esperanto which, he believed, was the agent that would eventually bring all war to an end, since wars came about owing to misunderstandings between peoples who could not speak each other's languages. He therefore insisted on talking Esperanto to foreigners, on principle. Gill was a real crank: a crank *pur-sang* of the kind I had lived among at Letchworth. But greatly to our surprise, Frankie and I discovered that he was entirely free from the sanctimonious overt saintliness which we found so uncongenial. Gill was actually a *covert* saint and one of the most tolerant men I have ever known. I never heard him condemn anyone for anything and he even regarded his own faults with leniency, which was pushing charitableness to a point extremely rare among the saints. He was also entirely without *amour-propre*. We engaged a village boy, Georges Raiwoit, to fetch and carry for us at work. Georges was an ugly imp who resembled a frog. He had an immensely wide mouth, a dirty yellow skin and warts, but he was highly intelligent and mischievous. Georges was often extremely impertinent to Gill who was never in the slightest bit annoyed by his bad behaviour, but rather led him on to worse extravagances of horse-play and hilarity. The mixture of *patois* and Esperanto in which they conversed was in itself grotesquely comic.

Soon after we had moved to Sommeilles, Edmund Harvey arrived to inspect us, bringing with him Mr Barrow Cadbury, one of the most influential members of the Society of Friends and a financial pillar of the Mission. Frankie and I happened to be at hand when they drove up, and after we had shown them over our new home Mr Cadbury asked to see a building being erected, and we accompanied our visitors to where Gill and Georges Raiwoit were supposed to be working. The site of the building was screened by trees, and when we turned the corner we saw to our dismay that Gill, who was a good gymnast, was walking away from us on his hands. His bare calves and sandalled feet protruded from his cotton overalls and were waving in the air and Georges was encouraging him with shrill yelps and screams of delight. Gill remained unaware of our approach for what seemed a very long time keeping his balance marvellously. Finally he turned right side up and recognised the visitors.

"Oh, how do you do, Mr Cadbury?" he said with perfect self-possession. Mr Cadbury returned his greeting, but it was clear that the spectacle was not what he had come to France to see and that he was disappointed. His friend Gill did not seem to realise that he should set an example of hard work to the young men over whose morals and discipline he was supposed to watch.

Though Gill was an admirable *Chef d'Équipe* he was not fitted to supervise the building work, if only because he would insist on talking Esperanto to the French. We therefore had Herbert Wright as our foreman, or *caporal*. Wright was only just over twenty but he was mature in mind and free of the hesitations and doubts of most men of his age. He was lightly made, freckled, with pale eyes and light-coloured eyelashes and he kept his mouse-coloured hair cropped very short. He was quick in making decisions and stuck to them once made. He hated the Quaker besetting sins of overt saintliness and hypocrisy. Otherwise he was fairly tolerant and, though often astringent, did not easily lose his temper. He soon became a warm personal friend of both Frankie's and mine.

Soon after we moved into the village some of the girls thought it would be amusing to play a practical joke on us and one day, when we went to lunch, leaving our tools in the hut which we were building, they came and hid our hammers. Wright guessed at once that the culprits were the girls aged from sixteen to twenty who had been hanging about that morning, so he rounded them up and said: "It is disgusting that you should behave like little children of ten or twelve when you are really women of twenty-eight or thirty." Our hammers were at once returned but his words created a coolness which lasted for some time.

We rose early and did a couple of hours work before breakfast. Gill, who approved of alcoholic drinks in moderation as much as he disapproved of meat—indeed he said alcohol was essential if vegetarians were to keep a sane outlook—used to get up while we were asleep and put on the kettle for our early cup of tea. Then he would walk from camp bed to camp bed, gently waking the sleepers and offering each of them, except one who was teetotal, a teaspoonful of cointreau as an inducement to get up quickly. At eight o'clock we came back to breakfast, had a quick wash in the fountain outside our garden door, and a breakfast which was almost always cocoa, sardines and bread and jam. I soon loathed the mixed flavour of cocoa and sardine oil. But unfortunately the Cadburys and the Frys made generous gifts of cocoa to the Mission stores and coffee was harder to come by.

After breakfast we worked for three or four hours until lunch, which was cooked for us by Madame Pierron l'Oste. It was a considerable economy employing her, as she must have saved double her wages by levying tribute from the village. Later I discovered that the Sommeilles *Équipe* cost far less than any of the others for food per head. The reason was that Madame Pierron let it be known what was required, and the villagers clubbed together to supply us with fruit and vegetables free of charge. I soon introduced wine into our diet and came to live almost entirely on wine, vegetables and bread. The bread was supplied to the entire district by the French Army and was wonderful stuff, since it tasted much better than English bread and never went stale. It contained rye, barley and tapioca as well as wheat.

After lunch we took a rest and then did a long afternoon's work, knocking off at six.

We soon got to know the village people. At first they would invite us to drink a glass of white wine, or of *prunelle*, and tried, on these occasions, to wangle priority, or ask for special favours. It was fortunate that Wright was our foreman at that time. He would always accept the proffered drink with alacrity and flatly turn down the request which accompanied it, making it clear that there were going to be no favourites and no privileges. Naturally, if there were any legitimate request or difficulty, Wright did all he could to help.

One early complaint did a good deal to make us popular in the village. One of the first of the one-roomed huts to be built was allotted to Veuve Leblanc, a rather tiresome old woman, who was intensely aware of her superior respectability, cleanliness and rectitude. She had got her hut early because she had refused to move and had been living in her cellar since the previous September. One day as we were finishing lunch, she arrived and made a formal complaint that her roof leaked and asked that we should repair it immediately. She added a number of caustic remarks about English workmanship. Wright went at once to investigate and Frankie and I went with him. It was quite true: there was a pool of liquid in one corner of the otherwise dry, clean floor. Wright looked at the ceiling, puzzled that he was unable to see any sign of moisture where it had dripped. Suddenly Frankie pointed to Madame Leblanc's large doe rabbit, which had been allowed out of its hutch and was hopping about under the table.

"*Tiens. C'est le lapin qui a pissé!*" he cried and then, dipping his finger in the little puddle held it out to her. "*Sentez, Madame, sentez! C'est bien votre lapin qui a fait çela!*" Madame Leblanc stood erect, virtuously indignant at the suggestion. But she sniffed and recognised that Frankie's intuition had solved the mystery. And at once her anger blazed out against the criminal. "*Sale bête. C'est toi qui me rends folle!*"

Everyone in the village was enchanted with this story and Frankie was the hero of the occasion.

"*Bonjour, Madame Leblanc. Est ce que votre lapine a encore fait pipi?*" M. Thomas asked the next morning, meeting her in the street.

I loved tiling and soon became skilful at laying the tiles or throwing them up to the tiler. Wright could throw so accurately that, kneeling on one knee on the roof, I could take a tile out of the air as it rested motionless, for a hundredth of a second, at the top of its trajectory, pop it into place and put out my hand to take the next one, almost without looking, knowing it would be there at the exact instant I was ready for it. We worked in teams, specialising to some extent. We could continue working in the wettest weather inside those huts which had the roofs on. There were not many wet days, but a great many sudden storms. I have never seen so many rainbows as that summer at Sommeilles.

The war was close at hand. All through the night, the windows rattled with the gunfire. Observation balloons suddenly went up over the horizon of forest and were hastily hauled down amid tiny black balls of bursting shells. Aeroplanes, almost always Maurice Farman biplanes, used to come over low down, one of them was not twenty feet over my head when I was tiling a roof near the top of the hill. French troops often rested in the village, either on the way up, or the way down from the line. Shortly after our arrival, the 162nd regiment spent a few hours resting in the village and I began talking to one or two of the men. Among them were several Russians. One, the gamekeeper of a Russian nobleman who had an estate in France, had been put into the French army as no passage could be got for him to return to Russia by Archangel. I had not forgotten all my Russian and talked to him in it. The soldiers were friendly and interested in our work. But I was soon too busy to take time off to talk to them.

Late that summer, the Argonne was the objective of a big German offensive and, while it lasted, the passage of army lorries was continuous and the village would suddenly be traversed by columns of marching men. Everything near the road was coated thickly with oily white dust. About six o'clock one morning, when I was working on a roof near the road, a column of troops came past, the officers in front, walking beside their horses, on which sat men in the last stages of exhaustion, who would otherwise have fallen out. In one of the ranks a crazy buffoon was wearing an opera hat instead of the French close-fitting steel helmet painted blue. When he caught sight of me on the roof, he took it off, tried to make a bow, and staggered on. The French losses in the *Bois de la Grurie* were appalling and, as the offensive dragged on, the little railway line which ran through Nettancourt was almost blocked with hospital trains crawling south. The incessant thudding of the guns, the flares visible at night, and the rattle of the lorries all night long got on the nerves of everyone in the village. One day, when I was working near the road, a whitish blue column of dog-tired, dust-covered men was passing with the continuous sound of hundreds of men marching out of step, when one of them called out to a group of village women, watching. Suddenly the self-control of one of the women broke. She screamed, she shouted, cursing first the Boches, then the war, then the men who made war and finally the men passing by, for fighting in it. She was beside herself, and to see and hear the distraught creature shrieking at the helpless column of soldiers was terrible. The soldier who had provoked her outburst was a hundred yards down the road and still she raved. Finally two other women got hold of her and dragged her away. But usually the self-control of the villagers was perfect. They felt a bitter hatred of the Germans, of those who made war and glorified it, and of those who, as *embusqués*, made money out of it and escaped it.

In some villages the young Quakers came in for a lot of criticism as *embusqués*. It was natural for the French to feel critical. Their men were fighting while we, healthy young men, were living in safety. In Sommeilles such hostility was broken down by two men: Frankie on our side and Georges Leglaye on theirs. Leglaye was sufficiently well informed to be able to explain that, though there was no military service in England, the Quakers, who believed war was wrong on religious grounds, had freely volunteered to help the French people. Frankie, on his side, broke down hostility by his warm humanity. Very soon everyone in the village came to love him. The hatred of militarism among the French peasants was intense. When the news came that Julien Thomas had been promoted sergeant and awarded the *Croix de Guerre* for exceptional gallantry at Verdun, Frankie congratulated Madame Thomas who replied:

"*D'abord on vous donne la croix de guerre; ensuite la croix de bois; avec deux mètres de terre.*"

Living with these clear-headed, bitter people who had no illusions left, I soon came to understand and share their point of view and to judge wars and the policies of Governments by what they meant in suffering. Later, I found it almost nauseating to return from the bitter, but invigorating, realism of the French to the shallow sentiment of the English. A typical example, which I remember, was an exhortation by Dr Winnington Ingram, the Bishop of London, that "everyone ought to take a bright view of death." If the inhabitants of Sommeilles had heard that appeal, their comments would have surprised His Lordship.

Yet sometimes I caught a glimpse of the beauty and romance of war. There had been a little storm of rain one morning while I was working at the Weber's hut below the church when, down the hill, on wet horses, with their sabres jingling, came a squadron of General Humbert's bodyguard. They wore Phrygian helmets, the shape of the cap of Liberty, but with the brass covered in pale blue cloth. Down their backs streamed horsetails, most of them black, but with one or two dyed red for variety. The troopers had their carbines slung over overcoats; the officers wore long blue riding cloaks. Most of them were young men, with Gallic hawk features and, at first glance, with the black tresses streaming from their helmets, they looked like mounted Amazons.

Nôt long after we had settled in at Sommeilles, Augustine Birrell paid us a visit, accompanied by Mr Bailey, an Irish Land Commissioner. They spent a night in the village in an empty hut which we had just finished and which we fitted out with a couple of camp beds for the occasion. Our visitors came to see us after visiting the British Sector of the front and staying at G.H.Q. They were surprisingly warm and friendly, but I found it quite impossible to discover how intelligent Mr Birrell really was—and no doubt he was quite as unable to form a judgment about me, if he ever entertained any curiosity on the subject. I could see that he was charming, witty and humane. But he had become a "character" based in part upon Dr Johnson, and this, and the difference of age, produced an unbridgeable gap between us. It was a relief when he went and we got back to ordinary routine.

Our visitors had been lent a car by the Mission and their driver was a remarkable young Scotsman called Robert Tatlock. He impressed all of us, and Augustine Birrell particularly, by his determination and drive and a love of hard intellectual argument not to be found among the Friends who distrust logic and live by the spirit. He was tired of his work in France and was busy pulling wires with the Home Committee to get himself sent to Serbia, where he was convinced there was far more important relief work to be done. I was to get to know him very well in later years, but what struck me most forcibly at our first meeting was the ease with which he had

FRANCIS BIRRELL AT SOMMEILLES

impressed himself on Augustine Birrell. Why was it, I wondered, that whereas I was treated as a pleasant ineffectual boy, full of half-baked ideas, Robert Tatlock was immediately picked out as a man to be taken seriously? The answer I arrived at was that Tatlock knew exactly what he wanted to do and was not concerned with emotions but with facts in the world as he found it. My approach to most things was still governed by my emotions. I felt no jealousy of Tatlock as I was without any formulated ambitions. I wanted, indeed, to be a writer, but whether I became a good one would depend on my development and not on my seizing opportunities.

As impressive as Tatlock, but in an entirely different way, was a member of the Mission whom both Frankie and I had known and met several times in London before the war, as he was a friend of Arthur and Hubert Waley. This was Reynolds Ball, a poet, a natural ascetic and a visionary and saint, not unlike Blake. Ball was not a Friend—his father was indeed a Canon at Norwich, but he was a convinced pacifist, I think on religious grounds. He reminded me sometimes of my Latin master, Gerald Warre Cornish who was killed a year later in the Battle of the Somme leading his men. In later years I was once or twice reminded of Ball by a look or phrase of T. E. Lawrence's.

Ball's absolute sincerity and saintliness had impressed itself on the heads of the Mission and he had been allowed to take up a sort of roving commission, though nominally he worked with the agricultural section. Actually he spent a good deal of his time bicycling about our area and ferreting out the poorest, oldest people, who after the invasion had taken refuge in hovels, outlying barns or huts in the forests and had been too timid or infirm to ask for relief. Some of those he found had been completely forgotten and were dressed in rags and starving. Ball would bring help to these unfortunates and see the mayors of their communes on their behalf and arrange that they should be looked after, or supplied with the necessary tools to look after themselves.

Ball came to Sommeilles for a night whenever his work

brought him our way and took great pleasure in Frankie's lively wit and streams of talk. He was human in spite of his natural ascetism, and Frankie had a story that Ball had once been found in the avenue at Sermaize, on the way back from a day's work in the harvest field, where he had been given too much white wine, embracing a young lime tree and declaring that it was so beautiful that he would not leave it.

We had one famous visitor, besides Augustine Birrell, while we were at Sommeilles. One day, when we were going out to work after lunch, a car drove up to La Fontaine and a little man descended who asked for Frankie. To our astonishment, it was J. M. Barrie. Frankie took him round the village and to see Georges Leglaye, but I saw no reason why work should not proceed as usual and made everyone go straight on with the job, which one or two worshippers of *Peter Pan* thought hard. If our visitor had been an author whose work I had admired, I should have been less of a disciplinarian. Barrie was, I think, staying with E. V. Lucas who was managing a hospital not far off. I had visited him shortly after my arrival at Nettancourt.

I disliked *Peter Pan* as a child and when I grew up it seemed to me morbid and unhealthy in a particularly unpleasant way. The sexual instinct which in a healthy normal man is aroused by the women painted by Rubens or Renoir, or in a homo-sexual by a beautiful adult of the same sex, emerges in Barrie as a baby's bedtime sexuality which revolts me. This watery perversion has come to be a national institution.

Far more important for me than any possible visitors were letters from my friends which showed me that I was not forgotten, and kept me in touch with a life very different from that of the Mission.

Lytton wrote:

July 14th 1915, 6 Belsize Park Gardens N.W.

I'm told that you've arrived safely at your destination and gather that you continue to face life with equanimity, for which the Lord be thanked. I have no notion of your manner of existence, how full it may be of horrors, mental or physical, what your companions are like (baboons or angels?), whether you are busy or idle, safe or in danger, silent or chattering . . . but I imagine a judicious mixture of all these. Are there any flies? And if so, how many have you killed? And, if you have killed untold millions, is your reputation enormous? I expect it is. And Frankie? Is he bearing up? I long to hear every detail: why is it impossible to talk? I wish I could whizz across in an aeroplane for a few minutes. Keep a good look out; perhaps one fine morning I shall.

Life here seems to continue in an agreeable manner: one can't help feeling rather guilty about it, with these surrounding horrors; but there it is. It's so nice and hot for one thing, and then there are so many occupations in this town. One can go from Hampstead Heath to the British Museum, from the British Museum to Gordon Square, from Gordon Square to Treviglio's, from Treviglio's to the Palace, from the Palace to the Café Royal, from the Café Royal to . . . in fact a beneficent Deity appears to have provided suitably for every moment of the day and night. You need not suppose that I am idling: far from it. I am working hard over Voltaire and Frederick, and enjoying the business—so far. It's really a great pleasure reading on and on, when the persons concerned are so extraordinarily sensible, and the fact that they're also fiends rather adds to the attraction than otherwise. (Devils perhaps would be a better word.) One gets such queer sidelights on the possibilities of the human soul. Tiens!

Probably you've heard from Vanessa or Duncan about our Ottoline visit last week-end. It was not particularly enchanting. Such fussifications going on all the time—material, mental, spiritual—and at the same time quite indefinite. *Dona nobis pacem, dona nobis pacem*, was all I could murmur. The house is a regular galanty-show, whatever that may be; very like Ottoline herself, in fact—very remarkable, very impressive, patched, gilded and preposterous. The Bedford Square interior does not suit an Elizabethan Manor house in the wilds of Oxfordshire. It has all been reproduced, and indeed redoubled. The pianola, too, with Philip, infinitely Philipine, performing, and acrobatic dances on the lawn. In despair I went to bed, and was woken up by a procession circumnavigating my bed, candles in hand . . . the rear brought up by the Witch of Endor. Oh! *Dona nobis pacem!*

There are various items of gossip, but I expect you've heard them too—such as they are. A curious scene took place the other night, as I read aloud my little Pasquinade to those principally concerned. It was well received—except by Clive, who remained plunged in silent disapproval. I was in terror—feared that an irreparable breach was opening, etc., but Vanessa assures me that this is not so. Have you seen his pamphlet? I do think it's amazingly bright.

I am slightly put about by a singular incident yesterday at the Café

Royal. That creature Shelley begged Iris to introduce me to her. She did so: the creature Shelley (who I thought was very pretty) then said "You're in the Navy, aren't you?" Whether she was drunk I don't know; but she then proceeded to make an assignation with me for tomorrow night. It looked as if she must have some definite object in view—but what? It's really rather intriguing. James tells me that she has had dealings with you, and perhaps she wants to talk to me about you. I can't make it out, and perhaps it's simply fantastic. But if anything transpires I'll let you know. In any case I shall be most discreet ... from every point of view. The worst of it is that I find it so difficult not to be utterly bored by that sort of woman.

I hope to write to you again quite soon. Give my love to Frankie. I hope you both occasionally remember that there exists an *être pensant* in a brown beard and tortoise-shell spectacles, who is your affectionate

Lytton.

At Sommeilles changes in our party came soon. Sewell went home to help his father at Whitby and was not able to return. Gill went on leave and decided to join the Friends Ambulance Unit, which ran a hospital train in Flanders. Wright was sent away to supervise building a hutted hospital. About the same time I heard that Edward had joined the Italian Ambulance Unit, organised by Sir Charles Trevelyan and Philip Noel-Baker. For a time I planned to join him.

When Gill and Wright left, Edmund Harvey paid us a visit to decide who was to be our new *Chef d'Équipe*, a matter of great concern to us. I was considerably surprised when our Leader took me by the arm and led me away to ask me how I would like to be *Chef*. I refused and said we should be much happier if we could have MacAlpine, who was a birthright Friend—and who was a capable and delightful Scotsman. Two days later, Harvey came back to say that MacAlpine had declined the job, so I took it on. Two pleasant fellows were sent out as replacements of those who had left. The two months which followed were the most interesting part of my stay. Doing both Gill's and Wright's work kept me busy. I kept the accounts, indented for rations, bought food locally as necessary, paid our French carpenters and saw to their needs, woke up our gang in the morning—without cointreau—which I could not afford, and, in theory, looked after our discipline, welfare and

86

health. I was supposed, by the London Committee, to read prayers, but I followed Gill's example and refrained.

There was no discipline, for we were all hard workers, and we kept fit, except for septic sores which were endemic in the village owing to some virulent bacteria in the soil. I discovered from Dr Hilda Clark that the only medicament which would make them heal was grey mercury ointment and treated all sufferers, native and British alike, with it. My use of it caused some comment, as it was the old treatment for syphilis and I was once told that it was dangerous and unsuitable. But it worked.

As foreman, I had to plan the building programme, see to the supplies of timber being sent up in advance of requirements, arrange the cartage of tiles from Nettancourt station, and make any modification in the programme imposed on us by the availability of material, or the changing needs of the inhabitants. I also remained the chief tiler and laid most of the roofs myself. I was not so good a foreman as Wright, as I was apt to be swayed by my preference for straightforward and good-looking people, to the prejudice of the crafty and the ugly. There was one girl, Marie Raffner, whom I found it very hard to refuse. She was about eighteen, very fair, with blue eyes and much more attractive than most of the girls in that part of France. She lived with a wastrel, drunken father, did all the work on their little holding, and supported her brothers and sisters by acting as the village carrier, carrying parcels and executing commissions when she drove her brown ox in a narrow tumbril in and out of Nettancourt twice a week. She had an affectionate, jolly way of speaking to the ox, and the long goad which lay on the side of the cart was only used to direct him to the right or left. She certainly got the best out of her beast, for he went at a very fast walk. Unfortunately Marie had chosen the wrong bit of furniture from *Le Bon Gîte*, a cupboard instead of a table, and she wanted me to arrange for her to have a second choice. This turned out to be impossible, but for some time I felt miserable because I admired Marie and hated disappointing her. Frankie teased me a great deal about her. There was no question of flirtation; Marie had not the time, or inclination, for anything of that kind. On the other hand my friendship with old Weber did lead to a little innocent flirting with his fleshy red-faced daughters.

Often we worked overtime until it was dark, if a truckload of tiles had to be unloaded at the station, or when a hut would not otherwise be ready to move into on the arranged day.

In a letter to Edward I wrote:

> The villagers are so sick of the whole subject of bereavement, ruin and sorrow, that they don't speak of it, and try not to think about it. Instead there is this village life which concentrates on gossip and the little things which go on from day to day. We provide an audience and subjects for laughter and discussion. That is really more important than providing them with houses.

It was just because Frankie provided them with a new interest in life and opportunities for gaiety that he was the most important person at Sommeilles. When I revisited the village in 1952, I found that long after all the rest of us had been forgotten his memory was still treasured by people who remembered him from nearly thirty-seven years before, when they were children. The charming photograph reproduced opposite page 82 was brought out and shown to me—a treasured possession of the children of Georges Leglaye.

Shortly after Augustine Birrell's visit, Frankie and I had a furious quarrel about Sir Walter Scott's merits as a novelist in which I must have been led into making some very wounding remarks, for we did not speak to each other for three days. I have always thought Scott a bore and Frankie's praise of him as one of the world's greatest novelists was coupled with remarkable ignorance and indifference to the work of modern writers, in which I had been soaked since infancy. To our companions, our behaviour appeared to be that of lunatics. For months we had jabbered incessantly about things which meant little to any of them and then, one fine morning, *apropos* of nothing, we had quarrelled like Tweedledum and Tweedledee. Some of the dear fellows were greatly puzzled. However, if Frankie chose to sulk, I would not apologise. *Kenilworth* was tripe. I found it a strain to keep my rage against Scott at white heat and, after three days, we made friends again suddenly over Balzac's *Les Splendeurs et Misères des Courtisanes* which Frankie had begun to read. It was the only quarrel I ever had with the least selfish of men, in a friendship which lasted twenty years, until his death. Curiously enough, this quarrel must have had an influence on him as, after my return to England, his letters were full of discussions of Dostoevsky, and in one letter he informed me that Conrad's *Lord Jim* was a work of genius. Later he amply repaid me by introducing me to Proust and to those comparatively low-brow writers Abel Hermant and Colette.

Our reconciliation was cemented by collaboration in a play which we wrote in two Sundays. It was a high-spirited production and the characters included several members of the Mission and Augustine Birrell. Frankie was confident that we should get it put on in the West End and should make our fortunes, and sent it to Denis Eadie, but I was always a bit doubtful as to its success. It was a real collaboration. First one of us would get an idea and dictate to the other, who would get excited and insist on interpolating matter of his own. In the final version, almost every speech was the work of both authors. Six months before, at Eleanors, Duncan and I had collaborated in writing a novel which never got finished, but we wrote alternate chapters and never achieved a unified style.

One day a pretty girl Germaine Dommartin, invited Frankie and me to go round to her grandmother's hut that evening. It was one of our single-roomed buildings, furnished with a stove, a table, a bed and two chairs. We were given glasses of *prunelle* and pieces of gingerbread and Germaine sang to us. Then old Madame Dommartin was led to say: "Ah! You should have heard me as a girl! I used to sing beautifully when I had my teeth!"

Frankie soon made her sing and, to our astonishment, the old creature could sing exquisitely and had a vast repertory of slightly improper eighteenth-century songs. Frankie completely won old Madame Dommartin's heart and she began to give a series of parties, inviting different friends of hers to come and meet him. We brought wine and biscuits and chocolate, others brought *prunelle* and we sat on the floor. Madame Dommartin sang and Frankie introduced games. None of the French villagers had played games since they were small children and they threw themselves with enthusiasm into hunt the slipper. In a letter written after I had gone back to England, Frankie wrote: "I spend most of my evenings playing kiss-in-the-ring and you'd be a great addition. At least that is how Dearden and I passed last evening with old Madame Dommartin."

One afternoon there was an immense excitement in the village. Something had obviously happened, for working on my roof I could see the inhabitants clustering in the main street, like swarming bees. Georges Raiwoit at once made off, but was sufficiently loyal to his employers to come back half an hour later to tell us what it was all about. Two of the six hostages, whom the Germans had taken on the morning that they captured Sommeilles, had suddenly come back. They had been sent to a camp in Germany and, nine months later, had been discovered to be useless mouths—hostages for a village which had been recaptured by the French a week after it had been taken. They had been sent to Switzerland, but had not been allowed to remain there. From Switzerland they had been sent to Paris and from Paris sent back to Sommeilles. Later I talked to one of them—old Michel Meunier. He was short-sighted and the lens of one of his spectacles had been shattered and the other one badly cracked. His chief grievance was against the Swiss, who had treated him astonishingly well, but who had refused to allow him to stay in Switzerland for the rest of the war, although he had had enough money saved up in France to enable him to live there for a year or two. The same harsh treatment had been accorded him in Paris. He was not allowed to stay, and had, almost forcibly, been sent back to Sommeilles, which he had last seen when it was in flames. I asked him about the camp in Germany.

"*On n'y était pas si mal là-bas. Les gardiens étaient hommes de famille—des types serieux. Seulement on avait affreusement froid l'hiver, et on avait toujours faim. Les Boches ne sont pas tous méchants."*

During the time that I was *Chef d'Équipe* I had occasional difficulties with the Committee and with two of the young men at our base. On the first occasion, when I sent in the accounts for money spent locally, I was informed that the Committee objected to money being spent on wine. I had always bought the cheapest red wine, which I regarded as a necessary food. I solved the problem of subsequent wine bills by including wine in a non-itemised bill for groceries. Once or twice there was trouble with the lorry-driver, who brought up our sectional huts and supplies of timber from Révigny. The lorry-driver wished to unload as quickly as possible, and on two occasions he brought companions with him and, with their help, dumped the load of wood in the main street. We then had to hire a horse and cart to move it where it was wanted which meant delay and expense. Wright dealt firmly with the lorry-driver the first time it occurred. When I succeeded him, he tried again. Luckily I caught him just as he and his companions had started to unload, and by a mixture of veiled threats and sarcasm I made them drive round the village, unloading the material on the sites where it was wanted. Those involved bore me a grudge and eventually had their revenge. In October the weather suddenly turned cold and, one frosty morning, our two French carpenters came to me shivering and asked me if I could get them some warm clothes. They had been working with us since the spring: their uniforms were threadbare and the cotton overalls they wore were no protection against the cold. They had no wish to remind the Adjutant of their Regiment of their existence, lest they should be recalled to their battalions. Next time I went to Sermaize the lady in charge of the clothing store looked out some suitable clothes for them. The car on which I came back could only take me as far as Révigny and I bicycled back, leaving the parcel of clothes to be sent out by the lorry. Unfortunately I told the lorry driver, with whom I left it, what it contained. The parcel did not arrive and a week elapsed before I discovered that the man had sent it back to Sermaize, with a complaint to the Committee that he could not reconcile it with his conscience that clothes given by Friends in England for the relief of the civil population should be used to clothe French soldiers. I lost my temper and injured my case by calling him a hypocritical little rat, and though I later submitted a claim that the Mission had a moral responsibility for the welfare of all the men working for it, the Committee decided against me. Fortunately Frankie and I had each brought a suit of civilian clothing. Mine fitted M. Heriot who was tall and thin, fairly well; Frankie's was a bit tight on tubby M. Mouflon. Dearden, Edwards and Penney contributed pants and vests and our carpenters were able to face the winter.

While I was with the Quakers, I lived an absolutely chaste life, having little desire to do otherwise—and so of course did Frankie. Some of us flirted a little with the village girls but it would have made our work extremely difficult if any one of us had embarked on a serious affair. None of us did more, I think, than take a kiss if it were offered, or expected. Moreover our lives were extremely public. However the Committee persisted in being inquisitive about our morals and sent a certain Tartuffe to live at Sommeilles for a fortnight to report on us. He went off on his motor-cycle every morning and returned at night. Just before the end of the war, a girl on a distant farm showed one of the American Quakers a number of letters which Tartuffe had written her. They bore out her story that he had seduced her by speaking of marriage and had then written to her to keep her quiet until he had left the Mission. The letters were shown to Frankie, who refrained from making their existence known, except to me and to one of the builders at Sommeilles on whom Tartuffe had reported unfavourably because of his innocent friendliness with Germaine Colas, a pretty child of twelve or thirteen.

V

IN October I decided to return to England, but was careful to leave the door open for my return to the Mission. Duncan had been asked to go to Paris to design dresses for Maeterlinck's *Pelléas et Mélisande* which was to be produced by Copeau of *Le Vieux Colombier* Theatre. When that was finished, he planned to work at a hospital with which his aunt, Miss Daisy McNeill, was connected, at Serey in the Pyrenees. I wanted to find out what these plans amounted to. Should Duncan be working for some time in Paris, I thought I might get myself a job for which I was fitted at the *Institut Pasteur*. If these plans came to nothing, I thought I would rather go to Serbia, whither Robert Tatlock had persuaded the Friends Committee to send him on an exploratory expedition. Maynard had also led me to believe that he could get me work as a Russian translator working in the War Office, making a résumé of the Foreign Press.

My experience at Sommeilles had given me confidence in myself and had also turned me into a pacifist. I had read Clive Bell's pamphlet *Peace at Once* and agreed with his main argument. Without sharing the Quakers' views, or even being convinced that war was always wrong, I was sure that Clive was right and that the war ought to be brought to an end as quickly as possible by a negotiated peace. It was ruining France, England, Austria and Germany and it looked like killing off the best of my generation in a military stalemate. When I went out to Sommeilles, I was equally ready to join the British Army. When I returned I was determined to have no part in the war. My opinions had been formed by what I had seen of the war and by the people I had been working among.

On my way home I spent a few days in Paris and saw one of the directors at the *Institut Pasteur*. He told me he was extremely short of skilled assistants and, after hearing my qualifications said he would be delighted to employ me. Before I left he gave me a letter to say that there was a place waiting for me, in case I should have any difficulty with the passport authorities, or the French police, when I wished to return. I went at once to The Cearne to see Constance, for Edward was still with the Italian Ambulance Unit on the Izonzo. Afterwards I saw Duncan and all my friends in Bloomsbury, paid a visit to Ottoline's country house at Garsington, and started a love affair.

In spite of that, however, I only stayed a fortnight in England, for I found, as I had hoped, that Duncan was ready to set off to work with Copeau. We left on the second of November, and, being still a member of the Mission, I was wearing my uniform and the French *Service de Santé* brassard. At Folkestone I found myself separated from our luggage and hurried through a corridor, after showing my passport. But Duncan failed to appear. At last he arrived and scrambled on board, just as the boat was starting. He had been taken before a British Major who had abused him for not being in the Army and had told him that he regretted that he had no power to stop his leaving the country. All this had upset and infuriated Duncan. When we reached Dieppe, we were taken before a French officer who seemed to be expecting Duncan and who told him he would not be allowed to go to Paris, but would either be returned to England as an undesirable alien, or put into a Concentration Camp. The whole episode seemed as unreal as a nightmare.

I asked to be allowed to stay with Duncan, but was ordered by the officer to continue my journey. I had just time to talk to him for a few minutes and was then hustled on board the train, feeling angry and bewildered. The train moved away slowly and then stopped, and Duncan, who had been left at liberty, saw that with a little exertion he could have caught up with it and climbed in. He was tempted to do so, but refrained, as his passport had been taken away.

On my arrival in Paris, I went to the Hotel de l'Elysée in

the Rue de Beaune and took the cheapest rooms they had, unheated and just under the roof. I decided to stay there until I heard definitely whether Duncan would be allowed to come to Paris or not.

The weather was icy. Meanwhile Duncan had had his passport endorsed: "deported as a pacifist anarchist," and had been sent back third-class on the boat the next day, though he had asked to pay his fare. At Folkestone the British Major had told him that he was sorry that he had no power to have him detained. Duncan arrived late and hungry at 46 Gordon Square where he found Clive's party reading a play by Dryden.

St John Hutchinson, who had signed Duncan's application for his passport, took up the case with the Foreign Office and Maynard took it up with the War Office. As a result the Major at Folkestone was reprimanded. The French authorities, however, maintained their objection to Duncan's going to Paris. Copeau had unexpectedly left Paris for Florence and Duncan could get no reply to his letters to him.

I remained in Paris with nothing to do until Duncan's case had been considered. I had very little money, ate little, and found difficulty in keeping warm. Lytton, who wrote frequently to cheer me up, sent me a Shetland cardigan which may well have saved me from pneumonia. But in one letter he redoubled my rage against the established authorities by telling me of the police prosecution and suppression of D. H. Lawrence's new novel *The Rainbow*.

Clive is trying to get up an agitation about it in the newspapers but I doubt if he'll have much success. We interviewed that little worm * * * * * * * * * *, who quite failed to see the point: he thought that as in his opinion the book wasn't a good one it was difficult for him to complain of its suppression. Damn his eyes!

I had suppressed a good deal of my anger at the treatment Duncan had received. But all my fury burst out at the news of this idiotic piece of persecution of Lawrence and for a day or two I was almost raving. There was nothing I could do about it except write a very angry letter to Augustine Birrell. I received an amiable reply, saying that he had, by chance, read

The Rainbow and thought it a very bad novel, but he did not attempt to explain what relevance his opinion had to the injustice being done to Lawrence.

In the same letter in which Lytton had told me of the prosecution and suppression of *The Rainbow*, he described seeing Lawrence and Frieda at a party at Dorothy Brett's studio.

There were a great many people I didn't know at all and others whom I only know by repute, among the latter, the Lawrences, whom I examined carefully and closely for several hours, though I didn't venture to have myself introduced. I was surprised to find that I liked her looks very much—she actually seemed (there's no other word for it) a lady: as for him I've rarely seen anyone so pathetic, miserable, ill, and obviously devoured by internal distresses. He behaved to everyone with the greatest cordiality, but I noticed for a second a look of intense disgust and hatred flash into his face . . . caused by—ah!—whom?

Lawrence and Frieda had also been seeing something of Clive and Vanessa and Jack and Mary Hutchinson at this time, but there is no evidence as to whether he dreamed about beetles afterwards.

The fortnight which I spent living alone in Paris gave me plenty of time to think not only about my attitude to the war, but to Established Authority. While I was at Sommeilles I had seen that France was being bled white and that a negotiated peace was essential if Europe was to be saved from ruin, and for that reason I had decided to take no part in fighting. But the two incidents which concerned my friends: Duncan's being turned arbitrarily back at the frontier and the suppression of *The Rainbow*, roused me to a pitch of hatred and contempt for Established Authority, and for the whole apparatus of Government. It became clear to me that Government is in itself an evil: no doubt a necessary one to avoid other evils—but that the less Government the better. For the Government is bound, by its very nature, to be blind, ruthless and stupid because stupid and brutal men love power for its own sake whereas sensitive and intelligent men only care for power if there is interesting work to be done.

I wrote a letter to Maynard in which I said that our Governors had got themselves into the war and into a fine mess in consequence. As a result they were calling upon him and others like him just as the Arabian Caliph called a Djinn out of a bottle to save him when he was in dire straits. Maynard and other Djinns might succeed in saving our Governors, but he was much mistaken if he thought because he had been useful during the war he could get his views accepted afterwards. The moment the danger was over, he would be sent back to Cambridge—the Djinn would be safely corked up in his bottle again. My letter expressed the crude views of an angry boy, ignorant of British political organisation. But Maynard was interested and discussed my whole attitude on my return, agreeing that there was a great deal of truth in what I had said.

One result of my meditations was that I decided that the reason why I should not become a soldier was not simply because of the desirability of an immediate peace but because it would be wrong for me to delegate the responsibility for my own acts. "Theirs not to reason why," seemed to express the very essence of the military profession. It might be all right for some people. But it was a position that I would never accept. I would rather, like Thersites, be a tick in a sheep's back than such a valiant ignorance as Ajax.

My letters to Lytton must have shown the crisis I was going through and the unhappiness I was feeling, for he wrote to me continually to cheer me up and make me feel I was not alone.

Mon cher, go to the end of your Rue de Beaune and look at the house at the corner, on the Quai, where Voltaire died, at the age of 84, having conquered both the Rulers of this world, and of the next—and where (though the inscription doesn't say so, I think) he had lived fifty years before as a young poet. Consider that life and take courage.

Actually my little attic was in the top of the building to which Lytton referred.

Lytton also wrote to Jane Harrison, who happened to be staying with Hope Mirrlees, at the same hotel as I, and asked her to be kind to me. I had already noticed both of the ladies in the writing-room downstairs. As a result of Lytton's letter, Jane Harrison came up, talked to me about my mother, whom she remembered at Newnham, and about her Russian translations, which were very much in her mind just then. For Hope Mirrlees and she were learning Russian and Jane suggested that I should accompany them to one of M. Boyer's lectures on the Russian language at the school of Oriental languages. At one of these lectures M. Boyer made his students read aloud a sentence or two of Russian. When my turn came, he complimented me upon my Russian accent, picked up from the peasant boys in Tambov, and I was held up as an example to the class.

Jane Harrison's rough warmth of manner and her intellectual enthusiasms, always brimming over, not only completely won my heart, but came as a moral restorative at a time when I was driving myself almost mad with helpless rage. She took me with her several times to visit various leading intellectuals associated with the summer school at Pontigny. Thus I met M. Charles Dubos and, I think, M. Gide. She also took me to visit the Russian author Remizov, a curious little dried up old man.

By the middle of November it seemed unlikely that Duncan would ever get permission to visit Paris and so I returned to Sommeilles, though not as *Chef d'Équipe*. Northern France was in the grip of an iron frost, but working hard I seldom felt cold. I was pleased, however, to be remembered by the stray cat which I had petted in the summer, and which now got into our hut every night and, ignoring all blandishments from my companions, came straight to me and always slept in the mouth of my sleeping bag curled up against the nape of my neck. The water in the fountain was frozen for some weeks and baths were impossible, and washing very difficult. Our working hours were much shorter, as they were limited by daylight. In the evenings Frankie and I wrote a second play called *The Hue and Cry After Genius* which was a satire on the Asquiths, Eddie Marsh and Ottoline.

One Sunday two or three of us went as beaters to take part in a wild boar shoot. We kept as far as possible in line, breaking through very thick undergrowth and driving the game across a ride in the forest where the postman and four or five of the peasant proprietors who had guns were waiting, with as many small boys holding dogs on the leash. I heard one wild pig rush away from me and it was soon greeted with a fusillade of shots. The ride was not wide and practically all the shooting was up and down the line. However, nobody was hit and three of the wild boars were wounded, brought to bay by the dogs and subsequently shot from fairly close quarters. In a shoot which took place after I left, fifteen boars were bagged and the whole village turned out to admire them when they were laid out in line. I am sorry to say I never ate wild boar, but Frankie reported it as good but tough. After the shoot old Onesime Commenil invited us into his house and gave us glasses of deliciously strong perry, of his own making. Other people made cider, but old Onesime always had to have things different from, and better than, his neighbours. He was a very keen sportsman. One day, later that winter, he was laid up in bed and Frankie took him a bottle of liniment. The old farmer, who may have been feverish, told one story after another about *la chasse*. Finally, as he described how a huge wild boar had charged him, he snatched up his old hammer gun, which was standing loaded beside his bed, and cried out: *"Justement quand le sanglier se ruait sur moi, je lui lachais les deux coups à la gueule!"* And suiting the action to the word, he sat up in bed and fired both barrels out of the window. Frankie came back from his errand of mercy feeling that he had had a lucky escape.

But my return to Sommeilles, delightful as it was to see Frankie again, was only a stop-gap. I was receiving many letters urging me to return to England.

Maynard wrote:

Why don't you come back? I am sure you ought to. The "danger" is very small and you won't anyhow escape it. The expense is less. You waste your time as it is. If you come back here, either you get a job, or you have a very good excuse for leading what life you like and an opportunity you may never have again of seeing if you can write. It's really absurd to stay out there and quite against reason. This letter is meant to be a cold and icy appeal to reason. So regard it. Your affectionate J.M.K.

I waited, however, till the end of December, as I had sprained my ankle badly. I then accepted an invitation from Dr Hilda Clark to spend Christmas at the Maternity Hospital at Châlons. She was slim, dark and fearless and was full of the love of adventure. I was greatly attracted by her. But besides the pleasure of driving to Châlons with a beautiful woman whose character and work I admired and respected, I was a good deal flattered by her invitation.

On Christmas day a party was organised in the enormous ward on the first floor of the old building. In it were ranged some thirty beds occupied by pregnant women. Their families had been invited and the ward was packed with women and excited children. The only access to it was at one end, by a narrow winding staircase and it was heated by an enormous iron circular stove which stood near the stairs and was almost red hot. Beyond the stove the nurses had introduced a Christmas-tree covered with lighted candles and decorated with cotton wool to represent snow.

One of the ambulance drivers, dressed as Father Christmas, with an immense beard of cottonwool, had just begun to gather up presents from below the tree, when his beard touched a candle and flared. He tore it off and the decorations on and round the tree caught fire. In a second there was pandemonium. With roars and screams of terror the crowd of visitors and children dashed for the narrow staircase. In their path was the huge, almost red-hot stove. Luckily Reynolds Ball and one or two others were near it and for a moment or two we had to fight the crowd to prevent the children from being pushed against the stove. In the meantime the women patients had clambered out of bed and were seeking to escape in their nightgowns. The nightmare only lasted a minute or two; it was ended by Father Christmas, who, although scorched about the face and having lost his eyebrows, tore down the flaming decorations with his bare hands and extinguished the flames with a bucket of sand. One of the English nurses had leapt on to a table and begun to ring a handbell. When the moment of panic was over, I looked up and saw her still ringing it wildly.

In spite of this horrible incident and the fact that on Christmas eve the Germans had begun to shell Châlons with a long-range Big Bertha and had dropped four shells into the middle of the town by the time I left on Boxing Day, I enjoyed my Christmas there very much, as I liked Reynolds Ball and Dr Hilda Clark. I wish, however, that I had stayed at Sommeilles and had seen Frankie at one of his happiest moments. He wrote to me:

I do wish you could have been here for the Children's party on Friday. It was God's own success. All the village turned up, even Onesime, which was, I felt, like having Royalty at one's ball. Excellent food was provided, then games and dancing, several couples being formed for *La Scoyotte*—self and Madame Machinet, Edwards and Simone etc. Finally the Christmas-tree with self in the title role, unfortunately recognised at once by the majority of the children present. Madame Rouillon Leblanc however was deceived. But it really was delightful seeing everybody so happy, young and old alike. All the gendarmes were there and masses of children I'd never seen before, who hadn't been invited and didn't belong to Sommeilles at all. Fortunately there were spare presents. The whole organisation reflected the greatest credit on Margaret Bulley. Young Geddes came with his fiddle: we furbished up the big room in the school till it really looked quite nice with evergreens and lanterns and flags. In the evening we settled down to a bottle of champagne, really a trifle too sweet, stood us by Madame Niçaise Prevost—and then, Margaret, Geddes, self and Miss Rackstraw went round to Madame Dommartin's. Geddes excited the old lady with his fiddle so much that she sang incessantly, more divinely than ever. I went along to Louppy next day and again appeared as Father Christmas. Also a great success and I had a glass of beer afterwards with the Curé and the Mayor. I don't know what is the public opinion of my performances, but for my part, I thought they left little to be desired. . . . My duties get more and more various. This morning Miss Allen came to see the various invalids, Germaine Colas has had a sore throat, leaving a cough. But Miss Allen hadn't time to see her and asked me to look at her throat myself. I found it rather an agreeable occupation and wasted as much time as possible over it, being delighted at being asked to do the sort of thing that gets one sent home. Georges seemed very cut up at not having said goodbye to you. So you might be particularly affectionate if you write to him. Also his grandmother died on Christmas Day which was rather galling for him.

VI

ASHEHAM is a small, late Regency or early Victorian farmhouse which stands in a flat, shovel-shaped depression at the north-west corner of the range of the South Downs which stretches from where, in the east, the Cuckmere River cuts through it at Alfriston to where, in the west, the Sussex Ouse cuts through the chalk between Beddingham and Newhaven.

The bottom meadow, in which Asheham stands, lay between high banks, on the slopes of which grew tall beech trees, and ran back into the main mass of Itford hill which rose from the farmyard behind the house to a height of five hundred feet. Asheham itself looked west across the river valley to Rodmell, a mile or so away on the first high ground on the other side of the water meadows. It has a plain front and a slate roof, but its most striking feature is its fenestration: double french windows with arched lights over them: the combination gives its façade a curiously dreamlike character, like a house drawn on a plate or by a child. Asheham was a little set apart, not quite of the real world, like the houses in Walter De La Mare's novels. It was haunted, though I never saw a ghost. Clive (the most unlikely of all the rationalists who stayed or lived in it) in company with Duncan and Harry Norton did actually see a ghost:—a figure passing from room to room and crossing the windows, as they walked up to the house when they knew for a fact that it was empty. They found it empty when they went in. Virginia wrote *A Haunted House* in the collection of experimental sketches and impressions which she published in *Monday or Tuesday*, a year or two after the visit I shall describe, and that lovely sketch evokes the ghost of Asheham, a house with a personal character as individual as that of a woman one has loved, and who is dead. For many years Asheham house has only been a ghost, for though it is standing its surroundings have been utterly transformed. An immense heap of spoilage has been dumped into the flat meadow in front of it, entirely shutting out the view. This is now overgrown with briars and bushes and young trees. Huge sheds, warehouses and a roasting oven with a tall chimney fill the old farmyard. Much of the down behind has been excavated. The great yellow lorries grind up to it empty along a wide concrete roadway and rumble away with loads of cement in paper bags. A siren blows. To visit Asheham house today is a rude lesson in the importance of economics. The girl who forty years ago was the most lovely figure in a ballroom, is met again serving as the cashier in a cafeteria. . . .

Places explain people. They become impregnated with the spirit of those who have lived and been happy in them. For a full understanding of Virginia, who spent her holidays and week-ends there for several years after her marriage, Asheham would greatly help. But the clue has almost gone—it is more a memory than a reality and in common with all the houses which Virginia made her own there was a suggestion in it of a timeless, underwater world.

Coming to Asheham in January 1916 from the *Zone des Armées* was extraordinary. It was a house filled with—after living with the Quakers I hesitate to use the word friends— it was filled with intimates. There was leisure; nothing urgent; sympathy quick to turn to laughter; complete freedom. For six months I had lived at close quarters with people with whom I had little in common. I found myself in an almost forgotten heaven. Vanessa, Clive, Duncan and I stayed at Asheham for about ten days. Norton and Lytton were there for part of the time; Maynard came for at least one week-end. The children were, I suppose, staying with their grandparents at Seend. We went up for walks on the Downs; the weather I think was clear and frosty, and Duncan and I practised a cruel sport on Vanessa, called crimping. Each of us would take one of her arms casually, as we reached the edge of the Down, and then we would suddenly rush with her down the precipitous slope, in spite of her cries for mercy. If Clive, Maynard, or Harry Norton were with us they would look after us with mild annoyance at finding the intellectual discussion interrupted by such childish horseplay.

I went once to look for a book in the small sitting-room which we did not use, and looked with surprise at a large photograph of Henry James, which stood, an oddly conventional object, on Virginia's writing table. I admired James's work myself greatly and had read many of his stories and some of his novels; both my parents were also great admirers of his, but I was surprised to find that Virginia shared our opinion. Henry James was mortally ill; he died about a month later.

Much of our talk was about the prospects of the bill introducing conscription, which all our visitors agreed that they would resist. Clive had been asked by Lloyd George, then Minister for War, to serve on a Committee which was to recommend safeguards for conscientious objectors. Many arguments were used against conscription, among them that the war which had been begun in opposition to militarism, was militarising England and taking away one of the outstanding liberties of the British people. Our objections were, in truth, all political objections—but that does not mean that they were not also a matter of conscience. We distrusted the military conduct of the war—and we were right to do so. Some of us believed that a negotiated peace was the only way in which European civilisation could be saved from ruin. Clive, in particular, supported that view with what seemed to me irrefutable arguments, and everything I had seen in France led me to agree with him. We all intensely disliked the Germans, but the price which would have to be paid for their humiliation and defeat seemed likely to be the sacrifice of a generation and impoverishment of Europe. Although I have completely abandoned my pacifist opinions (I took a commission in the R.A.F. V.R. in September 1939), everything which has occurred since the end of the First World War leads me to think that Clive and the rest of us were right.

Maynard was in an exceptional position inasmuch as he was

occupying a position of continually increasing importance in the Treasury, and was thus in possession of the secret facts with regard to the day to day conduct of the war. Much of what his closest friends said exasperated him, since they were ignorant of the facts and he was unable to use his knowledge to prove them mistaken. On the other hand his detailed information led him frequently to adopt a short-term view and he sometimes failed to see the major issues as clearly as his friends. When, in 1918, the policy of British intervention in Russia came up my mother, Constance, was right and realistic, and Maynard, with all the detailed knowledge of day to day secret information, was wrong.

Our holiday at Asheham came to an end and, within a few weeks, the bill for compulsory military service was brought in by the Government and became law. Sir John Simon resigned from the Cabinet and led the fruitless opposition to it. Two societies organised resistance to the Act: The Council for Civil Liberties and the No-Conscription Fellowship, organised by Clifford Allen, afterwards created Lord Allen of Hurtwood for his support of Ramsay Macdonald. I joined many of my friends in Bloomsbury in volunteering to help at the office of the National Council for Civil Liberties, other assistants at the office in Fleet Street were Duncan, Adrian, Vanessa, R. C. Trevelyan and James Strachey, who had just been sacked for his opinions from his job as sub-editor of *The Spectator* by his cousin the editor, St Loe Strachey. Some of us addressed envelopes and stuck on stamps; others wrote leaflets. One of them accused the Government of bringing in conscription in order to be able to prevent strikes and crush Labour. Lytton wrote the second half of it:

The Cat kept saying to the Mouse that she was a high-minded person, and that if the Mouse would only come a little nearer they could both get the cheese. The Mouse said: "Thank you, Pussy; it's not the cheese you want: it's my skin!"

This leaflet was printed but all but one or two copies were destroyed owing to the violent disapproval of Sir John Simon.

Under the Military Service Act, Tribunals were set up all over the country to decide on cases where objections were raised on account of great hardship, or of conscience.

There was no mechanism for recording the cases brought before the Tribunals, the treatment of applicants, the evidence brought forward, or the reasons given for the decisions made. The Council for Civil Liberties and the No-Conscription Fellowship therefore began to organise watchers who were to take notes of the cases. It turned out, however, that this was a task greatly beyond their resources. Neither body had the finances necessary to employ hundreds of shorthand reporters and there were not nearly enough volunteers qualified to undertake such work. Even had reports been taken, they would have needed an immense amount of sifting. One day a smallish, white-bearded old gentleman appeared in our office and he and I at once became firm friends. We were given the job of organising relays of watchers for some of the London Tribunals:— a task which we performed badly, as most of the voluntary helpers were unqualified. He was a master at Harrow called Frank Marshall and was an uncle of Ray Marshall, whom I married six years later.

When we were working in the Fleet Street office, what I may call the Gordon Square contingent: Vanessa, Adrian, Duncan, James Strachey and I often had lunch together. But when Bob Trevelyan came to work with us, he joined us, and unfortunately Vanessa thought him a bore. I remember her rushing out of the office and dashing through the traffic across Fleet Street, only narrowly escaping being crushed between a lorry and a bus and waving wildly to us from the opposite pavement, in order to escape Bob, who was following us down the office stairs. On that occasion we did avoid him and blew Vanessa up for risking her life in such a manner.

"I would far rather be run over than listen to Bob Trevy for another hour," she declared. "He has been talking to me without stopping all the morning, and I had no cotton wool to put in my ears."

On the first of February 1915, a party consisting of Oliver

Strachey, who had recently returned to England from India, Vanessa, Barbara Hiles, Carrington, Duncan, John Nash and I, went to the World's Fair at Islington. I only recall the occasion because Carrington and I left the others and wandered off round the sideshows, until we came to where the Tattooed Venus exhibited herself. She was a fine woman in her forties with a proud expression on her tough face. Her entire back, from the very cleft of her bottom to the nape of her neck and her shoulders and arms were marvellously emblazoned with mermaids, sea-serpents, ships in full sail, sailors, tigers, elephants with howdahs, British soldiers in scarlet coats and spiked helmets assailed by natives armed with assegais, all intertwined with whorls of red and blue and black so as to give the effect of a Paisley shawl inspired by the chapter headings in *Petit Larousse.*

Carrington was spell-bound and gazed at her in silence for a little while. Then, to my horror, I saw her wet her finger with her saliva and rapidly rub a spot on the living tapestry before us. The Venus turned on her indignantly and Carrington at once said: "I beg your pardon. . . . I forgot that you were . . ." She was obviously going to say "were alive"—but I broke in with some feeble flattery. Venus, however, felt that she had been insulted: her anger rose and her dark beauty was an extraordinary contrast to Carrington's white-heart cherry coloration and her very blue, deceptively innocent eyes. For a moment as the two women faced each other, they made a picture as unforgettable as that of the Westmoreland cottage girl and the wandering Malay, described by De Quincey in the Opium Eater. Babbling apologies, I hastily dragged Carrington out of the tent. I have seldom witnessed such a social *gaffe,* but Carrington was unperturbed and unrepentant. "It would be so easy for her to put the patterns on with a transfer," she said. "Then she could wash it all off whenever she liked, or if the circus was closed in summer." But the colours had not run and the pattern had not blurred under the test applied.

Julian Bell's birthday was on Friday, 4th of February. He was eight years old and we had a birthday party for him in the studio after Vanessa had come back with the boys and with Molly MacCarthy and her little daughter Rachel, from the pantomime. Perhaps it was something they had seen which led Julian to say, "I shall go round the world before I fall in love, in order to find out who is the most beautiful person in it."

Rachel MacCarthy replied: "Oh, but the prettiest people are never the nicest."

Julian replied with consummate tact: "Well Molly is pretty and she is nice, and Nessa is nice and she is pretty."

Vanessa with her usual logic and love of mischief asked: "But if you couldn't make up your mind who was the prettiest?" Julian replied perfectly calmly: "Nessa you are too confusing."

About this time Duncan and I were invited to a memorable week-end party at Garsington, the Morrells' country house near Oxford. I was to go there many times during the war years, but on this occasion the other guests were all young: Barbara Hiles, Carrington, and John Nash, and all of them were painters.

Garsington was on the slope of a hill. The approach was down a lane with farm buildings on the right hand side, screening it, so that the lovely dignified front of the Tudor Manor House came as a surprise. It was noble, even grand, yet it was the very reverse of ostentatious. Hiding itself to the last moment, the façade contrived from the front to look like that of a smaller house than it actually was. On the garden side its full extent and nobility were revealed and it dominated the delightful garden which sloped away from it and terminated in an oblong piece of ornamental water, converted by Ottoline into a swimming pool, screened by yew hedges which formed a background for statues and plaster casts.

Inside there were several large panelled rooms, which had, I surmise, been a mixture of genuine seventeenth century and

Victorian baronial styles before Ottoline descended upon them. She had transformed them, stamping her personality ruthlessly everywhere. The oak panelling had been painted a dark peacock blue-green; the bare and sombre dignity of Elizabethan wood and stone had been overwhelmed with an almost oriental magnificence: the luxuries of silk curtains and Persian carpets, cushions and pouffes. Ottoline's pack of pug dogs trotted everywhere and added to the Beardsley quality, which was one half of her natural taste. The characteristic of every house in which Ottoline lived was its smell and the smell of Garsington was stronger than that of Bedford Square. It reeked of the bowls of pot-pourri and orris-root which stood on every mantel-piece, side table and window-sill and of the desiccated oranges, studded with cloves, which Ottoline loved making. The walls were covered with a variety of pictures. Italian pictures and bric-à-brac, drawings by John, water-colours for fans by Conder, who was rumoured to have been one of Ottoline's first conquests, paintings by Duncan and Gertler and a dozen other of the younger artists.

Greeting us was Philip Morrell in riding breeches and rat-catcher coat with a glassy geniality gleaming in his eyes and his head thrown so far back that the high bridge of his nose was level with his forehead. And the pugs barked their welcome. At Garsington, Philip Morrell, posing as a farmer, exhibited precisely the kind of humbug which the Victorian novelists, such as Surtees and Thackeray, loved to make the subject of their good-tempered fun. He was addicted to double-breasted waistcoats which gave him a slight resemblance to Leech's drawings of Mr Jawleyford in Surtees' masterpiece, *Mr Sponge's Sporting Tour*.

But the humbug did not run all through. It was not in the man himself, but perhaps the result of his marriage. In spite of his uneasiness, even his falsity, I was often aware of a genuine shy interest, kindness and a sincere wish to help me. There were also moments in conversation when it seemed as though he hoped to pick up some hint which would enable him to understand the mystery of life a little better.

Besides Ottoline and Philip there were, living at Garsington, their daughter Julian, Juliet, a young Swiss girl who was her companion, and Maria Nys, the daughter of Belgian friends of Ottoline's who was being given shelter in the Morrells' home during the war. Julian Huxley married Juliet and Aldous Huxley married Maria.

Saturday afternoon was wet and, after lunch, Ottoline clapped her hands with inspiration. "All of you are artists, except Bunny, so you shall decorate the room in the Monastic Building."

She led us out to an adjacent building which I had taken for a barn and we followed her up a ladder to a long empty white-washed room above. The painters were allotted different bits of the walls and agreed that their subjects should be scenes of rural life.

They got out their paints, Ottoline went away, and we set to work—for I became a painter rather than sit idle. We worked hard and, by tea-time, we had all finished except Duncan, who had run into some snag. A gay and care-free evening followed, with Ottoline at her most charming and Philip Morrell greatly enjoying himself playing on the pianola.

Next morning the sun was shining. But Ottoline turned to Duncan after breakfast and said: "Duncan you must finish your lovely picture in the Monastic Building." He protested feebly but she was firm.

The rest of us were sent off with Maria, Juliet and Julian for a country walk. Once out of sight, however, I turned back and joined Duncan in his prison. I found him furiously angry and declaring that he would not touch a brush.

"Nonsense. She will keep you here all the afternoon too. The thing is to finish the picture quickly."

Duncan, however, was obstinate and not to be persuaded, so I picked up his palette and brushes and set vigorously to work on his picture. After I had been painting for a quarter of an hour, Duncan, who had been looking out of the window in a dudgeon, came to inspect the picture and his eyes lit up with interest.

"I say, that's quite a new idea; one might make something out of that." His mood had changed and he took up a brush. Working together we made rapid progress and the picture had been nearly completed, and quite transformed, when I heard the ladder creak. I had just time to drop the brush I was holding and cross the room to the other window when Ottoline's head appeared through the trapdoor.

"Ohhh, Duncan. . . . What a lot of work you've done. . . . Ohhh. It is exciting . . . you've changed it so much. . . . It's a masterpiece. . . ." Suddenly she caught sight of me. "What are you doing here, Bunny? The others are all looking for you. . . . Do go and find them. . . ." I was glad to obey.

During lunch she told us how Duncan had finished his picture and what a wonderful masterpiece it was, quite transformed from the day before. On a later visit I went back to have a look at the pictures again. To my surprise the works of John Nash, Barbara and Carrington and my original little daub had been white-washed over. Only the masterpiece by Grant dominated the room. Carrington, who had painted an extremely charming sketch, always regarded this discrimination, in favour of what was largely my work, as an outrage.

Maynard may possibly have felt some responsibility for persuading me to leave the Friends; at all events he convinced Duncan and me it was no good our hanging about in London and that we should have more chance of exemption from Military Service if we were working on the land. A cousin of Duncan's mother, a Miss Florence Ewebank, had just died; her house, garden and orchards were empty and neglected. It fell, I think, to Major Bartle Grant to dispose of them. It was soon arranged that Duncan should rent Wissett Lodge, that he and I should set up as fruit-farmers, and that Vanessa should come down for the summer and keep house for us, bringing Julian, Quentin and Blanche, the tall housemaid. I went down to Wissett with Duncan and met his father there. It was a remote little village in Suffolk, a few miles from the market town of Halesworth. A line of brick or weatherboarded cottages straggled along a road which followed a small stream. On the other side of the stream were Miss Ewebank's orchard of apples, interplanted with blackcurrants; Wissett Lodge was half a mile away on higher ground. Major Bartle Grant was not a militarist, but he was cross with Duncan for not joining the army and I expect he blamed me for it. He was polite to me, though not effusive, but in conversation with Duncan he always referred to me as: "Your friend Garbage."

The Major was a small man with many tricks of manner with which I was familiar in Duncan. He blinked his eyes a great deal while speaking and rubbed the end of his nose with the flat of his palm and uttered little snorts as an aid to self-expression. He regretted what Duncan was about to do; he may even have greatly disapproved, but he loved his son and did not wish to interfere in his life. So he was helping us to do what he thought was mistaken, possibly wrong, and certainly a breach of all his family traditions. The snorts and the Garbages were a slight relief to his feelings. I liked Major Grant, but he did not like me.

Wissett Lodge was a little early Victorian house with numerous small, exceptionally dark, rooms.* They were dark partly because the ceilings are low and the floors slightly below ground-level; partly because the walls and windows were smothered with rambler roses and climbing plants. A magnificent wistaria, the largest I have ever seen, almost completely blocked the windows of the drawing-room and of the large bedroom above. But even without the creepers, the house would have been dark, for it was dominated by an enormous ilex—a "plum-pudding tree" the children called it—which shut out all the light from the east. On the west, a huge fig-tree shut out the light. Wissett Lodge had none of the magic of Asheham, but it had charm and breathed out the spirit of Miss Florence Ewebank, for whom I soon felt a growing affection and regard, as I read her Bee Journal, her diary of work in garden and orchard and her notebook full of household and cooking recipes, and

* It has been modernised since I lived in it.

as I devoted myself to carrying on her enterprises. I have her Bee Journal and some of her notebooks still.

I began to work very hard at Wissett: the orchards badly needed pruning, the blackcurrant bushes were infected with "big bud." I dug all day and planned new operations late into the evening. I was young and strong and this was my first falling in love with working on the land. I made plans, scoured the countryside for bees, went to market-day auctions at Halesworth and bought chickens, ducklings, and goslings.

Duncan worked hard too, but I am glad to say that he often spent either the morning or the afternoon in painting. Our future was uncertain; it was highly probable that I should be uprooted from Wissett even before I had taken root—but ignoring such possibilities I worked with love.

One evening, late in March, as Duncan and I walked up from the orchard, we paused to look at the edges of the lawn, overhanging the pond. They were crowded with early daffodils.

"A practical man would turn those flowers to account," said Duncan. I started guiltily, for I prided myself on being the practical man of the pair and here was Duncan invading my province while I had been enjoying the beauty of the flowers with no thought of turning a penny.

"We ought to pick them all and take them into Norwich to sell," he added. I could but agree and flew to my authority: the three volumes of bound-up leaflets issued by the Board of Agriculture. There I found directions on the growing, marketing and packaging of daffodils. Duncan was obviously right and the prospects were made to look excellent.

After tea Vanessa and Blanche, who had just arrived, were pressed into the task of picking the flowers in the twilight, and later we sorted them and tied them in bunches. We had just over twelve dozen bunches with twelve blooms in each bunch. Next morning Duncan and I were up soon after dawn, packed our flowers in hampers which we fastened to the handlebars of our bicycles and set off to ride the twenty-four miles to Norwich.

We went by by-roads and lanes to Bungay, discovering new beauties at every turn of the road: old cottages with early spring flowers in their gardens, cart-horses with jingling brasses drawing the sacks of seed barley to the fields. And then empty pastures and pightles and the birds nesting and the first leaves breaking along the hawthorn hedges.

Later, when we caught sight of Norwich below us, we rested while Duncan tried to identify the landscape before us with pictures that Crome had painted. We bicycled gaily into the city but soon found that the flower-shops were well supplied and that the young women who served in them haughtily refused to buy. The stalls in the market-place were shutting up, but at last Duncan was directed to a small fruit and flower shop which bought the whole lot of flowers at a penny a bunch— twelve and sixpence. I had hoped to get at least threepence. However we were able to go and stand ourselves lunch on the proceeds. Duncan had the instinct of seizing any opportunity. By a stroke of luck we were in Norwich and there was the picture gallery, Castle and Cathedral to be visited. We spent a long time in the picture gallery, although most of the pictures were very bad, so that finally we had to come home by train. Our expenses had put us heavily out of pocket on the day. As we rode up to Wissett Lodge, I looked a trifle sadly at the flowerless garden and the stripped banks on each side of the ornamental pond. However, as a practical man I thought we had done the right thing, and I respected Duncan for his business instincts.

Besides the orchards there were several paddocks where we decided to keep fowls.

Soon we had quite a large flock of white Leghorns, including six birds from a prize-winning poultry farm. They were to be kept apart and their eggs set under broody hens. Unfortunately they flew like pheasants, and in spite of my efforts they were always getting mixed up with the other birds. When this occurred, it was a long business finding and catching the birds with yellow rings round one leg among about fifty birds almost identical with them. Duncan, however, had a brilliant idea. If we were to dye the tails of the pedigree birds blue, it would enable us to see at a glance if one of them had got into the wrong enclosure and we should be able to catch the right bird more quickly. We at once mixed some blue dye in a bucket and holding the birds firmly upside down, dipped their tails in it. The effect was lovely. With their big bright scarlet combs, white bodies and blue tails they looked like French tricolour flags as they sped about in their run on the green paddock. The idea was extremely practical and saved us a lot of trouble, but oddly enough it had an unfortunate result.

The Mauser family had long been retainers of Miss Ewebank. Until our arrival Mrs Mauser had acted as caretaker of Wissett Lodge and Mauser himself had done a minimum of work in the garden. But, with our advent, these employments had come to an end and the Mausers headed a faction in the village which looked upon our activities with an unfriendly eye. Every Sunday, groups of village people strolled up to Wissett Lodge and looked for a long time over the paddock gate to see what new folly we had committed. Our tricolour fowls turned out to be the last straw. Nobody laughed at them, or congratulated Duncan on his labour-saving idea. They thought it was a joke, but as they could not see the point of it became convinced it was a joke at their expense. We were making fun of them, of the birds, of serious poultry keeping. Hostility grew thereafter, but it was not felt by all. The land adjoining Wissett Lodge was occupied by Mr Dunnett, a friendly and charming old man who asked nothing of us and gave Duncan a sheepdog puppy with one blue eye, which he called Henry after Ottoline's brother, Lord Henry Cavendish Bentinck, who had recently bought a picture by Duncan. Mr Dunnett was liked by all his animals and, when one of his geese hatched out her eggs, the gander took wing and flew to where Dunnett was working in the hayfield, three meadows away. The bird set up a tremendous cry and presently flew back to the farm. When the loaded hay waggon was brought into the stackyard, Mr Dunnett went to where the goose was sitting and saw the goslings, just out of the egg.

The man in Wissett with whom we had most to do was a gipsy higgler called Cutts, as his services were essential to our existence. He made a good deal of money out of us, but I am sure he liked us and our unusual ways of doing things, as he had a very lively mind and was full of plans and inventions. Cutts drove us and our visitors to Halesworth station in his battered dogcart and if I bought or sold anything in Halesworth market he conveyed it for us in his four-wheeled coster's cart.

He was always swapping his ponies with other gipsies and he did not always get the best of it. On one occasion he took a lame pony to a fair, determined to get rid of it and eventually found a gipsy with a pony to swap, or sell. The man looked at Cutt's pony but did not ask to have its paces shown off, before he agreed to the exchange. Cutts was so eager to get rid of his own animal that he only gave a brief look at the other pony which was tied up against a wall.

The bargain was struck but when Cutts turned his acquisition round he found that on the far side it was eaten away with mange and blind in the eye.

We had many visitors at Wissett Lodge. Barbara Hiles arrived on a motor-cycle and took me round the neighbourhood, riding pillion behind her. Oliver and Lytton Strachey, Saxon Sydney-Turner and Harry Norton all came. But the most memorable visit was that of Ottoline. The weather was wet. The low-ceilinged little rooms would scarcely contain our magnificent visitor, who I think was uncomfortable. Duncan and I went out most of the day—working, and Heaven knows how Vanessa kept her entertained. Blanche reported that when she went into Ottoline's bedroom with a tray of tea in the morning, Ottoline was lying in bed with her face already completely made up.

I remember the feeling of relief when Monday morning came and Cutts drove his dogcart up to the door. Ottoline, who retired after breakfast, suddenly appeared in a dress which she had not worn before during her visit. It might have been designed by Bakst for a Russian ballet on a Circassian folktale

116

theme. Russian boots of red morocco were revealed under a full, light-blue silk tunic, over which she wore a white kaftan with embroidered cartridge pouches on the chest, on to which fell the ropes of Portland pearls. On her head was a tall Astrakhan fez. As we gathered round, with Julian and Quentin there to say goodbye, a blaze of sunlight fell unexpectedly upon the scene after the long wet week-end, and it lit up, with cruel accuracy, Ottoline's make-up which must have been done more or less by guess-work in her dark little bedroom. As she bent down to kiss Quentin, the little boy flinched and asked:

"Why have you got all that on?"

There was a moment's silence after this unanswerable question; then a deep gurgle, half-growl, half whine, from Ottoline, which passed itself off as a laugh—a rush of farewells from Vanessa, Duncan handed Ottoline up beside Cutts, she seated herself and waved and off they drove looking exactly like the advertisement for a circus.

On Sundays I used to work in the vegetable garden, so as not to outrage the Sabbatical prejudices of the villagers by being seen working in the orchards, and I was rather surprised when Harry Norton discarded the Sunday paper and came tripping out across the lawn, sat down near where I was working and talked to me as I dug. I had scarcely known him, but we soon became firm friends. Norton was tall but his shin bones were too short and he walked with ridiculously short steps. His face was round with a fine forehead, a short straight nose and he had a very bad complexion with acne, which, like his pessimism, was due to his leading a much too sedentary life. He wore glasses which magnified his brown eyes. Norton was a mathematician, a fellow of Trinity College, Cambridge, and he was working on what I believe is called the Cantorian theory of numbers. His intelligence was, I think, *purer* than any of the first-class intelligences of Old Bloomsbury. By purer, I mean less intermingled with emotions, prejudices and beliefs. No one could have claimed pure intelligence as a characteristic of Russell, or Keynes, or Dickinson, or Fry.

Nor were the intelligences of Clive, Lytton, Duncan, Vanessa, Desmond, Leonard or Virginia pure.

Of the older men Charlie Sanger and, of the younger, Harry Norton were the only ones with that very rare thing: an intelligence detached and impartial, which could not be swayed or corrupted by the passions, sympathies and habits of the body to which it belonged.

Harry Norton had come to Wissett because of his devotion to Vanessa, but Lytton came, I felt sure, as much to see me as to see any of the others. One afternoon, during his visit, we went together for a walk; the young corn was already in ear and nearly waist-high and as we walked in single file along the edge of the field so as not to tread it down, he began telling me, turning his head a little and talking over his shoulder, about a recent attachment which was occupying a great deal of his thoughts. Nicholas Bagenal, who was in love with Barbara Hiles, had just come out of hospital after recovering from a wound in the hip and Barbara had persuaded Lytton to play the part of chaperon during a week she wished to spend with Nick, before he went back to the front, in her father's cottage in North Wales. Lytton had suggested that Carrington should be a fourth member of the party. He had fallen in love with her and when the week was over had gone off with her on a visit to Bath and Wells. Lytton wanted to discuss Carrington's character and tell me all about their love affair but he did not at all want his attachment to come to the ears of Virginia, or of Ottoline, who he thought were certain to make mischief. So I was sworn to secrecy. I very rarely have let out a secret I should have kept, and I never referred to this confidence of Lytton's during his lifetime.

There was, at the time Lytton told me this, another reason for secrecy, which was that Carrington was afraid that if Gertler knew of her relations with Lytton he would be violent. Two years later, after Lytton and Carrington were living together at The Mill House, Tidmarsh, her fear proved justified. After a party given by Jack and Mary Hutchinson on the evening of 14th of February 1918, Lytton and Carrington left together and walked away into the blacked-out streets of London with their arms round each other, talking, and oblivious of a shadowy figure they overtook. It was Gertler, who sprang at them with hoarse cries of rage and attacked Lytton with his fists. Luckily Maynard and Clive were close behind and seized Mark and led him off.

A week after this incident, I happened to be dining with Lytton at the Eiffel Tower restaurant when Gertler came in, saw Lytton and hurried up and said: "I am so sorry about the other night. Please forgive me."

Lytton gave a little giggle and said: "It was nothing at all. Please don't worry yourself about it."

I don't think that was what Gertler wanted to be told. However, it was owing to my being present at this apology that I heard Lytton's account of the incident and of why Gertler had failed so completely to hold Carrington's affections.

I had written an account of what I was doing and why, to Godwin Baynes, who was a Major in the R.A.M.C. at a hospital in France. One day I received a reply from him which ended:

"Have Rupert and Nurse Cavell died in vain? I spew you out of my mouth. . . ."

I had known for months that I should be regarded by many acquaintances as a coward and a shirker, but Godwin's letter came as a shock. He had known me since I was a boy of sixteen. I had never kept back a thought from him; he had known my parents and my upbringing and he wrote assuming that I was a coward, only concerned with saving my own skin. For all that I knew I *was* a coward, for no man can say that he is not until his courage has been proved. But Godwin must have known that it was not fear which made me refuse military service, but the arguments of men whom I respected, and he might have guessed that what I had seen of the devastation of war in France had also led me to that course.

I was able to compare Godwin's attitude to me with that of Maynard to Ferenc Bekassy and I remembered how Maynard had then put personal friendship above patriotism and had insisted that his duty was to help his friend to join our enemies when he had been unable to persuade him to remain in England.* I wrote to Godwin immediately to say that I hoped his judgment was temporary and that his letter had not altered my feelings for him. But the latter statement was only a pious hope, which turned out to be untrue. As the war went on, I came to understand that whatever I might say, or wish, my friendship and respect for him was utterly destroyed. But I did not realise this fully until I met him again in person. His letter was an excellent moral tonic for me, though not in the way he had intended. I realised that I must expect to lose other friends. The first of them was his sister, Ruth. Godwin's breach with me would put her in an unfair position, for she also condemned my behaviour and did not like, or understand, my friends and my philosophy.

Meanwhile the first of our appearances before a Tribunal was upon us and the cases of many of our friends had already been decided.

Bertie Farjeon, who enlisted alone, after my refusal to enlist with him, had failed to come up to the medical standards of 1914 and had been discharged from the army. He now was called up and put forward a plea of conscientious objection which was accepted. As the Strachey home was still in Belsize Park Gardens, Lytton's case also came before the Hampstead Tribunal. I wish that I had been there, as it must have been an extraordinary spectacle. The Stracheys attended in full force. First came Pippa carrying a light-blue air-cushion as Lytton was, at the time, suffering from that distressing malady, the piles. Then James, Marjorie, Pernel and Oliver trooped in, followed by Lytton himself. The proceedings were, in any case, a farce, as Lytton's health would not have been good enough for him to become either a soldier, a farm labourer, or a factory worker.

In the course of the proceedings the Military Representative was inspired with a flight of fancy and asked:

* See *The Golden Echo*, p. 270.

"What would you do, Mr Strachey, if you saw an Uhlan attempting to rape your sister?"

Lytton looked at his sisters in turn, as though trying to visualise the scene, and gravely replied in his high voice:

"I should try to interpose my own body."

The cases of Clive, James, Adrian and Gerald Shove also came up. All of them were eventually given exemption on condition of doing work of national importance.

Duncan and I appeared before the Local Tribunal at Blything. Adrian, who had read law, presented our cases, but did it extremely badly, as though he was addressing a Judge in Chancery who would decide the case on points of law. Actually the the startled farmers were intensely suspicious of us because we had recently come to live in Suffolk. A tiny incident will exemplify the whole. Adrian mentioned that my mother had been a lifelong pacifist, who had visited Tolstoy in Russia. In dismissing our case the Chairman remarked that they had listened to much irrelevant matter. What difference could it make what town my mother had stayed in during the course of her travels? We did not bother to explain that Tolstoy was a person and not a place, and filed out, already beginning to discuss the appeal as we went through the doorway.

Several weeks later, we were summoned to the Appeal Tribunal at Ipswich. The whole atmosphere there was very different. This time Maynard had taken charge. Philip Morrell also came to give evidence on behalf of both of us, an action for which I have always felt the warmest gratitude to him. Edward, who had returned from the Italian Ambulance Unit to find himself unemployed, also turned up.

The Tribunal, though composed of men superior in intellectual calibre to the puzzled farmers of Blything, included such mutually antagonistic elements that the extremists on each side cancelled each other out. An indignant Nonconformist conducted an argument in fierce whispers with a Diehard Baronet in a Brigade of Guards tie, while the Chairman decided the case with practically no reference to his colleagues.

Maynard took an aggressive line from the first moment.

Carrying a large locked bag with the Royal cipher on it, he demanded that our cases should be heard as expeditiously as possible, as he had left work of the utmost national importance in order to attend and he had to be back at the Treasury at the earliest possible moment.

After Maynard had presented Duncan's case, Duncan was cross-examined by the Military Representative, a pleasant young officer, who had perhaps been sent back wounded, or shell-shocked, and whose heart was not in hounding cowards and shirkers to their deaths.

"I think I understand your scruples, Mr Grant. But you would not push your objection to war-work so far as to refuse to make a pair of boots, I suppose?"

Duncan, who had been sitting hunched up and dejected, looked up brightly at this question and replied with a trace of hauteur:

"Under no circumstances whatever, would I consent to make a pair of *boots*." Several of the Tribunal nodded approvingly. It had become a class matter. Duncan was a gentleman and objected to making boots, and they could enter into the blighter's feelings. The Military Representative saw that he had somehow made an unfortunate suggestion and said weakly: "Oh, I don't actually mean that you should make boots. . . . There are hundreds of other forms of war-work. . . ."

"I would never consent to make a pair of boots," repeated Duncan doggedly and it was obvious that even the Diehard Baronet understood his point of view. The members of the Tribunal began to discuss the case among themselves and the Chairman announced that Duncan had been awarded non-combatant service. At Maynard's insistence, he was allowed the right to appeal to the Central Tribunal. My turn came next. I put in a letter from the Prefect of the Marne, full of high praise for the work of the Friends War Victims Relief Expedition. I was at once asked whether I would go back to work with it. This did not suit me, so I replied that the work in the Marne was rapidly coming to an end—which was technically true as the Friends had moved into the Meuse—and the matter was not pursued. Philip Morrell testified to the sincerity of my convictions and the honesty of my character. The chairman smoothly announced that, like Duncan, I was awarded non-combatant service. I immediately demanded the right to appeal to the Central Tribunal, on which everything turned.

"It is quite foolish of you to wish to appeal," replied the Chairman. "Your case does not offer any exceptional features which would justify my giving you permission to appeal. On what do you base your claim to do so?"

It was touch and go and I saw that there was only one thing to be done, though even at the moment I felt a cad in doing it.

"I ask for leave to appeal because your decision is unjust and a violation of the intention of the Act of Parliament. I believe the Central Tribunal will reverse it."

The Chairman started and his face flushed, as though I had actually slapped it.

"Leave to appeal granted," he said angrily as we stared each other in the eyes. I had judged his character rightly. He was so honest and fair-minded a man that once his integrity was publicly impugned he would never be able to refuse the other side a hearing. It turned out, however, that my words proved true. Duncan and I were sent long questionnaires by the Central Tribunal which we filled up absolutely truthfully, after much searching of heart.

Duncan took the line that he belonged to a tiny minority and that his views differed *in toto* from the majority on almost every subject. His opinions would never be attended to, and he would never fight for those of the majority, particularly as he believed it was always morally wrong to employ violence.

I replied that I did not think that the use of violence was always wrong, but that I believed it was wrong to delegate one's right of private judgment and therefore it was impossible for me to be a soldier. The essence of a good soldier was to obey orders without question. Once that was agreed, he might be ordered to commit any atrocity.

The problem I raised in this reply has cropped up after the Second World War, since the punishment of war criminals depends on the view that the delegation of private judgment and of personal responsibility for one's acts is ultimately indefensible. But though my views were the basis of the prosecutor's case at Nuremberg, they were not the correct ones in 1916, and later on I heard from Philip Morrell, who had asked Lord Younger, the Chairman of the Central Tribunal about our cases, that whereas Duncan had at once been given exemption on condition of doing work of national importance, my case had been a very difficult one and that it was only because of my record with the Quakers that he had been able to give me exemption on the same terms as Duncan.

We were ready to do "work of National Importance"—in other words work on a farm, but it was very doubtful if we should be allowed to go on with the work we were doing at Wissett Lodge. We put forward the best claim we could, based on the sales of our blackcurrants, which had been unexpectedly profitable and had made up our losses on ducks and fowls, but it was disallowed. The Tribunal declared that though the Wissett Lodge holding might qualify as work of national importance, it was out of the question for us to be our own employers.

It had become clear, after the introduction of the blue-tailed Leghorns, that we were unpopular at Wissett and we decided that it would be preferable to go back to the neighbourhood of Asheham, where Leonard and Virginia were living, and where Vanessa had pre-war acquaintances among the Sussex farmers, rather than to seek work in Suffolk.

Vanessa therefore paid a flying visit to Lewes on market day, and was introduced by one of her acquaintances to a brisk young farmer who agreed to employ Duncan and me as farm labourers. She was then introduced to an elderly farmer who was able to let her a farmhouse called Charleston on the Gage Estate, which would be empty a fortnight later. She thus completed the essential business of our move in an hour or so in Lewes market and returned to Wissett to tell us that she had settled our fate and taken an old farmhouse with a lake in front of it in which the former tenant, an elderly woman, was standing thigh-deep fishing when Vanessa arrived to look at it.

The actual move which followed was not so easy. Charleston had to be furnished and made habitable; the children, servants, and ducks had to be moved from Wissett, to say nothing of the easels, scores of canvases, boxes of paints, packing cases of books and a sack of globe artichoke suckers. My bees were left to be moved the following April. At first there was an acute shortage of furniture and for some weeks Duncan and I had to sleep on the floor. owing to the lack of beds. For a long while several of the rooms remained empty and unused. Then some furniture was brought down from 46 Gordon Square, other pieces were bought in Lewes and these with rare exceptions were astounding objects, bargains which attracted Duncan or Vanessa because of their strange shapes and low prices. One object seemed to be a rough model for the Tower Bridge and was made to do duty as a sideboard. Both Duncan and Vanessa appeared to believe that the inherent horror of any badly designed and constructed piece of furniture could be banished forever by decoration. The strange blend of hideous objects of furniture, painted with delightful works of art, gives to the rooms at Charleston a character which is unique and astonishing.

It turned out that our employer, Mr Hecks, was urgently in need of one of us. It was therefore settled that I should go ahead and start work, living at the Ram Inn at Firle, until Vanessa could organise the move. This provided me with the opportunity for an escapade which got me into hot water. I was at the time having a rather intermittent love affair with B ****** and, as both she and her friend C ****** were full of curiosity to see Charleston, we decided to go down for the week-end between my leaving Wissett and my starting work for Mr Hecks, to have a look at it and a walk over the Downs. Unfortunately we made a late start on Saturday and only reached Lewes in the late afternoon. Instead of taking the train to Glynde or Berwick, we walked out. The road was long and dusty and it was evening by the time we came to the Beddingham turn. It then occurred to me that, as I was going to stay at The Ram for a week or so, it might be impolitic to arrive after dark, accompanied by two young women, twenty-four hours before I was expected. Far better, and more economical, would be to go to Asheham and seek the hospitality of Leonard and Virginia. They would probably give us supper and, if the house was full of week-end guests, we could sleep in a barn. We therefore took the right-hand road. It was twilight when we came in sight of Asheham house, but no lights showed in the windows. When we reached it, we saw that the Woolfs were away and that the house was empty. It would be poor spirited indeed to sleep in straw, surrounded by calves and bullocks, when the friendly ghosts of Asheham were mutely imploring us to come in! So, without much difficulty, I shinned up a drainpipe and let myself in at a back window. It was lovely to be at Asheham again and I was full of happiness. not unmixed with the burglar's thrill, as I let my companions in and we crept stealthily from lovely room to lovely room.

We dared not light a lamp for fear of attracting the attention of farm people, but ate the food we had brought with us in the growing dark. Then full of gaiety and mischief, we groped our way upstairs. Almost all the blankets were in a locked linen cupboard, but we made up one of the beds by the light from the uncurtained window, and retired early.

All that day I had been feeling a breathless excitement because of C ******'s physical proximity, and after I had kissed B ****** goodnight, I lay awake for a long while, obsessed with the longing to embrace her neighbour. But I thought that I should wound B ******'s feelings irremediably and controlled myself until at last, exasperated by my own character, I fell asleep.

Several years later C ****** told me that she had also lain awake for hours, excited by my presence and by my kissing B ******, and longing for me to be her lover. Of us three, only B ******, fully satisfied, was fast asleep.

There is a flower in our garden
They call it Marigold
And if you will not when you may,
You shall not when you wold.

Next morning we woke early and fearful of discovery, let ourselves out and stole away. We climbed the steep side of the Down behind the farm and when we reached the top, we ate our very frugal breakfast. On our left was Mount Caburn with the Sussex weald stretching beyond its feet; on the right we could see a little naval vessel patrolling the coastal waters, black against the sparkling blue. There was not a human being in sight, no sound but the larks singing, and we rose up and walked on full of the heady intoxication of impudent youth, over the short turf, still grey with dew, towards the risen sun.

VII

MY first sight of Charleston was from the top of Firle
Beacon. I saw a line of elms sheltering barns and stock-
yards; the top of a tiled roof—the farmhouse beyond. When
we had descended we saw it was the centre of slow-moving
farm life. There were old Sussex waggons tucked away under
the boarded granary, an empty pig-sty, bullock yards, and
across the cart track a fine large farmhouse, with an untidy
strip of lawn in front of it, and a great plant of pampas grass
by the gate. Vanessa's lake had shrunk to a pond in front with
a big willow tree leaning over it, on the far side. Pastures
sloped away beyond. It was peaceful and, though the footpath to Firle passed between the barns and the house, it was
remote and seldom visited. On the north side of the house was
a garden with ancient pear-trees and greengages trained against
its flint and mortar walls. At the first inspection I could see that
it was ideally suited to all of us. The children would find it a
paradise and could navigate the pond in an old rotting punt
and fall into it. We could keep ducks; my beehives could be
deployed in the old orchard; the walled garden was private.
There was a room for Clive's library and for Duncan to
paint in.

Vanessa had indeed been fortunate on the day when she
settled the lines on which our lives were to run for the rest of
the war, in a hurried visit to Lewes market. When we had
peered through the windows and explored all the outhouses,
we went on to Firle and I said goodbye to my companions.
That evening I spent writing a sonnet to C * * * * * * and a letter
to Duncan describing Charleston and asking Vanessa to confess to Virginia that I had broken into Asheham and to obtain
her forgiveness. This was a stupid mistake. I only knew Virginia slightly, but I ought to have written to her and Leonard

CHARLESTON

at once, direct. Unfortunately we had been observed leaving Asheham by one of the farm labourers and Vanessa was too busy to write at once. Leonard and Virginia were considerably perturbed by the news of the burglary before they learned who the culprits were and they were indignant with me for some time afterwards.

Meanwhile Duncan had been tackling the task of selling the apple crop and much of our livestock at Wissett and of packing up. Duncan wrote to me:

It is silly to mind so much. But anyhow whatever may happen *this* has come to an end. . . . The Highlanders have a form of bagpiping called a *Lament*. This letter is a Lament: a raving relief of my feelings. I've joined, so Nessa says, the ranks of the poets. But I'm convinced the very finest poetry is the most impersonal; that is to say, in poetry an expression of all apparent aloofness from the human feelings involved in a person who has suffered all feeling. I presume the sort of poetry I mean results from a certain state of mind I am most happy to find in myself, when I have the luck to get there which isn't nearly as often or as frequent as I could wish.

In another letter he wrote:

The buck has come to live in the house. You see we can't do without a rabbit. He has taken to living in the fireplace of the oven in the kitchen, which just fits him. Poems of yours drop off every sticky honey box. I am making a collection. . . . Nessa is practically recovered but only yesterday. She is fearfully pleased that you like Mr Hecks and Charleston. It is a great relief to have a second opinion.

And in a letter, a week later, he described the final departure.

You have no idea of the rush of things that there was to be done at the end at Wissett. We only just caught the train and were busy to the last second, emptying E.C.s, burying a dead chicken as well as countless other things and owing to your not taking your full complement of luggage we had twenty-five packages! The hens, ducks and rabbits and chickens were sent off in the morning. I hope you have got them, and please send Cutts the crate. . . . On arrival at Liverpool Street a very nice detective said we had much too much luggage and that some were pictures and there was a fearful fuss and they were weighed and we were found to have 19/– worth over our share besides Henry, who howled at the top of his voice when I left him with Nessa and to add to it all we hadn't enough money and I suggested leaving my watch as security and that offended the chief clerk and the result was that we had to leave it all behind and I must fetch it tomorrow. We also lost five packages, perhaps luckily, and they turned up here today. There were two bicycles, because Nessa had bought Mrs Lampshire's the day before for £3. I think it is a bargain but that wretched woman, having made the offer in a state of high fever, repented the next morning and sent Lampshire round to try and get it back, but the money had been sent off and so had the bicycle so it was hopeless and Nessa doesn't know of this, so please don't tell her.

We were forced latterly to engage the younger Mrs Mauser to clean the house and luckily she did it very well so that it will be unnecessary to get Dunnett to paint it again. I've seen the children and Flossie and Mabel. Clive arrived yesterday and this morning I saw Philip Morrell, Sheppard, Cecil Taylor and Maynard. This evening we are going to the Coliseum, but I hate London and long to come to Charleston. . . . Such a lot of luggage had to be left behind that we shall have to have another load. How can one get into Pond Place? Because the van had better call there on its way. Can you send me the key and is Ott's portrait there? And do you want any books from there? I must stop. Please write again. Do you want more money? Yr B.*

Mr Hecks, my employer, was a suave, dark young man with a pleasant manner. He only paid Duncan and me 12/6 a week and five pence an hour for overtime but he showed great consideration in dealing with us and neither of us ever had a rough word from him. He was married and had a small son. Living with the family was a nephew and a young man learning farming. He employed also a carter, two dairymen, an intelligent boy called Eric Stephens, and the two Jacks. The farm was part of the Gage Estate and only about 120 acres in extent but Mr Hecks had just taken another farm called Lower Tilton, nearer to Charleston, as well. Mr Hecks was building up a pedigree Friesian herd and New House was chiefly a dairy farm with some arable, and a stretch of water meadows down by Glynde reach.

* Adrian had nicknamed Duncan the Bear and I and some other friends of his called him by the name. Adrian himself was the Corbie and Virginia the Goat. Vanessa was called the Dolphin because of her undulating walk, but the name was rarely used.
Later on I called Duncan Misha, which is the Russian peasant name for all bears.

On the first day, I was put to work with the two labourers pulling and topping mangolds. The Jacks were men, aged about fifty, who lived together about half a mile away, the other side of the railway line, in a barn where they looked after young stock in yards. Jack Whitemarsh was black-haired, bowed with work; he wore a sack as an apron and gripped a broken clay cutty pipe in his black teeth. His dark eyes, looking out through inflamed lids, were full of malice and his dirty, deeply lined face wore an expression either morose and dejected, or savage and sardonic. His nose was aquiline, red from drink, with a fresh drop always hanging from the tip and its predecessor sparkling among the hairs of his moustache.

Later, I learned his origin: he had once been a master baker in London. Drink had been his downfall and he had abandoned wife and family to work as a labourer, and had been living in his present way for ten years or more. As the day I started work was a Monday, Jack Whitemarsh was savage, silent and morose and the only notice he took of me was to work faster, so that he forged ahead and I fell behind.

His mate, Jack Williams, was a Sussex man, bigger in build than Whitemarsh and far less educated. His face was stained scarlet below the dirt, his cheeks all flaming grog-blossoms, with a little broken-down pug nose in the middle and curiously innocent watery-blue eyes. He was slow of thought and of speech and that day was completely silent.

Next day Jack Whitemarsh had recovered from his weekend hangover and greeted me amiably and showed me how to sharpen my knife on a bit of tile. I soon picked up the technique of pulling and topping mangolds and was, after that, able to keep up with them. Soon Whitemarsh and I became friendly. He was a good talker, when in the mood, but always sardonic, and he never referred to our employer except in terms of blistering irony. The two Jacks worked hard and spent little on food, cooked their own meals and once a week washed a shirt or two and shaved. Then, on Saturday night, they bought themselves a couple of bottles of whisky and stayed drunk throughout the Sabbath.

They kept a tribe of cats and were fond of them. Women were what Jack Whitemarsh hated most and, after women, the world of riches and respectability. Duncan and I both liked him and, oddly enough, he liked us, perhaps because we were also, in our way, outcasts from Society.

A week after I had been working at New House Farm, a van of furniture arrived. Vanessa and Duncan followed and soon we had settled down to an ordered life at Charleston.

Duncan and I worked a seven and a half hour day, with a half day on Saturdays. But in spite of the relatively short hours, we found our work very exhausting. Owing to the submarine blockade, fat and sugar rations were inadequate for hard manual work. I overcame the lack of sugar, after the following July, by providing large quantities of honey from my bees. But the lack of fat, and of meat, told on us. I was strong and during the years I worked as a labourer I became very strong. I was all muscle, without an ounce of fat on me. My weight during the war was never over eleven stone. After the harvest of 1918, I remember carrying sacks of wheat—each weighing two and a quarter hundredweight—all the morning about fifteen yards from the barn to the granary without feeling physically tired at the end. But the longer I went on working as a labourer, the greater became the emotional and nervous strain and, by the end of the war, my temper became very difficult to control. The cause of this was partly psychological and partly physical. I came to believe that the war would certainly go on for another ten or twenty years. My diet was insufficient owing to the shortage of fat.

Duncan who was lighter and less muscular than I, suffered more. In the second winter he began to lose weight alarmingly and had a severe attack of rheumatism. He then was medically examined and exempted from working except in the mornings. But for the first year, we worked the same hours, usually at the same job. The great merit of farm labour is its variety and that most of it is in the open air. I greatly enjoyed learning some new skill, all the more because I had a certain aptitude. Yet much of the winter work was almost unbearable. One evening

Duncan and I took out a cart with a broken-spirited young cart-horse which had been broken too young, to get a load of turnips. There was a bitter north-east wind and sleet and snow began falling. We had to pull up the turnips with our bare hands which were soon numb with cold.

When we had each pulled a heap, we loaded them into the cart with forks and then pulled more. Darkness grew and the misery and wretchedness of the scene was summed up in the passive endurance of the young horse, coated with snow, while we tore at the turnips savagely. We were plastered with freezing mud and when we straightened our backs, the nausea of the pain of our hands brought a moment's vertigo. Duncan, who was suffering at least as much as I, expressed his feeling in a smile which was most comforting.

That winter was severe with a long spell of frost which stopped most work except dung-carting. When spring came at last, our sufferings were greatly mitigated. In April I paid a flying visit to Wissett and packed the bees. In May Duncan and I were set to work hoeing a ten-acre field of beans and we continued working in it, without a break, for over a month. The weather was perfect and the scent of the bean flowers was exquisite. We worked side by side, each hoeing one side of two rows and, as we hoed, we took turns in telling each other stories. Sometimes we related every detail we could remember about the lives and characters of our aunts and uncles and cousins and their friends, digging out all the family scandals and disgraces that we could. The month that we passed, gossiping while we worked industriously in that bean field, was one of the happiest I can remember. Duncan's company was always an immense relief and I found the work far less endurable later when he was only working half days.

Threshing is a beastly job, particularly in a wind and if there are thistles in the corn, and we always seemed to be put in the dustiest places and our eyes became inflamed and our throats parched. One day we were threshing the last of the wheat. Old Prince, who took the milk float full of churns in to Glynde station every morning, had a hard day of it, for he was harnessed to the round-about which provided the mechanism that worked the elevator and, by the end, was stumbling round in an exhausted dream. The stack was full of mice and, when we got near the bottom it was a massacre. Mr Hecks's white fox terrier was pouncing here and there, quivering with excitement, and, when he looked up, there was a mouse's tail hanging absurdly from the corner of his mouth. All of us were continually interrupting our work to slash at the mice with our prongs and, when a rat appeared, there were shouts and the men dashed about in pursuit. Sometimes, when a sheaf was lifted, two or three mice would fall from it in mid-air. After a while, the dog could eat no more and vomited up a stomach-full of mucous glued-up mice and then came back brightly to the fray, eager to fill up with them again.

Finally the last sheaves were lifted, the humming ceased, and some of the crew of the threshing machine began rolling up the belt, while others got out the canvas covers for the drum. Our work was over for the day and Duncan and I took our bicycles out of the cart shed and set off home. Once we were round the bend in the road, an odd look came over Duncan's grimy face and he got off his bicycle. I pulled up beside him and asked:

"What's the matter?"

Duncan looked at me shyly, as though he had something to confess, and then began to grope about with his hand inside his shirt; withdrew it and produced a little mouse. While the rest of us had been slaughtering them in dozens, Duncan had picked one up and secretly had saved its life by slipping it inside his shirt. We looked at the bright-eyed little beast; then he put it in the bottom of the hedge and we rode on again, Duncan happy because I had not scolded him for failing to play his full part in the slaughter.

One winter's day Duncan and I were working digging out an open drain across one of the pastures when we heard the bellowing of cattle and warning shouts coming from the high road on the other side of the next field. It was market day and

Mr Hecks was sending several beast to Lewes market, among them a cow which was being got rid of because she had proved unmanageable after being separated from her calf. Suddenly the shouts redoubled and we saw the cow smash her way through the roadside hedge and come trotting towards us across the field. Behind her Mr Hecks and Ransome, the under-cowman, came running. But the cow was determined to get back to her calf and charged the post and rail fence, breaking the top rail and then jumping over the lower ones. "Let's head her off," exclaimed Duncan, throwing down his spade. "Better take our spades," I advised, remembering the cow's reputation, and Duncan picked his up. The animal was trotting towards us as we ran to drive her back into a corner, separating as we did so. But suddenly, when she was about twenty yards from Duncan, she put down her head and charged him at full gallop. I began to run towards him, but soon saw that I was too far away to be of help. Duncan stood stock still waiting for the cow, apparently paralysed with surprise. Just as she reached him he lifted his spade, as though it were a cricket bat, and struck the charging cow a perfectly timed blow upon the side of the nose with the flat of the blade. The force of his blow knocked the cow's head sideways, so that her horns just missed him. Only her shoulder struck him and sent him reeling. The cow had given a bellow when he struck her and did not pause in her rush until she reached the far side of the pasture and disappeared through the fence with the sound of splintering wood. Duncan was unhurt, having given a performance which would have gained him a reputation in the Spanish bull ring. A moment later Mr Hecks and Ransome came up and congratulated him, saying that the charge of such a cow is more dangerous than that of a bull, as she is far more difficult to dodge.

The cow was left for the rest of that day to her own devices, but the following week she was roped, loaded into a float, taken to Lewes where the butcher who bought her, preferring to take no chances, had her slaughtered in the cart.

I had no experience to match with Duncan's, though I used to work with a mare which the Army had got rid of because of her viciousness. Ordinarily she was quiet enough and she would even consent to draw a farm cart if it were empty. But once it had been loaded, she refused to pull and if one incautiously took her by the bridle, she would sit back on her haunches and strike out like lightning with her left foreleg. On one occasion, when I was hauling at her head, she nearly got me, actually tearing open my loosely buttoned coat. She had been loaned to Mr Hecks to breed from, by the Government, and there was general relief when he returned her as useless. I worked enough with horses to become familiar with them and once, when I was in London, seeing a horse go down on the wet asphalt, I ran out and sat on its head while the carter unharnessed it. I afterwards felt greatly surprised that I should have done something so simple and useful without a moment of reflection.

One day I got back to the farm after the dinner hour, to find a ghastly scene. Mr Hecks's riding mare, which had been shut up in the stackyard, had become excited by the cumbrous gambols of some cart-horse colts and had run into the barbed wire fence and cut an artery in her hind leg, just below the hock. The whole of the Hecks family was out for the afternoon and Eric and the cowman were standing helpless while the bright blood came in jets from the wound. I at once ran into the farmhouse and was lucky enough to find a yard or two of white elastic in Mrs Hecks's workbasket. With this we improvised a tourniquet which stopped the flow. The mare, a sweet creature, stood perfectly still while I did so, though she was trembling violently. We then gave her a pail of water, which she drank eagerly. But when the vet came, he found that she had cut the tendon so badly that she would always be lame, so she was shot.

Another experience with one of my employer's horses was the subject of the following sketch written many years ago.

It had been a hard winter. A soaking wet January, during which I had been employed in keeping the furrows open to drain the sown fields of wheat and oats, so that the grain should not rot in the ground, had been followed by three months of ruthless frost. It was the most severe winter I have ever known in England. The cattle could not go out into the fields; if they were turned out they found nothing. They had precious little to eat towards the end. . . . The haystacks were used up; there were only a few rotten or frozen mangolds in the pies; cake was dear.

For the most part we gave them what they would normally have had as litter—cavings, bean-haulm and straw, all put through the chaff-cutter and made a little more palatable by having a little cake and a few pulped up mangolds added and sometimes half a gallon of treacle in a bucket of hot water sprinkled over it.

When we went dung carting we used to be followed by flocks of starving birds, so weak that they could hardly hop out of the way of the shovel, or the horses' hoofs.

Every day my first job had been to attend to Old Prince. Once upon a time Prince had been a hunter, then a carriage horse; for years now he had taken the milk float to the station. That winter he broke his knees, then he developed a fistula on the shoulder. It had been cut open to drain and the wound did not heal. I washed his knees and the wound on his shoulder every morning, while Old Prince stood stock still as if he had been made of wood. He was just that flea-bitten white, with faded dapplings on the hind quarters, we have all loved in the old favourites of the nursery. Every morning he was a trifle thinner until at last he was a mere skeleton. It was the weather; besides there was no hay fit to eat, and he only got a handful of oats. Carter grudged him the oats.

I wasn't surprised when one morning, I remember it was the twenty-third of April, I heard that Old Prince was dead. Eric shouted the news at me as I crossed the yard and I walked through the orchard to have a look at him. It had snowed during the night and the snow still lay thinly on the ground and, on the snow, under an apple-tree, lay poor Old Prince, a flea-bitten white lump, hardly distinguishable from the thin carpet of dirty snow pock-marked by water dripping from the twigs.

I was looking at him and thinking that I should have been saved a lot of trouble if he had been shot three months before, when Mr Hecks walked out. He was neat and natty, as dapper as a jockey. He wore a check waistcoat, a dark riding coat, tan riding breeches, and one could see one's face in the glowing tints of his boots and gaiters. The snow drew away from the edges of his polished boots in awe.

My employer was genuinely upset.

"Garnett," he said, "you see poor Old Prince is dead. He has served me and my father for more than twenty—yes, for nearly thirty years. Old Prince was older than I am. He was the first horse I ever sat astride of and I feel very sad to have lost him. I cared more for Old Prince than for any of the beasts on the farm. There was never a trace of vice in him. Often I used to give him a lump of sugar and, as you know, I wouldn't have him shot, but all our efforts to pull him round were in vain. I suppose we must all die sometime, and I only hope when my time comes there will be someone who will feel my loss as much as I do that of poor Old Prince."

I said nothing and Mr Hecks continued: "It only remains now, Garnett, for you to bury him. Dig him a grave in the stackyard, on the left-hand side near the hedge. That is where I have buried all the beasts that served me faithfully and well. I like to think of them there all together, you may think it sentimental, but I like to think of it. We bury the calves—if a cow slips a calf—and that sort of thing—on the right-hand side. Put Old Prince's grave on the left——"

We walked over to the stackyard and my employer added suddenly:

"I don't care how long you take over it, Garnett, as long as you do the job *well*. Dig the grave six or seven feet deep."

I thoroughly enjoyed digging the grave. It was a slice of luck. The work was pleasant, a bit out of the ordinary and I was alone. I made a really good job of it, first of all peeling off the turf and rolling it up in neat little rolls, such as you see when they are laying turf on a golf course. These I set on one side and then dug down. By twelve o'clock I was up to my elbows in the grave. The weather had cleared up, the wind had dropped and the sun was blazing. Spring had come that morning. When I looked out I saw Mr Hecks coming up to me.

"What a lot you have done, Garnett," he said. "And I am afraid all your work is wasted." Then he caught sight of the little rolls of turf. "Who taught you to take turf up like that? That's splendid, we can use that turf. Mrs Hecks is always complaining of that patch outside the dining-room window; you shall put that turf down there for her and make a good job of it. That's splendid. But I'm afraid the rest of your work is wasted, Garnett. I went down to Gibraltar and saw the foreman there and sold him the hide for a guinea; he'll come up and skin him this afternoon; I rang up the kennels and they want the flesh. They said they would send down for the meat. Fill up that hole when you get back from dinner." The claims of sport had proved greater than those of sentiment and it was right and proper that the old hunter, whose ears always pricked at their music, should go to the hounds.

After Old Prince got past work, a white pony called Tommy was used to draw the milk float. He was kept at Lower Tilton, for there were half a dozen cows in milk there, as well as those of the New House Farm herd. Tommy became very fond of Tom, the boy who drove him with the milk churns to the station. I have seen Tom go to the pasture three fields away from the farmhouse, carefully shutting the field gates behind him though there was no stock in them. The pony ran up and let Tom put a halter on him and get on his back. Tom then raced him back to the farm, Tommy jumping each of the gates with Tom sitting him bareback and holding on by the halter. There was no bit in the pony's mouth and it was one of the prettiest bits of riding I have seen, all the better because it was done on the sly, with no thought of bravado. Tom was indeed careful not to be seen riding like that by anyone who would report it to Mr Hecks, for he would have got into trouble for risking Tommy's knees.

As the war went on, I found that I could cope physically

with the farm work and I became indeed a skilled labourer. At the same time I became more and more an automaton. In June 1918 I wrote to Constance:

It is the hay season and for eleven hours I blink with hayseed in my eyes on the stack. I don't think or feel or do anything but blink and pook hay to Jack Williams. He is conscious of the stack. Its shape, its curves, its symmetry all depend on him. At intervals there is a "whoa!" from below and the pony stops, the elevator stops and we drop into the hay. At once I am asleep—I am conscious perhaps of a thought or two, then I am snoring. Suddenly I realise that the elevator is rattling and Tommy is walking round swishing his tail. I stagger to my feet and at once begin pooking hay. So you see a day is nothing and at the end there is only the surprise of finding oneself twenty feet above the ground, walking gingerly upon a knife-edge a foot wide, instead of standing on the broad staddle of faggots with which we started. There is another life—but I am too tired to attend to it.

The farm work was the background and that, and the uncertainty and misery of the war, combined to make me irritable and deeply pessimistic in spite of the "other life"—the continual interest of living at Charleston.

It was impossible not to brood continually on the war. The deaths of Edward Thomas who was killed in April 1917, and of Pauley Montagu, who disappeared into the desert without trace, were the two losses which meant most to me. Thomas's death was made the more dreadful because it was during the war that he had realised himself as a poet—and his poems brought him continually back into my mind. My sorrow took the form of anger and hatred for the whole unwieldy mechanism of society—hatred of the frenzied nationalism which had led the rulers of Europe to sacrifice the lives and happiness of millions for phantoms of Honour and Power. A whole generation of Europeans was being wastefully, wilfully and incompetently butchered by statesmen who had not the courage to make peace and by generals who had no idea in their heads except to drive armies into seas of mud and barbed wire to attack the enemy at his strongest point. The rivalries of the generals and the chicaneries of Lloyd George inspired me with the rage of Thersites in *Troilus and Cressida*. Indeed I believed everything that Thersites declared about the Greeks was true of the Allies—and no doubt, equally, of the Germans. Ajax was the very type of British general and I "would rather be a tick in a sheep's back than such a valiant ignorance." The knowledge that the majority of my countrymen would have thought I was a tick, if they had ever learned of my existence, was not particularly consoling. Meanwhile Ajax, and that "old dog Fox" Ulysses had killed Pauley and Edward Thomas. Giblin would probably be killed too.

VIII

IN my spare time I worked in the garden and looked after my
bees, translated French, or Russian, and sometimes wrote a
little myself. Then there were many visitors. Clive, naturally,
was with us whenever possible. He brought with him not only
such *douceurs de la vie* as Manilla cheroots and bottles of wine,
but stories of the Great World, which enabled us to feel that
we were in touch with it and to laugh a great deal. Clive had
been roped in by the Military Service Act and had found a
niche for himself at Garsington, where he soon became the
most popular figure on Philip Morrell's farm. His boundless
good nature and humour and acceptance of life as it is, are the
qualities that the working classes like best in a gentleman. The
men could imagine that they would have been like Clive if
they had had the opportunity; the women wanted just such
qualities in a husband or a lover. When he was in the hay or
harvest field there were jokes and laughter and the work went
quickly.

Gerald Shove was less successful. His natural inclination to
take the blackest and grimmest view of farm life did not com-
mend itself either to the wage slaves whose exploitation he
inveighed against, or to Philip, whom he regarded on principle
as a capitalist bloodsucker. Nor was Gerald of much practical
use. He was put in charge of the poultry—after which there
was a sudden falling off in the number of eggs. When Philip
tried to investigate, Gerald reeled off the contents of an advertisement for a famous egg-producing nostrum which he had
somewhere come across, and told Philip that he could not
expect fowls to lay without it. Greatly impressed by this expert
knowledge, Philip ordered half a ton of it—but no more eggs
were brought in after its arrival than before. Some months
later, when Philip got tired of being told that he was an

exploiter, Gerald and Fredegond left to work on a farm with Adrian Stephen which was run with nothing but conscientious objectors for labourers. There Gerald tried to get up a strike— purely as a matter of principle—most embarrassing for Adrian, one of his closest friends.

After Gerald left Garsington it was discovered that the laying boxes were choked with eggs, most of them rotten and that the sacks of patent food had not even been unpacked.

Vanessa was more conscientious in her dealings with Philip. Some rabbits had been sent from Wissett, and soon after our arrival at Charleston Vanessa had supplemented our food supply by keeping a large number, for whose feeding and management she made herself entirely responsible. In October 1918 she decided to get rid of them. During a visit to Garsington, she discovered that Philip was thinking of starting to breed rabbits and he eagerly bought Vanessa's stock. Duncan was also away from Charleston, taking his week's annual holiday and I was alone when I received a letter from Vanessa asking me to pack up the rabbits and dispatch them to Oxfordshire.

When I went to look at the hutches, I was astonished to see that although Vanessa had bought the best does of the Flemish Giant breed procurable, they had changed their sex and that the hutches were occupied by numbers of aged buck rabbits with immensely long claws and withered testicles. The farm boys working for Mr Stacey at Charleston were also rabbit fanciers and had taken advantage of Vanessa's absence to substitute worthless animals from the surrounding district for Vanessa's pedigree does. So I was only able to send Philip three rabbits, after all.

According to Clive, Philip was not the only victim at Garsington. One of the chief ornaments of Ottoline's garden and terrace was a peacock, which Aldous Huxley had named Argus. He was an old bird and towards the end of 1917 he was seen to be ailing: he broke out in green carbuncles where patches of feathers had come off and it was no surprise to Clive when one morning he had disappeared. There was a house party for Christmas. Clive was invited to dinner and was horrified to see that Argus was being served up roasted. He had the moral courage to refuse his helping and Ottoline showed that she was greatly displeased by his squeamishness. Gertler was sick almost at once and some others afterwards. Ottoline declared that it was an epidemic of appendicitis— but Dorothy Brett, who was particularly ill, had had her appendix out years before.

While Clive kept us abreast of the doings of the social world in London and of the news of Garsington, Maynard, our other most frequent visitor, told us of the war and of the political world. When Maynard arrived for a short visit, he told us his news on the night of his arrival and we did not see him again until lunch next day. He brought with him an immense number of official and other papers, breakfasted in bed and spent the morning working. He liked tearing up papers after he had dealt with them, and all his life, prided himself on having filled his wastepaper basket before lunch.

When he came down, he always showed keen interest in all our doings and gave Duncan and me advice about any difficulties which had upset or disturbed us.

After tea perhaps he would suggest a walk on the Downs. On one occasion there was a strong wind blowing from the south-east and when we reached the top of Firle Beacon the sound of the guns of an offensive which had just started in Flanders was very loud.

Someone remarked on the bombardment and I said:

"Well, there's a south-east wind."

"The wind can make no difference," said Maynard. "Sound waves travel through the ether."

"What was that you said?" asked Clive who was up-wind and could not catch the remark.

"Sound waves travel through the ether," repeated Maynard.

"No they don't," I said angrily. "Sound waves travel through matter by knocking the molecules together."

"That isn't what my physicist friends tell me," said Maynard blandly.

"Well, you're wrong," I shouted, no doubt, rudely.

"What's that?" asked Clive again.

"Bunny says the Cambridge physicists are wrong about the diffusion of sound," said Maynard with no trace of annoyance.

Clive, who was probably not much interested, made no comment, and Duncan's expression showed that he hoped I would not continue to make a fool of myself. I was so angry that I dropped a little way behind the others. It was only several hours later that it occurred to me that I should have replied: "The wind is blowing the words out of your mouth and Clive cannot hear unless we shout." What maddened me was that Clive and Duncan went out of their way later to soothe my feelings ruffled by Maynard's exposure of my having made an elementary mistake in physics.

Such an incident was not unique. Maynard picked up knowledge with lightning rapidity and occasionally got it wrong and would bluff it through if possible. He was, however, usually the most gentle and harmonious of our visitors. After lunch he would often go into the garden carrying a small piece of carpet and spend an hour or two on his hands and knees weeding the gravel path with his pocket knife. He worked slowly and removed every scrap of weed. It would have been easy to tell the length of his visits by the state of the path. If he had stayed for a week there would be four or five yards weeded. Often I used to go and sit near him and the desultory conversations which I had with him then gave me renewed confidence that one day the strains and agonies of frustration would be over and that I should achieve something worth while.

Degas, one of the last survivors of the great French Impressionists, died in 1917 leaving a wonderful collection of pictures. Early in 1918 the news came that it was to be sold in Paris, and Duncan wrote and obtained a catalogue of the sale. It seemed to him to be a wonderful opportunity' for the National Gallery to acquire pictures by the great Impressionists and Maynard was persuaded to fall in with Duncan's scheme.

By a coincidence, the sale of the pictures occurred during the last week of March 1918, when Maynard had to attend an inter-ally conference on finance in Paris. After his departure the news suddenly came of the German break-through south of the Somme and of the rout of the British Fifth Army under General Gough. The situation was obviously extremely grave and Paris itself appeared to be threatened. But at Charleston we were wondering how the news from the Front would affect the sale of the pictures. Clive came down on Thursday, the twenty-eighth of March, after a visit of several days to London. At dinner we had two bottles of claret and listened gaily to Clive's gossip. He had gone out to dinner with Cecil Taylor and Sheppard who declaimed first in Greek, then in Italian, reciting the opening of the Inferno, and finally in French, much to the astonishment of those dining at other tables in the restaurant.

Suddenly we heard the front door open and, a moment later, Maynard, whom we had thought in Paris, walked in. He had crossed the Channel that afternoon and Austen Chamberlain, who was staying the week-end at Five Ashes, had given him a lift from Folkestone, dropping him at Swingate.

"I've got a Cézanne in my suitcase. It was too heavy for me to carry, so I've left it in the ditch, behind the gate."

Duncan and I jumped up and ran out. It was a clear moonlight night and we ran all the way down to Swingate and, breathless with excitement, retrieved the bag and carried it back in triumph between us.

Maynard had eaten little during the day and was very hungry. Dinner was brought back, another bottle was opened and while Maynard ate and we sat round, he told us the story of his adventures from the beginning.

In order to put through Duncan's scheme, Maynard had first won over one of the permanent officials at the Treasury, Mr Meiklejohn, whose opposition might have been dangerous. He had then gone to see the Director of the National Gallery, Charles Holmes, and drafted a letter which Holmes agreed to send Maynard. Holmes was naturally astonished and delighted at this roast pigeon unexpectedly flying into his mouth and agreed to see Lord Curzon, one of the Trustees, whom he successfully won over to the plan. Next morning Maynard went to see Bonar Law, showed him Holmes's letter, told him that Lord Curzon supported the proposal and that he favoured it himself. Bonar Law was much amused by Maynard's enthusiasm and said it was the first time Maynard had been in favour of expenditure of any sort. He thereupon initialled a draft for 550,000 francs. Maynard at once put it through and obtained a passport for Holmes. The British party consisted of Austen Chamberlain, Lord Buckmaster, then Governor of the Bank of England, Maynard, Geoffrey Fry, his assistant, and Holmes himself, who had shaved off his moustache and assumed a pair of spectacles so that he should not be recognised by any of the Paris dealers. The subject of the sale and Holmes in his disguise interested the other members of the party far more than the financial business—of arranging further credits for the French.

Bidding was done through Knoedlers who were outside the ring of Paris dealers. Duncan had indeed advised Maynard to "be as professional as possible in the buying and get at the right people . . ." On the second day the auction was exciting as they had to bid against the Louvre for the *Baron de Schwiter* by Delacroix and were successful. But Holmes, in spite of Maynard's urging, had refused to buy any of the Cézannes and came away from the sale with £5000 unspent, which had to be returned to the Treasury. He could have bought two El Grecos with the money. However he had secured four pictures by Ingres, two by Delacroix, two by Manet, a small Gauguin and a number of drawings.

Maynard himself had spent less than £500 for which he bought a little still life of apples by Cézanne, a little picture of a horse by Delacroix, a lovely drawing by Ingres, and several large charcoal drawings by Degas. He gave a drawing for a decoration by Delacroix to Duncan. Prices at the sale had been low as the Germans were shelling Paris with a long-range gun, though Maynard had never heard any of the explosions.

There had been the greatest excitement and apprehension during his visit and at one moment everything was being got ready for evacuation of the city by the Government. But the military news with which Maynard returned was good. The Germans, after having completely routed our Fifth Army, were being held owing to their utter exhaustion after three days of continuous fighting without food, or sleep. Their supply organisation had broken down. But it seemed clear to us that if the Germans failed, so would any Allied offensive that might follow it.

We were all delighted by Maynard's having put through Duncan's plan so successfully and in a letter which I wrote to him I said:

"Nessa and Duncan are very proud of you. . . . You have been given complete absolution and future crimes also forgiven."

The explanation of this sentence is that among many of his friends, particularly Lytton, Clive, Norton and Sheppard, there was a fear that "Pozzo", as Lytton and the Stracheys called Maynard, after Pozzo de Borgo, was going to the bad. By that they meant that he was sacrificing his principles to his ambition and that he would lend himself to carrying out the plans of the most unscrupulous politicians. His friends did not hesitate to tell Maynard what they thought and he was sometimes rude and irritable when they did so. With Vanessa, Duncan and me he was very seldom irritable, for I think he felt sure of our love and loved us without reserve.

Shortly after the purchase of the pictures, there was an extremely painful scene at 46 Gordon Square. One evening, when Vanessa was in London, they were sitting up late after dinner talking over the refusal of the Emperor Karl's Peace Overtures which had been published that day. Maynard came into the room, after working late at the Treasury, and hearing what they were talking about, treated their views with the utmost contempt. Later the conversation turned on conscientious objection and Maynard declared that he did not believe anyone had a genuine conscientious objection. If he said this to exasperate Vanessa and Norton he certainly succeeded. When they expostulated he said several times:

"Go to bed. Go to bed."

Sheppard became angry at this behaviour and said:

"Maynard, you will find it is a mistake to despise your old friends."

When Maynard had gone to bed his friends discussed his character. Vanessa took a gloomy view. She thought that Maynard had reached a critical point in his life and that the strain of prolonged overwork might have injured the quality of his brain, or at least have made him disinclined to use it. Indeed he might be so far on the downhill path that nothing would save him. Harry Norton thought that Maynard's behaviour was due to complex psychological reasons. For example, he was sure that the reason for his bad table manners —Maynard would help himself from the nearest dish with his own knife and fork when dining with his friends, instead of passing his plate—was that it flattered him to believe that he was so much liked that they did not mind how he behaved in small ways. His schoolboy insolence to them that evening was another instance of the same thing.

Sheppard, who seems to have been the angriest, attributed it to Maynard's nonconformist ancestry. He believed also that Maynard had a touch of what the French call *folie de grandeur* —an overweening sense of his own importance. Later, when I visited London, Sheppard told me that he had overheard Maynard call Jessie the cook up the basement stairs and say to her: "I'm going to dine with the Duke of Connaught. Isn't that grand?"

On hearing this anecdote I said that any one of us might have said the same. The remark was slightly ironical, at his own expense, and partly because it was a piece of news that would greatly interest Jessie who would certainly think it grand. Sheppard maintained that Maynard really did think it was grand. If he had not done so, he would have told Sheppard about it when he opened the invitation, instead of which he had left the room to boast of the grand event to Jessie, knowing that he could not do so to him. "It's nonconformist snobbery. They are like bugs in a rug."

It is easy to see now that these criticisms were partly the result of the intense strain of the war. Maynard was the object of attack because he was in a particularly difficult position. He had risen with rapidity to a post of great responsibility and importance, and he was aware of hundreds of secrets which he could not divulge in order to justify his opinions, when they were challenged by his friends. Impatience and irritability were the natural consequences. It is perhaps significant that Duncan, who knew Maynard better than anyone, never added a word to the chorus of criticism. I think he alone understood and made full allowance for the difficulty of Maynard's position.

This account of the war-time differences between Maynard and his closest friends may appear to some readers to be a superficial matter which I should have been better advised to allow to remain forgotten. I have included it because I think their critical attitude at this time was a factor of great importance in Maynard's career. One of the chief characteristics of his great intelligence was the capacity to see both sides of a question, and the criticisms and anxieties of his friends led him to a stricter examination of his own motives and of the policies which he had to advocate as a servant of the Government, than he would otherwise have made. It was because his friends kept him aware of the danger that he might, for the sake of a brilliant official career, be a party to bringing about terrible evils, that he finally took the course he did in resigning his post rather than accept the reparations clauses of the Peace Treaty. That resignation led to the writing of *The Economic Consequences of the Peace* which was the foundation of his subsequent fame.

The habit of going beneath surface appearances, of analysing and detecting far-reaching consequences, was native to his mind. But the criticisms of his most intimate friends encouraged him to criticise and justify the work that he was doing during the war and made his ultimate resignation necessary for his own peace of mind.

And I am quite sure that even though Maynard was often acutely irritated by the criticisms of his friends, he looked upon Duncan, and to a lesser extent Vanessa, as the keepers of his conscience.

Shortly after this painful scene at 46 Gordon Square, Maynard came down to Charleston for a week's rest. He was alone with Duncan, Vanessa and me and during the whole of his visit he was so delightful that I think he was trying to make amends for it to Vanessa. Not one of the vices which they had been discussing was in evidence during the whole of his stay. Even his greediness was kept within pleasant bounds.

I was, for reasons which I shall explain later, in an emotional condition which must have made me extremely difficult to live with at this time, and I don't know how Vanessa and Duncan managed to put up with me. One Saturday or Sunday during Maynard's visit, when we were having lunch, Vanessa told us that she had secured old Mr Ford to come over from Firle and work two evenings a week in the garden.

I forget what I said in a burst of anger. That it was unnecessary, unkind, intolerable. My words were passionate and a moment later I had rushed from the table to hide my feelings.

Maynard came after me and found me trembling with emotion under an apple-tree.

"Come, Bunny, sit down and tell me just what you are feeling and why."

For a little while I hesitated, perhaps because I was ashamed, but Maynard had such a gentle troubled look, there was so much kindness in his eyes, that swallowing my tears, I explained it all.

Vanessa was giving me free board and lodging: I had no money and could only earn twelve shillings and sixpence a week working on the farm, or fifteen shillings if I did six hours overtime. How could I respect myself unless I worked in the garden, pruned the trees and supplied honey for the table? But it was all no good. She wasn't satisfied. She was getting a gardener. I was a complete parasite and I should never be anything else. And the tears, which I had been trying to restrain, poured down my cheeks.

"I thought it was something like that," said Maynard and putting his arm through mine, he led me up and down the garden and when I had recovered myself, he urged me to think again. Surely it was a mistake for me to imagine that after working eight hours a day, or ten or eleven in the weeks of hay-making and harvest, that when I was tired out, I could do all the work necessary in the garden as well? Nobody could do it and if I insisted that Vanessa should not employ old Ford, it meant that we should be short of vegetables and that I should be depriving her of any hope of flowers.

"How can you ever go away for a week-end, or read a book, or write yourself?"

"But I mustn't go away. I mustn't waste my time trying to write. I can't write anyway." And again I was unable to speak. Maynard just squeezed my arm with his and walked up and down with me and then tried again.

"Look how well you have done with your bees. You have already paid me back ten pounds out of the twenty that I lent you to buy hives. And that reminds me: I want you to send a dozen sections to my mother in Cambridge. . . . You must try to look at it from outside, Bunny. There are thousands of young men like you, all in the same boat, because of the war."

"They are not parasites. I am."

"What do you think Vanessa would say, if she heard you?"

I was silent.

"She would tell you not to be such a goose."

I looked at Maynard and saw such distress in his face that I said:

"All right, then. I'll try to be more reasonable."

Having missed half of his lunch and spent about half an hour with me, Maynard went indoors to resume his morning's work—for the pouch with plans for financing our Allies, or persuading the Americans to relieve us of some of the burden of doing so—or something of the sort—had to be sent off that evening. I began digging in the garden.

If I had told Maynard then that he was the kindest, most

lovable man I had ever met, he would have said that I was being unfair on his friends and he would have been right. Many of his closest friends in Bloomsbury and in Cambridge had, in their own characteristic ways, much the same mixture of intelligence and of goodness.

Perhaps it was not an accident that they had all known each other very well and shared the same philosophy.

Lytton paid us a week's visit in August 1917 and another visit for several days in the spring of 1918. He had finished the four biographical studies which make up *Eminent Victorians* and was looking for a publisher.

Every evening, during Lytton's visits, we would gather in the garden room—with the french window open in summer and huddled round a log fire the following March. Vanessa sat with a piece of sewing, Duncan and I tired out by hard work on the farm. But whereas I was eagerly absorbed in every word, Duncan always fell asleep, and at the first suspicion of a snore I used to pinch him, so that Lytton should not become aware of it. On the first visit he read us *Manning* and *Florence Nightingale*. On the second *Gordon* and *Doctor Arnold*. Vanessa was somewhat critical:—not of Lytton's treatment of his subjects, but of his style which she thought was too much in the Victorian tradition and too full of clichés. I was first amazed at being taken back from the values of a world at war, but soon realised that Lytton's essays were designed to undermine the foundations on which the age that brought the war about had been built.

The life of Gordon, and still more that of Florence Nightingale, had indeed many direct applications to the conduct of the war of 1914–1918. When the book was first published, the likeness of the Crimean War to such sideshows as the campaign in Mesopotamia must have struck every reader. It was in Lytton's mind when he read and in mine as I listened. But so far as we were aware then, no Miss Nightingale had appeared to criticise and condemn the minds of our Generals and the working of the military machine, and to force our Governors to listen. Only later did we hear of the existence of T. E. Lawrence whose genius recalls that of Gordon at one moment and Miss Nightingale at another. Thus as I listened to Lytton and occasionally gave Duncan a pinch, the thing which struck me most was the topical relevance of the *Eminent Victorians* to the condition of the moment. Even *Cardinal Manning* was an apt illustration of how men rose to power and their passion for it. In *Doctor Arnold* I saw how English education moulded men to accept convention and prefer almost any sacrifice to losing caste by thinking for themselves. I felt sure that there were many of my generation who would recognise the same implications in *Eminent Victorians*, and I could not doubt the book's success.

Lytton would often make devastating comments on people he did not like, but he had an astonishing patience and sympathy with those he did. He often had an intuitive understanding of what I was feeling. I remember going out for a stroll with him one summer's evening when I was feeling absolutely desperate. My thoughts were: "The war will go on for ever. I am turning into a mere clod. In ten years I shall be like Jack Whitemarsh: an embittered cynic who once knew a few interesting people, but I shall never achieve anything myself." But I did not say a word of this to Lytton, and we walked for some time in silence. Suddenly Lytton said:

"Don't despair. There is no reason. Remember that Sterne was an ordinary country parson till he was forty-five. Then he sat down and wrote *Tristram Shandy*." I repeated those words to myself very often.

Shortly after we had gone to Charleston, Carrington wrote several letters to me asking me to search for an empty farm or cottage where Lytton could live. But it was not till nearly a year later that she found The Mill House, Tidmarsh, a few miles from Pangbourne. Lytton had practically no money, but Maynard, Harry Norton, Saxon Sydney-Turner and Oliver Strachey each contributed twenty pounds a year which enabled them to take The Mill House.

Maynard's and Lytton's visits were for me always a great

VANESSA BELL IN THE GARDEN AT
CHARLESTON

LYTTON STRACHEY

pleasure; it was otherwise with those of Roger Fry. Roger was in an odd way physically very like Edward, though they became less like as Edward grew older and more massive. But in the middle years there was a strong resemblance. Roger's hair, the line of his nose, jaw and neck, the roll of his eye and the cock of his eyebrow all reminded me of Edward and, perhaps because of this, I sometimes felt the impatience that a young man so often feels for his father. Roger wore also the kind of clothes which Edward had been accustomed to wear in middle life: a brown Jaeger shirt, a homespun loosely cut jacket and trousers which soon lost their shape, sometimes a tie of shantung silk. Both Roger and Edward had moreover much the same attitude to life. They were intolerant of the British Public, the bourgeoisie, the villa residents, and of the British indifference to art. They both not only disliked the British way of life with its shams, hypocrisy, respectability and censoriousness, but they denounced them in almost the same words, in tones of pitying exasperation. Both felt the same deep contempt for the British business man. Both had the same attitude to conventional morality.

But though they had these views in common, their intellectual differences were enormous. Edward was intuitive, illogical and in many ways ill-educated. He had little use for theory and could seldom bolster up his opinions by inventing one. He arrived at his opinions, especially his aesthetic ones, by instinct and by sympathy. He was intensely sceptical and never more so than when confronted by theories of aesthetics. He did not believe there were any rules and preferred that there should be none.

Edward was not an egotist. Although he regarded himself as a rebel, there was deep down in him a fund of conservative common-sense. In all these respects Roger was his opposite. Thus Roger, who was one of the most intellectually fertile men of his generation, never stopped inventing theories which he was incessantly abandoning, modifying and superseding. He was astonishingly credulous and would believe almost anything which was not obviously incompatible with his basic philosophy of life. Sometimes he seemed unable to dismiss any theory as nonsense until by accepting it he had discovered its weaknesses. Indeed he was inclined to regard it as "unscientific" to reject any hypothesis outright, however lacking the evidence for it. And for however short a time Róger had held a theory, he was always amazed if one disagreed with him. Both his likeness to Edward and his unlikeness made me unduly critical. It would be easy to tell stories of Roger's credulity and egotism. It is not so easy to explain or illustrate his genius, unique among the men of his generation. He stimulated the brain more than almost anyone I have known. After an evening spent listening to Roger, I was kept busy for several days finding out what I thought myself. But more important than the stimulating effect of his ideas was his intellectual example. When Roger approached an idea or a new work of art he divested himself of all prejudices and all defensive armour. He had an extraordinary sensibility to pictures and a capacity for divining the intentions of the artist which no other critic I have known has approached. And he had almost as much understanding of a writer's intentions in literature. His judgments fluctuated and developed, but his example taught me to try to strip myself naked of prejudice before judging a work of art. Only if one did that were one's vision and judgment one's own. Unfortunately at the beginning of our acquaintance Roger rather disliked me and I reciprocated. His dislike was not in the least because of my sceptical attitude to his ideas but for more personal reasons of which he may have been almost unaware. He had the deepest regard for and devotion to Vanessa and was mystified by her tolerant affection for me and he was inclined to think I was a parasite who did not appreciate her. Thus there was perhaps a touch of unconscious jealousy in his feelings for me. Duncan he greatly respected as an artist of genius, and loved him as a friend. But during the war years he never suspected that I might also become a creative artist. When I had done so, he performed the kind of reassessment of which so few men are capable and his whole attitude to me completely changed.

Long before that occurred, however, I had come to like and admire him and to value his extraordinary restless intellectual energy.

The following conversation cannot pretend to be verbally accurate but the substance of it owes nothing to my imagination.

ROGER: I can never get used to the fact that the vast majority of people, once they have been taught to believe a thing, actually see what they have been taught to believe and not what is really there. For example, everyone believes that lightning occurs as an electrical discharge in the clouds and strikes out of the sky on to the earth. I expect you believe it, Duncan. Everybody sees it happen in that way during a thunderstorm. As a matter of scientific fact in just as many cases the flash is from the earth into the sky. People don't know that this is so and so they never see it occur.

DUNCAN: That must have been what happened to me when I was struck.

ROGER: When were you struck?

DUNCAN: I was running back to 46 Gordon Square in a thunderstorm after posting a letter. There was a tremendous flash and I was struck on the tongue. I see now that the lightning must have travelled through my body and the flash must have left the earth from the tip of my tongue.

[*As Duncan said this Roger's eyes goggled with delight at the idea and his mouth fell open.*]

ROGER: Well, Duncan, I don't say it's *impossible*—but I suppose you might have been mistaken.

DUNCAN: There is no doubt that I was struck. My tongue was paralysed and I could not speak to Blanche when she opened the door. And the shock almost stunned me.

ROGER: It is not *impossible*, of course. Saliva would be a good electrical conductor, but it cannot have been a heavy discharge or your mouth would have been burned.

DUNCAN: It was very painful.

VANESSA (*laughing*): Why do you tell us such nonsensical stories? Nobody believes that you were struck by lightning in Gordon Square.

ROGER: Did anyone else see the flash? So far we have only your evidence. Of course it is *not at all impossible*, and the most likely hypothesis is that it was a brush discharge. But I was really using the universal failure to see what happens in a thunderstorm as an illustration of people looking at pictures. The vast majority of English people, when they look at a picture, do not see it at all. They see what for some reason they have been led to expect ...

Roger greatly enjoyed a game of chess and was a much better player than I. We often played together and usually he beat me fairly easily. But if I made an unexpectedly good move which put him in difficulties, Roger would always try to find a way of altering the course of the game. He would pick up one of my pieces, start an exposition of what I might have done, and put the piece back on the wrong square. I was never quite sure how far he was aware that he cheated at chess. But Julian told me, some years later, that Roger frequently did the same thing with him so as to avoid being beaten. Occasionally something of the sort occurred with money. Once, years later, Roger, Duncan and I took a taxi from Hammersmith. Duncan and I got out at Gordon Square and Roger went on. As I was getting out, I handed Roger a pound note and said:

"I suppose that is about my share, isn't it?"

Roger took it, muttered: "Let me see . . . I haven't worked it out. I expect it is about right! . . ." and put it in his pocket.

"What on earth did you do that for?" asked Duncan indignantly as the taxi drove off.

"Just as an experiment. I wanted to see what Roger would do."

"You deserve to lose your money if you make experiments like that," replied Duncan.

There was indeed a constant stream of visitors which must have been a strain on Vanessa and the servants, and difficult to feed in the days of shortages though people brought their own butter and sugar.

Besides my mother, one visitor who came to see me was Lyndhurst Giblin whom I had loved since I was four years old. It was the third of August 1917, and he was a Major in the Australian Army Corps just about to go out to France, where he took part in the prolonged Ypres offensive which finally got bogged down at Passchendaele. He had come down, full of warmth and friendliness, to reassure himself that I was not having too bad a time as a conscientious objector! He also wanted to find out what I had turned into since my schoolboy days. He was very large, with close-cropped hair, rugged features, tanned to pale mahogany, very slow in speech, and untidy in unbuttoned tunic and badly wound puttees. Thus he sat in the Garden Room, pulling at his pipe and taking small sips of beer, confronted by Vanessa, to whom, with a sure instinct, he began to speak of his old friends at Cambridge, Lowes Dickinson, Wedd, and Clapham. He had been at King's.

Giblin had heard of Maynard and wanted to know all that we could tell about him. His visit helped to make me see the world impartially and to restore my confidence. Giblin's future did not seem likely to be a long one, but he was severely wounded in the thigh that autumn and then made an astonishingly quick recovery. During his convalescence he married Eileen Burton. On their honeymoon Giblin thought it wise to give his wounded leg a thorough test in a walking tour on the South Downs and, early in 1918, he and Eileen dropped in at Charleston to call for me and I walked with them to Alfriston where we had dinner and stayed the night. After his return to France, Giblin and his Australians helped to hold the Germans after the *débâcle* of the Fifth Army and he found time to write me a long letter describing the broken troops and ravaged countryside.

Besides the fairly constant visitors of our own, we saw something of those who stayed at Asheham. At Christmas 1917, Saxon Sydney-Turner, Barbara Hiles and Carrington were there and I went over and stayed the night. There was snow covering the Downs and, after dinner, we tobogganed down the side of Itford Hill on two large teatrays in the moonlight until after midnight.

Noel Olivier and James Strachey also stayed at Asheham on two occasions and again I went over to spend an evening and enjoy the pleasure of seeing her. She had become by that time a qualified doctor, specialising in the illnesses and upbringing of babies. She had always been mature beyond her years but she ripened into a very amusing woman, unselfconscious of

159

her beauty and with the glowing warmth one finds only in those women who have inspired many passions.

I had met Virginia Woolf at intervals since I had first got to know her brother Adrian in 1910, but it was not until I was living at Charleston that I got to know more than that she was a very beautiful woman, tall, with large green eyes, a lovely forehead and aquiline features, who flashed in and out of our company and was on the most intimate terms with Vanessa. Both sisters might have been models for the sculptors who made the doorways of Chartres Cathedral. But though they were very much alike, their beauty contrasted. Vanessa was the Virgin, with Quentin an infant Jesus in her arms; Virginia a Saint or Angel, with none of the beauty of maternity. In company there was as much contrast in their behaviour as in their looks. For whereas Vanessa was reserved and domestic, disliking going outside the circle of her intimate friends, Virginia was a woman of the world who enjoyed making excursions into Society and bringing back stories of her encounters.

Perhaps the greatest difference between the sisters was in their voices and manner of speaking. Vanessa's voice is clear and even. She speaks, particularly when she is giving her opinions, as though she were reading aloud in accents of balanced beauty the sentence of the court. Only when she is provoked by an interruption will she flash back, but even then, her voice is quiet and controlled. Virginia, holding a cigarette, would lean forward before speaking and clear her throat with a motion like that of a noble bird of prey, then, as she spoke, excitement would suddenly come as she visualised what she was saying and her voice would crack, like a schoolboy's, on a higher note. And in that cracked high note one felt all her humour and delight in life. Then she would throw herself back in her chair with a hoot of laughter, intensely amused by her own words.

Vanessa lived in a closed room; when Virginia came over from Asheham she brought the wind off the Downs into the house with her. She had a warmth and good-fellowship which set people at their ease; she had the gift for sudden intimacy which I had found so charming in D. H. Lawrence when I had first met him. Her voice and her glance were filled with affection, mockery, curiosity, comradeship. She would put a hand on one's shoulder and as she propelled one about the garden, between the flower beds, she would ask some reckless question which flattered and disturbed. Her interest was exciting and left one tingling with satisfied vanity or doubts about oneself.

She was particularly interested in young people and children so that her visits from Asheham were a signal for rejoicing on the part of Julian and Quentin who had secrets to share with her. Thus she was always led aside and from the corner of the walled garden where they were ensconced came her clear hoot of laughter—like the mellow hoot of an owl—and Julian's loud explosions of merriment, protests and explanations.

Virginia was a wonderful raconteur—she saw everyone, herself included, with detachment, and life itself as a vast Shakespearean Comedy. She loved telling stories at her own expense—some of them as ribald as anything in Chaucer—for all her personal vanity was forgotten in the storyteller's art. But alas, while I was living at Charleston I almost deliberately avoided having a friendship with Virginia, for it would have been impossible without confidences and in the home circle she had the reputation of a mischief-maker. We were all on edge enough owing to the war without running any unnecessary risk of letting Virginia embroil us with each other. Thus it was only later on that I became on terms of close friendship with Virginia and then our friendship grew steadily, until, when my hair was streaked with grey, I became not Bunny, but her dear Badger. By then she had for me long ceased to be a possible mischief-maker and became the very opposite—a woman on whose sympathy and understanding I could rely when I most needed support.

Her work always interested and excited me. She is one of the very few writers I have known who was never satisfied to repeat herself but was always experimenting and developing and in that respect I have tried to follow her example. There was much of the same reckless imagery in her conversation that gives such individuality to her novels. Such things as her description in *Jacob's Room* of Southampton Row:

> Chiefly remarkable nowadays for the fact that you will always find a man there trying to sell a tortoise to a tailor. "Showing off the tweed, sir; what the gentry wants is something singular to catch the eye, sir—and clean in their habits, sir!" So they display their tortoises.

Leonard Woolf usually came with Virginia, a lean man with the long hooked nose and burned-up features and ascetic lips of a desert dweller rather than those of the typical Jew. Leonard had spent ten years shaken by fever and burned by the tropical sun as a District Magistrate in Ceylon. He was very quiet and liked to sit silent until others had finished giving their opinions when he would say in a low voice which vibrated with the passionate desire to appear reasonable, that he disagreed with every word that had been said and that he believed that the exact contrary was true—after which he would give a little laugh and the argument would begin in earnest.

Unlike Maynard, who always wore town clothes in the country, Leonard was always beautifully dressed. His oldest, raggedest coat had the distinction of a Duke's and there was such a perfect harmony in all he wore that he has sometimes reminded me of a fruit tree covered with lichen. A spaniel was always at his heels, for he loved animals and prided himself upon his complete understanding of their characters.

Leonard and Virginia came often to Charleston, sometimes by bicycle, sometimes walking over the Downs, for nobody in our society had yet bought, or learned to drive a motor car. Often they brought a guest who might be staying. Once it was Sydney Waterlow, whom I remember particularly, as he had figured not long before in a charade in which Duncan impersonated him with a cushioned corpulence and important manner and a large black velvet bow drooping from his lip as Waterlow's cavalry moustache. These features were very recognisable, but the real man was unexpectedly friendly, talked to me about the art of writing, drew me out and told me that Katherine Mansfield was his first cousin.

Sydney Waterlow was an old friend of the Stephens, of Leonard and of Maynard, who became involved in a bitter vendetta with him for the duration of the war, on the subject of the Sicilian orange crop. The morale of the Sicilian troops depended on their oranges finding a buyer, and the only willing purchasers were the Germans and Austrians who paid high prices through Swiss intermediaries. Sydney Waterlow was determined to stop this leak in the blockade and told stories about German troops throwing oranges into the British trenches as a proof that our blockade was ineffective. The only way of stopping the Germans getting the oranges was to buy them ourselves and let them rot in Sicily, as we had not the shipping to move them. Maynard believed the money could be spent better in other ways and for two years in succession defeated Sydney Waterlow's pet scheme. Finally, however, he gave in and the 1918 crop was bought. So in the winter and spring of 1919, the oranges rotted in Sicily and the Germans and Austrians went without when the war was over.

Our visitors made it far easier for Duncan and me to go on working as farm labourers peacefully. But there were unsettling influences, breeding discontent and despair. In Duncan's case there were continued projects and efforts to obtain his release from farm work so that he should be able to paint. The first of these efforts was made by the French Government, who not so many months before, at Dieppe, had deported him from France. The French were anxious to earn dollars and had sponsored a project for Copeau to take the *Vieux Colombier* company for a season to the United States. One of the plays in their repertory was to be *Twelfth Night*, with dresses and scenery which Duncan had done before the war. Another was to be Maeterlinck's *Pelléas et Mélisande*. Copeau therefore got the French to make an application for Duncan's release on that account. It was refused. However, Duncan designed the dresses for *Pelléas et Mélisande* and Vanessa and Barbara Hiles cut them out and made them at Charleston. But were they used, or were they torpedoed on the voyage to America?

Another possibility, which was mooted several times, was that Duncan should be chosen as a War Artist like John, Nevinson, Roberts, Kennington, Wyndham Lewis and many others. In the end he was invited to become one, but discovered that the position of Official War Artist carried with it the rank of Major in the Army and that there was no way by which he could be a War Artist unless he were in uniform. So he refused the offer.

In my case there was the possibility of working again with the Quakers. Robert Tatlock, who had so much impressed Augustine Birrell at Sommeilles, wrote to me on his return from Serbia. We met and he spent the evening telling me an intensely romantic story of his adventures which might have been conceived by Conrad. He had found himself on the Dalmatian Coast during the *débâcle* of the Serbian Army, among thousands of men who would soon be starving. On the horizon was a British battleship. Tatlock succeeded in getting in touch with the British Fleet, boarded Admiral Troubridge's flagship, and as a result food and transport were sent up in time to save the survivors. Three years later, when I knew Tatlock very much better, he hotly denied that he had ever told me any such story. But I believe it was true and that he had forgotten it as the result of a nervous breakdown in Vladivostok which took much of the early fire out of him. After that meeting, Tatlock went out to Russia and, later, to the United States on a lecture tour to raise funds for the Quaker relief work in Russia.

As the result of Tatlock's recommendation, and my own smattering of Russian, I was invited first to go out to Russia as a Relief Worker and secondly to take charge in the London Office of all the reports from the Russian and Polish Relief Workers and make them available to the Press. The term Public Relations Officer had not then been invented. These possibilities were very attractive to me, but each of them matured at a time when I felt uncertain that Mr Hecks would continue to employ Duncan if I left and in each case I temporised and delayed acceptance until the offer was withdrawn.

The Russian Revolution and its developments filled me, Constance and all of our friends with the greatest excitement and hopes for the future. It added also greatly to my unrest. At first it was difficult to get news. Arthur Ransome, almost alone among foreign correspondents, was reliable. The newspapers were full of lies and exaggerations. Thus it was not till I met Tatlock that I learned that there had been practically no injury to the buildings of the Kremlin. Occasionally we got news of some of our old friends. After the Revolutionists captured Tsarskoe Selo they sent one of the Imperial carriages every day to drive Vera Figner round St Petersburg where she was greeted by cheering crowds of happy people as one of the heroines of the Revolution.

We were at first ardent supporters of Kerensky, until we realised that his policy of continuing to keep Russia in the war was self-destructive. The Russian people needed two things, the immediate end of the war and the division of the great estates among the peasants. Any government that hoped to survive must give them those immediately whatever the cost in territory or dishonour.

Directly Constance heard the news that Lenin had returned to Russia she wrote to me: "I feel certain Lenin will capture power. I wish we knew what he will do with it."

Neither Constance, nor Edward, nor any of their Russian friends were Communists. They all hoped for some form of Democratic Government, and I shared their views. But Constance and I realised that it was madness to attempt to continue the war with a crumbling army, lacking munitions and equipment and with officers and a General Staff that the troops did not trust. In the civil war which followed, our sympathies were with the Red Army since the victory of the Whites would certainly have meant a Military Dictatorship which would probably have been worse than the Tsarist Autocracy. We were thrilled by the way in which Trotsky played his cards during the negotiations with the Germans at Brest-Litovsk, and it was indeed that amazing piece of impudent propaganda which captured the interest of many of my friends in Bloomsbury and inspired great hope of Russia. The Bolsheviks with extraordinary cleverness had stolen much of the substance of President Wilson's Fourteen Points and, on the question of self-determination, had got all the Subject Races of Europe to look to them as their champions. It seemed then as if a revolution, spreading from Russia, might sweep through Europe bringing the war to an end. Such a movement seemed to us far more likely to bring about Peace than more butchery like that of the Battle of the Somme. Nobody yet knew how the Bolshevists would turn out in practice. It seemed likely that even Lenin and Trotsky did not know themselves. After all, some of them, such as Lunacharsky, the Minister of Education, were men of culture. And when we heard that Djerzhinsky had been put at the head of the Secret Police and Prison Services our hearts rose. He had spent a great part of his life in prison: it seemed obvious that he would sweep away the cruelties and abominations from which he had suffered and make Russian prisons the most humane in the world!

It would have been inconceivable to us then that he should have used his experience to make them more terrible.

The Quakers had sent a mission to work among the famine-stricken refugees at Buzuluk, near Samara, in Eastern Russia. One of the first and most favourable accounts of the effects of the Russian Revolution that we heard was from my friend Reynolds Ball, who had worked with such devotion among the forgotten victims of the war in France when I was at Sommeilles.

While I had been working as a farm labourer he had been in Russia and, hearing of his return, I invited him to come for a week-end to The Cearne. He had, by what accident I know not, lost most of his teeth; one upper front tooth remained. His lean face was haggard, his angular body thin and uncared for. Except that he still shaved he did not seem to have given a thought to his appearance during the years of war, but this neglect accentuated a curious radiance so that he seemed a saint, come from suffering in far deserts to speak to us of strange spiritual experiences. He had fallen in love with the starving Russians among whom he had been working and he felt a deep sympathy with the state of mind of the common soldiers, returning from the war, who set out to create a new society after the Revolution.

Ball who put William Blake highest among the poets and prophets loved the streak of mysticism in the Russians, the faith which believed it was possible to create a materialistic Heaven upon Earth immediately. He spoke of the spirit of the peasants and soldiers meeting for the first time in a local Soviet to organise a New Society from first principles. Constance could visualise all that he described but she saw, far more clearly than I did, the dangers that would be run and the cruelties that must inevitably follow. Ball's indifference to his own welfare, his emaciation and his saintliness greatly distressed her. During the whole of his visit she was busy in making him cups of coffee, stewing a tough and stringy fowl for him to eat, moving about the kitchen and the scullery while Ball leant against a doorpost talking to her, unaware that her unwonted activities were in order to induce him to eat a few more mouthfuls before he set off on the new Quaker Mission.

"I always have a cup of coffee at this time in the morning with a sweet biscuit. You must keep me company," said Constance untruthfully. Ball accepted the cup and the biscuit without noticing them and said: "The Russians have an instinct, or a telepathic power comparable to that of bees swarming or birds gathering for the annual migration. They all talk at once, usually at cross-purposes, they seem all to be quarrelling and then after hours of disagreement, they all suddenly become convinced of what they must do and set about carrying it out. I wonder if this power could ever be awakened in English people?"

"Pass your cup," said Constance. It needed all her self-control not to dash into the argument and she longed to deny the existence of such an instinct, to ridicule the idea of telepathy and to point out that decisions taken in such a way must always lead to terrible results and to declare that a mob was always governed by the evil passions of the most evil individuals in it. But with something like heroism, she swallowed her words. If she let him talk, he might be induced to eat another sweet biscuit. It was a strange and touching scene. Only a few months later the news came that Ball had died of typhus, contracted while working among famine-stricken children in Poland, and Constance grieved for him more than any of his friends and she never forgot him.

I heard the news of the British landings at Murmansk and Archangel from Maynard who was staying at Charleston. He was enthusiastic about the prospects, prophesying that the Bolsheviks would collapse and that we should soon join hands with the troops of Admiral Kolchak advancing through Siberia and those of General Denikin coming up from the Crimea.

I told him that we had not the slightest chance of success and that our attempts at intervention were wicked and futile. The fact that a dear old friend of my parents, Nicholas Tchaykovsky, had allowed himself to be made the figurehead of the British intervention did not shake my conviction that the mass of Russians would support Lenin because he had given them peace and would break up the great estates. I was very angry with Maynard but he refused to get annoyed with me. Instead, he listened carefully to what I said and asked what my mother's opinions were based on. I did not shake him in the least at the time but I believe that I sowed a seed of doubt. Certainly he very soon realised that I had been right. At that time he knew extremely little about Russia, though he had discovered some eye-opening stories during his work at the Treasury. One was that beeswax had priority over all other munitions of war imported to Russia, as the votive candles of the Russian Orthodox Church were made of beeswax and the Tsar's Government regarded it as essential to satisfy the demand. Maynard had discovered also that a British factory had been working full time for years producing cartridges which were shipped to Russia but were of the wrong calibre. The Russian military mission in London knew the facts but had made no protest as its officers were only concerned to keep up the tonnage of munitions. If the tonnage dropped they might lose their jobs in England and be sent to the front.

My knowledge of Russia was greatly increased at this time by reading Mavor's *The Economic History of Russia*, which is by far the best book on the long political struggle between the Central Government and the Russian people from the time of Peter the Great until 1914.

I was also steeped at this time in Russian Literature and was trying to learn Russian again. In the large picture of the interior of the dining-room at Charleston with Vanessa and me sitting at the table which Duncan was painting at that time. I was engaged in translating *The Dream of a Ridiculous Man* by Dostoevsky, who proved an author too difficult for me. Many of my letters to Constance at that time are full of questions about Russian grammar. I gave my attempt at translating Dostoevsky to Constance when she was about to translate the story for inclusion with *The Honest Thief*, but it was no use to her whatever. I was able to help her more usefully a year later when I abridged and rewrote in my own words the *Biographical Sketch of Anton Tchehov* which precedes her translation of *Tchehov's Letters to his Family and Friends*. Constance was delighted with the vigour and freshness which I put into it. In the early months of 1918 I did a similar job by making an epitome of the main principles of kitchen gardening contained in Professor Gressent's *Le Potager Moderne* to which Constance had been introduced by Kropotkin many years before. Gressent's book is enormous, exhaustive and out-of-date. What is valuable in it is the exposition of the proper use of manure, the manufacture of compost and the rotation of crops, all of which I included in a small compass adding other material of my own. When I had finished it, I sent it to Edward and it was accepted by Selwyn and Blount and published at 1/6. Much of it was drawn from my experience at Wissett and Charleston. It was my first published work.

The chief cause of my desperation, in my last year working as a farm labourer, was a love affair, which for a few months took me away from Charleston every other week-end.

It was late autumn, and for most of the time I was loading dung in wet weather. My fork caught in the cows' rotting afterbirths thrown on to the muckheaps, the wet dung splashed on to my face, covered my hands, seeped through the eyelet holes of my boots and, as I worked, I was obsessed by the thought of a woman's body in a blue Chinese heavy silk chemise, and of pale blue eyes under dark lashes, suddenly lighting up. I could think of little else and my thoughts came between Duncan and me, as none of my other love affairs had done. A week of filth, long hours in the rain and hard work contrasted violently with the luxury of scented baths, silken embraces, leisure and a life completely devoid of any kind of work or duty, but it did not unsettle me so long as I felt sure that our relationship would continue. But after the end of the year I was never sure of her from one week to the next.

She excited a high degree of physical love and also an *amour de vanité* inspired by the contrast in our conditions, by her intelligence, her coldness and her apparent detachment. She, on her side, was grateful to me for providing her with a distraction from a constant preoccupation. But, after a little while, the intensity of my desire for her became my undoing. That bored her. My mistake is one of the themes of *Petrouchka*. She preferred the Moor. There were two or three idyllic Sundays in winter, when, rising late, we ran out into sunlit beech woods and everything was forgotten, except each other, as we played knee-deep in the rustling leaves. But the relationship grew doubtful as spring came and by April I realised that I was losing her and, with her, everything that seemed then to make my life endurable.

At the beginning I had lived each week on her letters, long, gossiping and filled with a grim, dry humour. Then they grew fewer and I realised that I bored her. A telegram came to postpone meeting and three weeks went by without a word, during which, from my miserable world of broken daydreams, I turned on Duncan in moments of uncontrollable rage. On the third week-end I went to The Cearne, and Frankie, who had come back to England because his father was ill, came down.

On Sunday evening he said: "I was told that I should find you in a suicidal condition. It just shows how wrong everyone is about other people's love affairs."

His words seemed to paralyse me. Everyone knew but I, and the devil of wounded vanity entered into me. I did not sleep that night. Next day Frankie persuaded me to take French leave from Mr Hecks to go and see her. It was fatal advice. She was annoyed at seeing me, coldly angry at my first word, desirable and beautiful and absolutely out of my reach.

I babbled almost meaninglessly, and she told me that all my feelings for her and hers for me were pretence, and before I knew what I was doing I had caught her by the neck and thrown her on to the floor.

My momentary impulse was not lust but murder, and, stunned by the horror of what I had wanted to do as much as by what I had actually done, I walked about the streets in a state of collapse and hysteria. I had found within myself passions which I had never expected. I was capable of a longing to commit murder and rape; I was sadistic and necrophilous. The only agony which I did not feel was jealousy. And worse than my desires was their disgusting and irredeemable vulgarity. As I walked back from Glynde in the darkness a nightingale was singing by Firle Tower; and the contrast between the beauty of nature, the loveliness of the spring night and the misery and hideous feelings in my heart, made me break out into another storm of tears. In the following weeks I saw that somehow I had to overcome the evil passions that possessed me, that poisoned the hours working on the farm and haunted me, waking or sleeping, with nightmares.

One morning early in June when we were planting cabbages Duncan said to me: "When I first got to know you, I do not think you ever had a bad or ungenerous impulse."

When he said this I realised that for weeks I had not had a single unselfish or disinterested one. I recovered my sanity but I had learned something, and my disillusion remained—and not only with my own character.

For all of us there is a breaking point: as a result of fear, or physical or mental torture, or starvation, or, as in my case, merely of the collapse of day-dreams, and when that point is reached we become, not animals, but the ancestral ape-man who begot us all. The layers of culture, of civilisation, our capacity for reasonableness, tolerance and unselfishness are all veneers. "Scratch a Russian and you find a Tartar." And then—if you scratch a Tartar, you find what? A cave man, or a monster. It seemed to me then, and often since, that the virtues are, by their nature, superficial. The most virtuous are those whose outer crust is too strong to be broken.

Those who have been prisoners of war and suffered in concentration camps can understand the self-disillusionment which follows such discoveries.

At the end of 1917 Lytton and Carrington had gone to live at the Mill House, Tidmarsh, near Pangbourne, which was originally planned to be a house where Lytton should live, and friends who paid the rent between them could go for weekends. A month after the agonising scene which ended my liaison, I received an invitation to visit Tidmarsh for the weekend in a letter from Carrington which contained a postscript saying that I should find the person I most wanted to meet staying there. Only one person could possibly be meant and it seemed obvious that *she* wished to see me and, knowing of my friendship with Carrington, had asked her to arrange it.

I asked Mr Hecks for Saturday morning off and I was just able to catch a late train which took me as far as Reading. As I walked out the eight miles to Tidmarsh I was in an emotional turmoil of anticipations. What would she say? How should I behave? It was impossible that she could wish to renew our liaison—and to see her would be an agony. Yet she could not have taken so much trouble to see me unless she wished to say a few friendly words and heal the memory of our horrible parting. But suppose Carrington, in blundering goodwill, had invited her without saying that I should be a fellow-guest! That would be too ghastly. If that was the position I would walk out of the house and sleep under a haystack.

NEW HOUSE FARM

THE MILL AND MILLHOUSE, TIDMARSH

It was late at night and Lytton and Carrington were alone when I arrived.

"I knew you would come tonight," exclaimed Carrington. "I was certain of it. Lytton wouldn't believe me. I have kept supper for you." She made me sit down to eat.

"Where is . . . my fellow-guest?" I asked as soon as I decently could.

"Upstairs," said Carrington.

I picked up my rucksack and went upstairs and Carrington followed to show me my room.

"Which is *her* room?" I asked, for it was torture to wait another moment. I must find out if I was there with her knowledge, even at her wish.

Lytton had come out on to the landing and looked at me with surprise. "Why, who do you think is there?" he asked.

I stepped forward to open the door but Carrington seized my arm. "Stop! You mustn't go in!" she exclaimed.

"Well, who is it, then?" I asked, bewildered.

"Mrs Swanwick," tittered Lytton who was mystified by the whole affair. This was an idiotic joke, for Mrs Swanwick was an elderly feminist and socialist.

I freed my arm from Carrington and was about to rush into the room when the door opened and a young man whom I had seen once before in my life stood in the doorway.

"He must be her lover! That is why Carrington is trying to stop me going in!" flashed through my mind.

But the young man was so incongruous a figure—so terribly unsuited for the part, that I realised that I must be slightly mad and I pulled myself together sufficiently to greet him civilly and then retire to bed.

But it did not occur to me that I was the victim of one of the singularly brutal practical jokes which Carrington sometimes played upon her friends. I could not imagine that she was capable of such a piece of brutality as to have planned the whole incident. Yet that is certainly the explanation. My obtuseness was fortunate as I don't think I should have easily forgiven her, and my relations with both her and Lytton might

173

have been spoiled. As it was I bore Carrington no ill-will, persuading myself that I was mad and that my obsession had led me to create the whole situation myself. Curiously enough her cruel joke was a better moral tonic than any sympathy; it helped me to break my idiotic habit of wishful day-dreaming and see myself as others saw me.

The scene upon the landing had been a violent emotional shock and Mr Marshall must have wondered what was wrong with me.

However, I spent a very happy week-end, mowing the lawn with a borrowed scythe, reading *The Turn of the Screw* and having long talks with Carrington as I helped her cook, or wash-up.

My innocence of her trick and the violence of my feelings which must have been apparent, softened her heart towards me. For from that time onwards she was much more friendly, and invited me to the Mill House at fairly frequent intervals.

The Mill House was built on to the end of a big weather-boarded water mill, and the mill stream, banked to a higher level, bounded one side of the garden. I do not think the mill-wheel was still in use, but the building above it was a corn-chandler's busy warehouse.

The stream and the weather-boarded water mill over the mill-wheel is the subject of one of Carrington's best pictures.

The black weeks in the early summer did not last. The company of Julian and Quentin did a good deal to make me feel happier, but what most changed my mood was the news that Vanessa was going to have another child which I could not doubt would be as delightful a creature as its brothers. The thought of the child filled me with delight: an affirmation of a belief in life at the time of blackest despair. I gave up eating my tiny ration of butter and added it to Vanessa's and Duncan I think did the same. This action was not sentimental on our part: it was because there was very little butter in those days and the child would need all it could get. There was fortun-ately plenty of honey by then, and once as I watched Vanessa eating the butter I said to myself: "I have not become wholly horrible."

IX

CHARLESTON was at first a rambling old farmhouse, full of badly planned passages and small rooms. There was, on the garden side, a long cool dairy room with solid slate slabs round the walls to set the shallow pans of milk for creaming; on the way to it was a pantry and another larder or a stillroom with a slatted door. Slowly the house took on another, but equally living character. One after another the rooms were decorated and altered almost out of recognition as the bodies of the saved are said to be glorified after the resurrection. Duncan painted many of the doors with pictures on the panels and with decorative borders round the frames. In every leisure moment he was at work. After breakfast, on a Sunday morning in summer, when the visitors were sitting around among the empty coffee bowls and the crusts of toast, already discussing the war, Duncan, dressed in old blue cotton overalls with a tear in the seat of the trousers through which a bit of lighter blue shirt was hanging out, unshaven and with his shock of dark hair presenting a curiously concave surface to the sky, was trundling a wheelbarrow, then asking me to help carry some old rusty milk churns that he was intent on removing to serve as the bases of a line of plaster casts which he wanted to have standing under the apple-trees in the walled garden, then involved in conferences with Vanessa in which careful measurements were being taken. They were always wrong. Duncan, like a sailor, was always quietly occupied with some task of his own invention. "Creative activity was his passion; he was never satisfied with what he had ready-made; he longed to make something new." Those words written of Tchehov were equally true of Duncan and it was not the only resemblance between the two men whose temperaments were curiously alike.

In his schemes Duncan was always seconded by Vanessa; they painted together in harmony, perfectly happy while they were at work, and rarely resting from it.* Thus Charleston was transformed.

Then Clive took possession of one room with his shelves of books, boxes of cheroots, Rose Geranium bath salts and a gun-case; the children filled others with toys; and, as they grew larger, fishing rods, butterfly nets, boats and an air-gun made their appearance. Julian was eight when we went to Charleston and eleven by the time that it ceased to be my home. He was a very beautiful young creature with a face and eyes as cleanly cut as sculptured marble. He had a strong will; and, often involved in wrong-doing, he would defend his misdeeds in endless arguments upon first principles with his mother. I soon came to love him and we had many interests in common, not shared by the other grown-ups. Thus he acquired from me a passion for wild nature and natural beauty and for birds, beasts and fishes.

I gave him *Bevis* on his ninth birthday and introduced him later on to the other works of Richard Jefferies which remained favourites all his life. *Marsh Birds Pass Over London*, an anticipation of the bombing of London which he did not live to see, was inspired by *After London* and in the opening poem of *Winter Movement* he salutes Jefferies as his master.

When I had an hour to spare I used to teach Julian a little elementary science: biology, the evolution and principles of heredity in animals and plants, their physiology and anatomy; the elements of physics and astrophysics, the calendar and the weather; the difference between igneous and sedimentary rocks; the ages of the earth; choosing the bits of knowledge I thought most important in order to give a brilliantly intelligent child an accurate conception of the earth and solar system. Sometimes we sat at a table and I showed him a book, or drew a diagram. More often my lessons were conversations when we went for walks and their text the things we came across: the rings on the stump of a felled ash, a dewpond, or worm-casts

*I write of it in the past tense but it still goes on unchanged.

176

on the lawn. Such conversations did me, perhaps, more good than they did him, yet he remembered some of what I told him after the very knowledge of it had faded from my mind.

Quentin was two years younger, a chubby Della Robbia angel with red-gold hair and innocent eyes devoid of the glint of devilry that sparkled in Julian's. He was a loyal and devoted assistant in Julian's mischief, but his sweet serenity of character often brought him off unscathed. One afternoon Julian got into a fight with two farm boys, worsted them and rushed in breathless, having forgotten his Man Friday, who was straggling along unconscious of evil, half a mile behind. He was spied, however, by the farm boys who, seeking revenge, ambushed him, one on each side of the path. When Quentin drew level one of the boys threw half a brick with all his force. It missed Quentin but hit the other enemy beyond him on the side of the face. Quentin came in and told us about it. It did not occur to him that an enemy had met with his deserts, for he was full of concern for the unfortunate victim of the accident. The whole incident was characteristic.

In summer Julian and Quentin often went naked, adding their beauty to the Charleston flowers and orchard. They would scramble over Maynard, ride each other horseback and fall into the pond. Vanessa sometimes followed them about stealthily, a Kodak in her hand. Duncan painted them. One summer I had to pose naked, close to the footpath leading to Firle, kneedeep in the old sheep-dip as an unhaloed St Christopher with Quentin riding astride upon my shoulders. In the picture I am portrayed as greenish in colour below the waist, but with a torso of golden copper. It is accurate for I had been harvesting for weeks wearing heavy trousers and only a tattered shirt.

Early in 1917, Amber Blanco White's two young daughters came to stay for a time. The eldest was a quick-witted brat with black hair and roving eyes who immediately became passionately devoted to Julian. The younger was a gnome with an absurd piping voice. The effect of the girls on the two boys amused us. They had been irresponsible and indifferent as to

177

whether they appeared ridiculous. But female admiration made them aware of the effect of their actions on their audience and Julian adopted the manly airs of their protector.

At the end of that summer Vanessa decided that a governess was necessary and went to London to look for one. She returned saying that she had had the astonishing good fortune to engage a young woman with the face of a Sassoferrato Madonna. She would serve as a most wonderful model—and I was teasingly warned that I must behave myself: it was not for me to upset her by trifling with her affections.

The Madonna proved to be a young woman who had been educated in a French Convent, and whose face wore a look of permanent peevish discontent. After the first day Vanessa was so bored with her conversation that she begged me to go and talk to her in the evening. Somehow our Madonna must be kept amused and I was, obviously, cut out for the job. I refused, and was roundly attacked for not bearing my share of the burdens of the household. I said I preferred to dig the garden, or chop wood for the fires. In a fortnight Vanessa's peevish Madonna had driven us all desperate. Then, one afternoon, she returned from a walk with the children covered with mud, soaking wet and furiously angry. Julian, to rid himself of her company, had pushed her into a deep ditch full of water and had run away, and she had extricated herself with difficulty. Her dress and shoes were ruined. She left a few weeks later. Julian was, of course, in deep disgrace, but it was impossible for Duncan and for me to hide our gratitude for his action.

Molly MacCarthy brought her children to stay and one evening they announced that they had got up a play for our benefit. The little wretches had been listening to conversation at table and the central figure was Ottoline, involved in some emotional entanglement and played by Rachel MacCarthy. The enchanting little girl, as lively and innocent as a squirrel, was not cut out by nature for the part. But Julian, as producer, had coached her carefully from memory, and her imitation, at second-hand, of Lady Ottoline's menacing growl and drawling whine, and the airs of aristocratic majesty which she put on, sent us into fits of laughter, though Molly, I think, was wondering what might not be coming next.

Molly came to Charleston several times and I became devoted to her. I have never had a conversation with one of our summer migrants—let us say a spotted flycatcher—but I am quite sure that if such good fortune were to befall me, it would be very like a talk with Molly. I should say something ordinary and at once the little brown bird would have vanished from off the railing where she perched, darting to catch a passing butterfly in mid-air and then, almost before I had time to wonder where she was, she would be back glancing at me gently out of a bright eye. Indeed Molly had, in that sudden flash of absence, caught a butterfly or a bee which she would bring unexpectedly and a little shyly into the conversation. After a few broken sentences and the words: "Oh, do you think? . . ." another flash, capture and reappearance would take place. But soon I saw that the butterflies and bees were not taken so delicately out of the air at random, but that each was part of a jerky progression—illustrations in a train of thought, two-thirds of which remained unspoken. Too banal to go into that—and Molly's mind jumped a page or two. One had to be quick-witted and gentle as a bird oneself, or she might impatiently give up and fly away. But alas, as the years went by, these qualities had to be combined with a loud voice, as deafness grew upon her. When she first charmed me, I thought that I often distressed her by my dogmatism, or my materialism, but she never gave me up as hopeless, or a bore.

The running of such a large household, with a stream of visitors, must have been a difficult and exhausting task and Vanessa had many worries with servants since her mainstay, Mabel, left to get married and her sister Trissie only stayed a few months before she married the son of rich old Mr Stacey who farmed Charleston and half a dozen other farms. In 1918, Mrs Brereton, found for Vanessa by Roger, came to help, bringing her daughter Ann, an attractive child who could hold

179

her own with Julian in a rough and tumble wrestling match. They were good for one another. Vanessa also engaged two savage black-haired sloe-eyed women as servants.

If Vanessa was in continual difficulties in getting servants for Charleston, owing to their habit of getting married, Constance was exceptionally lucky. Her Emily was a young woman who had lived for several years with our French friend Louis-ette Bréal and had been the nurse of her youngest child, Philippe, and looked after the elder two, Hermine and Michel. When she came to my mother, Emily was an attractive woman of about thirty, full of adventurous spirit, with a passion for gardening and outdoor life. A tent, or a gun, a new variety of lily, or a new breed of domestic fowl brought a sparkle to her eye and a flush to her cheek. She loved Constance and was happy at The Cearne; she only left after the war because she had fallen in love with the son of a neighbouring farmer who turned out to be worthy of his good fortune. George Lang-ridge has all the old traditional skills. He can milk and lay a hedge, thatch and split chestnut poles, plough and build a stack. He has also an instinctive knowledge of where to put his hand on a litter of fox cubs, or find a badger's sett, and like many men who have worked as farm labourers all their lives, he has a passionate interest in and understanding of everything to do with foxhunting. Emily and George Lang-ridge are old people now but they still love work and have an eager interest in all they do. Their visits are the occasion for a series of yarns about the past and Emily still laughs and blushes and is embarrassed if I mention peacocks.

Meat was short during the war and the rabbits in The Cearne garden were too plentiful. Constance therefore bought a shotgun and Emily shot the rabbits and served up dishes of *civet de lapin*, *gibelotte de lapin* and *terrine de lapereau* which she had learned to cook in France. The neighbouring keeper had gone to the war, Emily was of an adventurous tempera-ment and the *lapins* were sometimes replaced by *perdrix aux choux*, or even by *faisan rôti*.

One day Constance and Edward were sitting in the garden

in the evening when they heard a shot and presently Edward saw Emily coming into the garden carrying the gun and walking with a peculiar waddle. She came up to them in great distress.

"Oh, I've done something so dreadful," she exclaimed. "I've shot the Trevereux peacock," and, as she spoke, she drew the very much crumpled but still gorgeous bird from beneath her skirts. "I suppose I must go and own up and I shall be prosecuted and sent to prison. It was quite an accident. You see, he poked his head out from behind a tree and, in the poor light, I thought he was a pheasant."

Fortunately Edward was there and he told Emily to pluck the bird immediately, burn all its feathers and never breathe a word of what she had done.

Unluckily I did not visit The Cearne for some weeks but I was told that Emily's peacock pie was the most delicious dish she had ever cooked—far better than pheasant. Unlike Argus of Garsington, the Trevereux bird was young and he had died a violent death.

During and after the war, several bungalows were built round Cearne Bank Farm and Gracie's Cottage, which were eventually inhabited by friends of ours. This resulted in a community which Edward always called Dostoevsky Corner, though actually its spiritual atmosphere was almost as reminiscent of *Cranford*, as of *The Possessed*. The most important of its inhabitants was Sybil Rudall who had lived with us when I was five years old.

When she left us, she had gone to Russia and had taught English in several families. In one Polish château where she stayed, the two watch-dogs were eaten in their kennels by wolves one winter's night and in the morning there were only their blood-stained collars at the ends of their chains. She went on a tour to Germany with one of her employers—Madame Koch, an operatic star. When they returned, Sybil was made to wear a petticoat into the lining of which hundreds of cigars had been stitched, as they went through the customs.

"I felt very queer," said Sybil. "And I must have looked

very queer too with my skirt bunched out like that. But they took no notice of me."

After she returned to England, Sybil married Charles Wilson, a distinguished Persian scholar who taught at the London School of Oriental Languages and spent his spare time translating the Persian poets and walking in the woods. There was something faun-like and Victorian in the shy elderly figure carrying an umbrella whom one met under the beech trees.

Sybil's presence was a great pleasure for Constance and she was also able to read Russian aloud to her.

After Constance went nearly blind, she still went on working at Russian translation—but working with an amanuensis who read the Russian aloud and to whom my mother dictated the English.

Juliet Soskice was one of the earliest of my mother's helpers, and her visits to The Cearne were always a great pleasure to me for she had so much warmth and humour and irresistibly jolly good sense. She loved life and accepted it and liked people as they were, not wanting them to be different. And that attitude, rather rare among Constance's friends, was an agreeable relief to me.

Natasha Ertel, however, was Constance's principal assistant. She had married an Englishman, Mr Duddington, before the war. Natasha had the same capacity for working long hours at high pressure as Constance, and when she came down to The Cearne for a couple of days and a night they sometimes scarcely stopped for meals. Later on Constance would read over what she had dictated, turn it over in her mind and make corrections. Sometimes she felt the exact word had escaped her and worried over it for days until finally it would come to her.

Under her married name Natasha Duddington has done much translation from the Russian on her own.

She was strongly anti-Bolshevik from the first and her adopted sister, Lenotchka Goncharov, who had been an actress working under Stanislavsky at the Artistic Theatre in Moscow, had married an officer serving with Denikin's army. After its defeat, Lenotchka and he set off in a cart and drove hundreds of miles through the country of "the free Cossacks" and the nomad Khirgiz and succeeded in joining Admiral Kolchak's force just before their precipitate retreat across the whole of Siberia to Vladivostok.

Duncan and I got up to London at intervals;—sometimes alone, sometimes together, to see an opera. One evening, as I walked with a party down Endell Street from where we had dined, an air-raid warning sounded, and when we reached Bow Street I was astonished to see a crowd of the very poorest people pushing their way into the Police Court for shelter. Some of them looked like criminals and it seemed to show a touching faith in the authorities. But perhaps they knew that its stone passages and cells were very solidly built. The upper classes meanwhile were pushing their way into Covent Garden Opera House quite unconcerned and there were no empty seats in the stalls.

In the middle of the second act the noise of heavy explosions and a racket of guns broke out and drowned the music. The conductor—I think it was Sir Thomas Beecham, laid down his baton, turned to us and said: "Will any members of the audience who wish to leave do so now. The company and I will then continue." Not more than half a dozen people scurried out while we applauded and the opera was concluded with noises off. When we came out we found the last wave of Gothas had passed and that Southampton Row was full of fire engines. As usual the bombs aimed at Euston, St Pancras and King's Cross had fallen in and around Queen's Square. Saxon, who had rooms opposite the Children's Hospital was living in the centre of what appeared to be the bullseye. I enjoyed that evening all the more because of the interruptions which had made me feel at one with several hundreds of my countrymen.

Another visit to the opera was the occasion of a meeting which I found embarrassing. During the *entr'acte* I was standing in a corner of the bar when suddenly I heard a joyful shout of "Bunny!" and an enormous Major, or perhaps Lieutenant Colonel rushed up to me. It was Godwin Baynes. He demonstrated the warmth of his feeling by putting his hands upon my shoulders and addressing me in a very loud voice. I saw some of the crowd glance at us with surprise and, I thought, with a touch of distaste, as Godwin led me about the foyer with his arm on my shoulder trumpeting his delight at seeing me again. He had changed his mind about the war and was filled with admiration for the stand which Siegfried Sassoon had just made in refusing orders. It appeared that Bertie Farjeon and I had been right in becoming conscientious objectors, and he declared that we must get together and talk things out.

It was a relief when the bell rang. I found it difficult to listen to the music, as I was feeling miserably unhappy.

I could feel no response to Godwin's warmth, and I could not understand him. He had called me a coward—perhaps rightly—and had spewed me out of his mouth because he disagreed with my unpopular opinions. Now, simply because he had changed his own, he was throwing his arms round my neck. I could not wipe out the past so easily. What had happened was irremediable and though I realised I should have to pretend to be on the old footing it was impossible for me to be so. I had loved and trusted and admired him and he had destroyed my faith. It was unthinkable that Duncan or Maynard, or Frankie or Lytton should have behaved in such a way to an intimate friend because of a political difference.

What a contrast with Giblin!

Godwin had insisted that I should meet him later on and I did not shirk doing so. He was bubbling with pacifist ideas; I shared them, yet, coming from him, they embarrassed me and I was thankful when we parted. We met again once or twice in later years. Rosalind had left him and he came to dinner with a new wife after I had married Ray. By that time I should have been delighted to have rekindled our old friendship— but there was no spark left in the ashes.

In September 1918 I had an evening in London before going for a fortnight's holiday to Cornwall with my parents. I went alone to a performance of the Russian Ballet and was absolutely enchanted by *The Good Humoured Ladies* devised by Massine for music by Scarlatti. Massine as the waiter and Lopokhova as the servant girl at the inn both danced divinely and played cruel tricks at the expense of an ancient couple, played by Monsieur and Madame Cecchetti who were actually very old, having trained two generations of Russian dancers, but whose performance was as graceful as that of their pupils. By a lucky chance Ottoline caught sight of me and carried me off after the performance, to visit first Massine and then Lopokhova in their dressing-rooms. Massine was a slight figure, with very black eyebrows which nearly met and large almond-shaped black eyes, who looked to me more Italian than Russian. His face was oval and strikingly intelligent. At that moment he was in a state of extreme physical exhaustion with sweat starting through the greasepaint and he reminded me of a thoroughbred being led to the unsaddling enclosure after a gruelling race. Some months later he went to see Duncan at his studio after a matinée and was so exhausted that he had to stop and rest half-way up the stairs. Yet he danced the can-can in *La Boutique Fantasque* with immense energy that evening. The nervous exhaustion was perhaps as great as the physical.

We were soon joined by two tall, extremely elegant young officers with fair hair and rosy complexions. They were Osbert and Sacheverell Sitwell, whom I met for the first time. Osbert was self-possessed and talkative, Sacheverell seemed even shyer than I.

To find myself suddenly in Lopokhova's dressing-room—I had been spreading dung only that morning—was so incredible that I simply stared at her in dumb worship, as though I had been wafted by Ottoline into heaven. What an exquisite little head! What lovely arms! What a fascinating, extraordinary nose! Yes, I could see that like Papagena in *The Magic Flute*, she was more bird than woman.

But Ottoline was saying goodbye.

I spent the last fortnight of September 1918 with my parents and Nellie in a farmhouse on the north coast of Devon, just on the county boundary with Cornwall. The bathing was tricky except at the right state of the tide, as there were very strong currents and Edward and I had to be careful.

Duncan wrote to tell me of Trissie's wedding and that she had liked the brooch I sent her.

You must write something in Cornwall. I wish you would write about the youthful band, tossed and shattered by the war. . . . Virginia has been here most of the day. . . . The Webbs had been staying with the Woolves and from her accounts seem too terrible, not that she thought so. Lloyd George sent for them and asked if the Labour Party would mind if he made peace at once with Germany at the expense of Russia. Unluckily it seems against it.

Harry Norton came over for a night and greatly impressed Constance, but depressed her even more by his pessimism, which I shared. Both he and I regarded the end of the war as extremely unlikely and were certain it could not be reached by a military decision.

Just before the end of my holiday, I walked over to Clovelly, where Noel Olivier was having a holiday.

It is an extraordinary little beauty spot with steps descending to the sea instead of a village street, and on the steps were perched one or two elderly Royal Academicians (or would-be R.A.s) standing under green umbrellas on telescopic stands and painting sickly pictures of the scene. Noel seemed to me to be immensely enjoying the company of her inferiors. This was one of the carping criticisms that some of the older members of Bloomsbury frequently made about each other and which always infuriated me, partly because I was, no doubt, regarded by some as one of the inferiors in question. Yet I could not help feeling the same thing about Noel, because I could see no point in the jovial elderly men, who, having tied coloured handkerchiefs round their heads, adopted piratical airs as they flirted very mildly and drank shandy-gaff with young women.

Noel may have seen my irritation, for when night had fallen she suggested a bathe, and we swam out slowly, side by side, out of earshot of the horrors of Clovelly. The sea was dead calm as we rested floating in the water, and she began to talk about herself and her feelings for the people who had been in love with her. All my annoyance died away. I felt that I understood her and accepted her uncritically. She was the nearest I had ever had to a sister, and I felt perfectly confident that she would make her own life as she wanted it, though her way was not mine. We swam back slowly to the beach. The elderly pirates had finished their last little bed-time tots of whisky and had gone to bed.

After I came back from my holiday Vanessa went to London for a fortnight at 46 Gordon Square and Duncan also had his annual holiday, so that I was left with Mrs Brereton and the children. Duncan wrote to me almost every day as he knew how depressing it could be to be left to work alone.

(Postmarked October 6, 1918.)

I spent a very quiet Sunday beginning to decorate Maynard's room. Vanessa lies on the sofa and gives advice. We had lunch at about 2.30. Sheppard in a light blue dressing-gown, very amusing and perfectly charming, Maynard and Norton and Nessa. After lunch Maynard ordered a Landau and horse to fetch Nessa for a drive. At that moment Clive and Molly arrived and we took Molly and Maynard for a drive round the Regent's Park down Baker Street, through Hyde Park and back by the great Squares of Mayfair and Oxford Street. It was a most curious sensation. Everything looked totally different from usual, and the little boys laughed at us.

We are all sad today because Robbie Ross suddenly died yesterday after being out to lunch. He took aspirin and never woke up. I only saw him last Wednesday when he was so charming to me that I feel I might really have got to like him more and more.

(Postmarked October 9, 1918.)

We are just talking about you and Nessa has been condoling with you at your solitary evenings and Sheppard is amused to hear you probably spend your evenings with Mrs B. over the fire. Two charming letters have arrived from the children. Julian says you had a fit at dinner on hearing about the Peace Proposals. Well it's all very exciting but I remain rather stunned and absolutely unresponsive, except to Sheppard's wild excitement and the general good humour which surrounds us. I don't really dare to think of Peace, it seems a joke.

187

Nessa is given leave to drive in a barouche, a curious old-fashioned vehicle with a glass front (enclosed driver) and goes shopping in the mornings.

Roger came to lunch and Virginia and the two Sitwells came to tea. It was a charming party. I think the Sitwells are perfectly charming. Nessa is going to ask Osy to Charleston. I think you will like him. They are both over six foot high but I now remember that you know them. Please forgive me. They are going to give a party tomorrow. It was to have been given as a farewell party to Robbie on his departure to Australia. He did not know whether he ought to have put it off, but having taken no steps yet, there is no possibility of putting them off.

Osy is charming with the old men. Once he went to his dentist in mufti and saw an old man in the waiting-room staring rudely at him, so he said to him: "Can you tell me, Sir, why I am not in khaki?" Oh, shall we ever live in Peace?

(Postmarked October 10, 1918.)

As a matter of fact I'm sitting in Tanza Road waiting for Adrian and Karin to come in to supper. I've just been to see Gertler's pictures in his studio with the inevitable Koteliansky sitting in the background, silent as usual but I thought more friendly. I'll tell you about the pictures when I see you.

I'm very sleepy as we were all up till three this morning after a party at Osbert's in Chelsea. It was a charming party and I didn't at all want to come away, but we stayed as long as we could and were the last to leave. Nessa came in her barouche and it took us all back which was very luxurious. We went to *Scheherazade* first. I went with Jack and Mary to a box. Jack kept telling us in a raucous whisper to stop talking, but I am getting so used to Society that even the worst social dilemmas pass me by only perceived with a bland smile. All the smart set were there, terrible creatures and all exactly alike. And Ottoline really resplendent in her yellow Spanish gown with little Lopokhova in blue in tow.

Of course Ot. came. We had the most delicious food imaginable. *Pâté de foie gras* and melting cakes, the best brandy, muscat grapes, but I won't make your mouth water. I was very greedy but I loved the younger generation, they are very friendly. It's too horrid you weren't there. I really think you would have liked it too. Here they come so goodbye. I'll see you soon. I go home for Sunday and then freedom is over.

Soon after Duncan's return the Peace Proposals seemed to fizzle out and we settled down to another winter of farm work. There was, however, a change in my position. Mr Hecks had bought a Fordson tractor and, after its first novelty was over,

I was put on to drive it and soon was spending my days in ploughing. I enjoyed the work immensely. Indeed, though I often complained of farm work, it was not the work I disliked but the uncertainty of my position. I could have been perfectly happy working on my own farm.

In the first days of November, a change came. A wild excitement spread. It was obvious that something was happening in Germany. The enemy was unexpectedly cracking.

On November the eleventh Duncan and I went down to the farm, and just as we were starting work Cowman came out and told us the news of the Armistice. Mr Hecks was in Lewes, but that was a trivial detail.

"Come on," and in a few minutes we were on our bicycles, pedalling hard to catch the first train to London. By the time we arrived, it had already gone mad. The streets were thronged with crowds, singing and laughing, dazed with happiness. Lorry loads of girls—munition workers in their working overalls, straight from Woolwich Arsenal, or the factories, their young faces stained bright yellow with the fumes of picric acid, were driving slowly along, singing and yelling. Some of them exchanged catcalls and badinage with passing soldiers, but most of them seemed to be in a religious trance. There were more than the usual number of motor-buses—in some places the roads were blocked with them. They no longer ran on their accustomed routes, but loaded with a full and permanent complement of cheering passengers, they explored new neighbourhoods, such as the squares of Mayfair and of Bloomsbury, at the whim of the driver. Every taxi had half a dozen passengers inside and a couple more on its roof. Duncan and I made our way to Gordon Square where we found Sheppard and Maynard. Rather to our surprise Jessie produced some lunch. Later Mary Hutchinson told us that everyone would be welcome at Monty Shearman's flat in the Adelphi. It was central and after wandering about among the crowds, Duncan and I went there in the afternoon.

Already the rooms were packed with people, most of whom we knew. But the company was constantly changing, as people came and went. Those I remember are Lytton and Carrington, Osbert and Sacheverell Sitwell, Mary and Jack Hutchinson, Diaghilev and Massine, Henry Mond and his mother, Lady Mond, Lawrence and Frieda.*

I had not seen Lawrence for three years, and in a rush of pleasure went up to speak to him. He looked ill and unhappy, with no trace of that gay sparkling love of life in his eyes which had been his most attractive feature six years before. I greeted him warmly, but he only nodded, said: "So you're here," and went on talking.

Frieda gave me a squeeze and a look of pleased astonishment in her yellow eyes which made up for his lack of warmth. A moment or two later Carrington and I were dancing in a crowd of others as Henry Mond played on the piano. A little later I went back to Lawrence, and he was ready to talk to me. Soon a number of people had crowded round us.

What he said was something like this, though I do not suppose that a single phrase reproduces his actual words.

"I suppose you think the war is over and that we shall go back to the kind of world you lived in before it. But the war isn't over. The hate and evil is greater now than ever. Very soon war will break out again and overwhelm you. It makes me sick to see you rejoicing like a butterfly in the last rays of the sun before the winter. The crowd outside thinks that Germany is crushed forever. But the Germans will soon rise again. Europe is done for; England most of all the countries.

* In *Portrait Of A Genius But ... The Life of D. H. Lawrence 1885–1930* Mr Richard Aldington states, on the basis of what Lawrence wrote in the autobiographical novel *Kangaroo* that on Armistice Day "In the evening he and Frieda sat alone together and sang German Folk songs and Frieda wept."

In a review in *The Daily Telegraph* I pointed out that I had met them both on the evening in question, at Monty Shearman's flat, and controversy ensued. Mrs St John Hutchinson however had also a vivid memory of seeing Lawrence there then and Sir Osbert Sitwell makes the same statement in his autobiography. Nor did I visit Monty Shearman's in March at the time of the débâcle of the Fifth Army when Aldington met Lawrence there. Lawrence and Frieda were in the Adelphi flat on November 11, 1918, but I think it possible that as the party lasted all the afternoon and till late at night, Lawrence and Frieda may have left it in time to catch a train to Newbury and get to Hermitage late that night. Frieda's tears are natural enough in view of Lawrence's reception of the news.

This war isn't over. Even if the fighting should stop, the evil will be worse because the hate will be dammed up in men's hearts and will show itself in all sorts of ways which will be worse than war. Whatever happens there can be no Peace on Earth."

There was a sombre joy in the tone in which he made these fierce prophecies of evil, and I could see that he was enjoying being the only man in the room who was not rejoicing because the fighting was over. It was the last time that I saw Lawrence, or spoke to him. The impression he made on me was so painful that I did not try to seek him out during the year in which he remained in England, or on the rare occasions when he came back for a brief visit. I did not want to see him again. But I was delighted when he wrote a warm and friendly letter three years later when I got married, and I know he was very much pleased when I wrote to tell him how much I admired *Lady Chatterley's Lover*.

Evening had fallen. "Let's go out to Trafalgar Square," said someone, and a little later a party of us was in the Strand and was being split up by the surging crowd. I had just time to say good-bye to Frieda and then found myself separated from all my friends with Lady Mond holding my arm. She was a big, good-natured blonde, a German Jewess of about fifty. In Trafalgar Square everyone was dancing, and we also began to dance and soon joined up with a ring of about a hundred people, singing and dancing and beside themselves with joy.

> Whence come ye, merry maidens, whence come ye?
> So many and so many and such glee.

Most of them had come out of munition factories and were dancing because their work was over.

Lady Mond and I were absolutely at one; we might have been created for each other, like the ephemeridae that enjoy one short hour of ecstasy dancing over the surface of the stream before they drown. Then we fell in with some of our party and followed them gaily back to the flat. On the threshold of the flat we parted forever. I never made an effort to see the good lady again and even if she remembered me next morning she did not know my name.

In the flat I met Lytton, who said that he was going back to Gordon Square. I stayed on, but the evening began to lose its charm, and my last memory is of seeing Henry Mond banging on the keyboard of the piano with a tumbler of whisky clenched in each of his fists.

I went back to Trafalgar Square where Canadian soldiers had torn down some horrible hoardings covered with war slogans and had lit a bonfire with them against the plinth of Nelson's column. The temper of the crowd was enchanting. Lawrence was wrong. All were sick to death of hatred and were purging it out of their hearts in an outburst of universal love. Love and goodness were all about me and the same pure happiness animated us all. But though I was in love with the crowd I had no wish to become involved with any individuals, and I soberly made my way back to 46 Gordon Square. We sipped some wine and when Jessie produced sandwiches I discovered that I was ravenous. Bloomsbury was assembled and there was some talk of what the world would be like. Maynard said:

"What is really important is that we can't go back on this. Whatever may develop neither side can start the war up again. The troops would not fight and the people would not work." This was a more common-sense argument than Lawrence's and with it in my mind I went to bed and fell fast asleep.

I went back to the farm early next day, made my peace with Mr Hecks, and worked a little, out of pure good nature. When I thought over the events of Armistice Day it seemed to me rather an odd augury for the future that I should have begun as a slave engaged in forced labour, and before its close should have been dancing with the wife of a millionaire Cabinet Minister in Trafalgar Square. I had shared with tens of thousands of people in a spontaneous overwhelming orgy of happiness, goodness and love.

Although, in theory, Duncan and I were bound to go on working until we were demobilised, in practice we did little or no work after a few weeks. So long as Mr Hecks did not complain to the Central Committee no action was likely to be taken, as there was no real check on us. The Servile State had not yet been organised.

My future was uncertain. Duncan had suggested that I should become a picture dealer; Frankie had suggested a bookshop and a nebulous plan was formed of our hiring a small gallery and selling books and pictures, and making it a meeting-place for people interested in the arts.

The Armistice and the liberation of Northern France brought big developments of the Quaker Mission. The manufacture of sectional wooden huts had been started at the sources of timber supply: in the Pyrenees and in the Jura. Frankie had become a close personal friend of the Sous-préfet of the Meuse, who had much say in the work of the Mission. Frankie had also become deeply involved in its internal politics, and as a result of free elections to the Committee, many changes were made which quite altered its character.

Frankie was also much concerned with the welfare of the large number of young American Quakers who had come out to work for the Mission. Many of them were young men from the Middle-West, completely ignorant of Europe and of European culture. Frankie saw that it was an opportunity to broaden their outlook and educate them. Indeed it was more than an opportunity which should not be missed: it was a duty.

One of the ways in which he planned to do this was to start a magazine which should keep all the scattered groups in touch with one another's work. The plan was accepted and Frankie was the obvious choice as editor. He picked as his assistant a young American called Leslie Hotson and carried him off to Paris. All this meant that Frankie would not be available to start a bookshop for about a year.

About the middle of December I wrote to Constance:

Dearest Mother, I am sure you think me rather a sneak not to have come this week, but I couldn't have come without being one. . . . Vanessa had a chill last week and kept in bed several days. Now she seems much better and is up and about. I went away for the week-end to

Lytton's. His book is now in the sixth thousand and I found him surrounded by all the lives and works of reference about the Prince Consort. Carrington began a portrait of me. James has become a medical student at St Thomas's Hospital a bit late in life. . . . Maynard is going to the Preliminary Conference of the Allies and then will retire into private life and go back to King's.

Clive is writing a book called *Civilisation*, but I don't know what it's about.

I have just received a voting card from Tom Pargiter who is a local signalman who has put up as a Labour Candidate. Duncan and I both have votes and shall vote for him.

Duncan went out to drive the ducks off the pond and fell out of the punt into the pond while pursuing them. He had to find his way out in the dark and presented a miserable appearance. He was well laughed at for his misfortune. Your loving son, David.

Soon after this Vanessa asked me to stay on until after the baby was born. Clive had often to be away, Duncan wanted to go to London, and I could be useful cutting up logs. She added that it would give her confidence to know that I was in the house in case anything went wrong.

I wrote to Constance:

Christmas Day. Charleston.

Dearest Mother, Vanessa had a daughter born at 2 a.m. this morning, so I am very glad I was here. It is a queer little creature, very lovely and full of independent life. I went for the doctor about nine and sat up till it was over and then was able to have a look at it. It weighed seven and a half pounds, being put in a cardboard box on the kitchen scales. Clive is very glad it is a girl; so will Virginia be for she thinks highly of her own sex. Vanessa doesn't and is probably rather disappointed.

It is a curious emotional experience waiting for someone else's child to be born.

Maynard is spending Christmas here and I have had a rapprochement with him. He will leave the Government service after the Peace Conference and is now fighting Mr Hughes tooth and nail over German indemnities and I believe will beat him easily. Maynard has just refused an income of ten thousand pounds a year and a knighthood, the first on the grounds that it would not be a sinecure and he won't work at what he doesn't want to. You see there are respectable traits in his character. I shall probably come to The Cearne on the first of January. I am sure you think I am a horrid kind of son to neglect you at Christmas and hardly even write a line. Even after the nurse arrived I was really wanted. Besides

194

sawing up logs and running errands there was something in being here which was of value.

Well, even if you feel rather cold to me, please believe I love you—love you in just the same way as these nuzzling little creatures do soon after they are born and probably much more. Your loving David.

At first all went well. I paid a visit to The Cearne; Duncan went off to stay with his parents, and Roger paid a visit to Charleston which was followed by one from Lytton.

Maynard left for Paris where preparations for the Peace Conference were in progress.

The baby did not gain weight. She was a little creature, lively enough but she slowly shrank to skin and bone. Once when Duncan heard her mewing miserably, without the strength to cry, he began to hum a tune of Beethoven's and she stopped at once to listen.

Suddenly things took a turn for the worse. Julian and Quentin had been taken to stay at Asheham, as Mrs Brereton had gone away for a holiday, and Leonard wrote that he was afraid that they were too much of a strain for Virginia who had been having alarming headaches. The only place to send them was 46 Gordon Square and Clive had to go to look after them there. When I returned to Charleston, Vanessa was still in bed and it was clear that the baby was desperately ill. The old doctor from Lewes was a fool and, after feeding the baby on orange juice which gave her green motions, began dosing her with dilute carbolic which seemed likely to kill her.

I asked Vanessa if I might send a telegram to Noel, begging her to come at once. Noel telegraphed that she was not able to come herself, but was sending a friend, Dr Marie Moralt, in whom Vanessa could have complete confidence. Moralt arrived the same day and, after an awkward interview with the Lewes doctor, took charge.

The baby was being starved and the carbolic was likely to be fatal. Moralt advised a grey powder or two and a change of diet to Glaxo. After two or three days of careful nursing the baby was out of danger and began to put on weight. Freed from agonising anxiety, Vanessa was soon herself again.

195

However Moralt kept her in bed and stayed on for two or three weeks, and I stayed too, going into Lewes on errands, cutting up logs, and talking to Moralt in the evenings. She had been ill and depressed, and the change was doing her good.

As soon as the baby was flourishing, the question of her name became the subject of continual debate. Clive favoured Susanna; Vanessa preferred Claudia; Roger demanded Helen. All Bloomsbury sent in suggestions and I, in order to be helpful, made out an alphabetical list of every female name I could remember or imagine. I came across it not long ago and found that among the Cs I had put down Canada.

Fortunately that suggestion was ignored. Soon after Vanessa was strong enough to get about, she went into Lewes and registered the child as Helen Vanessa. A month or so later she paid a fee and altered the name to Angelica Vanessa.

X

I WAS in need of money and it occurred to me that though I could not write well enough to please myself and finish my novel, I might be able to write badly enough to turn out a novelette which would sell. I sat up one night at The Cearne writing out the synopsis and then, after my return to Charleston, wrote it in every spare moment. I enjoyed putting in every cliché that I could remember, deliberately basing my style on that of serials in women's papers. The heroine is a drug fiend, met in a night club. 'She was fresh as a rosebud, still touched by the morning dew'.*

I finished the main work in a week, but spent another week tidying it up, had it typed and gave it to Edward. He sent it to an old acquaintance of his, T. Werner Laurie, who wrote back accepting it.

He gave me an advance of fifteen pounds on a royalty of three halfpence a copy. Acting on Edward's advice, I published it under a pseudonym. The whole edition of *Dope Darling* by Leda Burke, which I think was 15,000 copies, sold out, but it was not reprinted.

When my novelette was finished I left Charleston to live with Edward at Pond Place and to work for a few months in a bookshop in Museum Street in order to get some experience of bookselling before Frankie returned.

I had been found my job by Sybil Wilson because the owner of the shop, a German who was still interned in the Isle of Man, had a deep respect for the scholarship of her husband. The shop dealt only in Oriental Literature and I was surprised to find that nobody in it could as much as spell out the titles of any of the books in Oriental languages upon the shelves. Mrs Halberstadt leased the whole of the building. The flat on the first floor

* See p. 45.

was let to a famous professional billiard player, above it were Mrs Halberstadt's rooms.

The manager of the shop was a naturalised German who had had no knowledge of the book trade until he had taken over, after his friend Halberstadt had been interned. He was a dog fancier and he and his English wife lived in Purley where they bred chow dogs. It was indeed Mr Schmidt's interest in the history of the breed which had led him to visit the oriental bookshop and make friends with its proprietor.

Schmidt was a typical German, energetic, conscientious and always aware of his own surprising rectitude. He did, indeed, work hard in the bookshop, but the chows came first. There had been a slump in them during the war, but he was looking forward to better times. During the lunch hour, he visited various black market butchers and came back with parcels of unsaleable meat which were the source of a morbid odour that clung to the shop. One day, soon after my arrival, as I pulled out a book from one of the lower shelves, I became aware of something soft and richly scented stuffed behind it. It was a brown paper parcel and a glance revealed maggots.

"Ach! It is two veeks dat I had lost dat leber for de dogs," exclaimed Mr Schmidt when I drew his attention to it. Nor was this the only occasion when his habit of hiding dogsmeat behind books led to unfortunate results. One day an elderly Hindu Brahmin came in and asked if he might look round, and I directed him to the shelf of Sanscrit texts. Suddenly there was a horrified exclamation. He had taken out a volume of the Rig-Veda, but with it came a blood-stained roll of newspaper which burst open scattering lumps of beef. Schmidt hurried up exclaiming: "Mein dogs' meat!" and grabbed the meat off the floor. Then, noticing our customer's expression, he said:

"You Mohammedans don't like dogs—not so?"

The Brahmin with an expression of murder on his face stepped quickly out into the street. It was bad salesmanship.

One day some question of Chinese arose and I mentioned Arthur Waley. "Vot! You know Mr Waley!" exclaimed

Schmidt with incredulity. "Yes, he's a friend of mine," I replied.

"Pah! A friendt of *yours*! Vy, Mr Waley is a great man!" said Schmidt, severely, for he was a firm believer in what the Americans call a "class-stratified society."

Mrs Halberstadt, who looked like an angry marmoset, sometimes came down into the shop. She would follow every movement I made with her wounded eyes and would creep about, trying to eavesdrop unseen while Schmidt or I talked to the customers. But she always *was* seen and her odd manner made the customers uneasy. It had not occurred to her that we might not be dishonest. One morning, when I arrived, there was a fearful racket going on, Mrs Halberstadt was weeping and exclaiming: "My gold dessert service. Every piece of it solid gold. Stolen."

Schmidt was shouting at her:

"If you haf a burglary, you go for the bolice. You call in Scotland Yard."

"No. No. Not the police. Not with my husband an alien. They might confiscate the stock of books. . . . All my gold plates, stolen!"

Mr Schmidt was infuriated. "If you say you haf a burglary, then I go to Scotland Yard. I vill not be zuzbect to steal gold blates dat nobody has never seen! Haf you ever seen dem?" he asked me, suddenly becoming aware of my presence.

"No. I never heard of them before."

Mrs Halberstadt made a supreme effort to appear calm and addressed herself to me.

"Before my marriage my name was MacMason. The Mac-Mason River in Canada is called after my father. He made millions in Alaska and gave each of us, his three daughters, a solid gold dessert service—plates, forks, spoons and fruit knives all of solid gold." Suddenly her self-control broke down and through her tears, she screamed: "Stolen in the middle of the night. And that man says he knows nothing and that they never existed. It is very odd, very peculiar indeed."

"You say dat again and I fetch the bolice!" cried Schmidt

furiously. Suddenly I realised that I was not witnessing a first night's performance of this drama. It had all been said before.

However, as she persisted and as the business of the shop was suspended, Schmidt went out and made good his threat. An hour or so later, a young detective came in. We heard again the story of the MacMason River and the gold plates, and Mrs Halberstadt and he went upstairs.

She did not reappear for several days and we heard no more about her loss.

After I had been at the bookshop a couple of months, a young man called Harry appeared and was greeted with joy by Mrs Halberstadt. He had been her husband's assistant four years before but had enlisted and had come through the Gallipoli and the Palestine campaigns without a scratch. General Allenby was his hero—almost his God.

I had been reading the French unanimists with delight and I wrote a description of the landing in Suvla Bay, founded on Harry's experience, closely imitating the methods used in *Mort de Quelqu'un*. It was an interesting bit of experimental writing but when it was finished I decided that the subject was too horrible for such theoretical treatment. Harry was given back his job and shortly afterwards Mrs Halberstadt sacked me.

My old friend Harold Hobson, who is an electrical engineer, had spent the war years in supplying power to mines and factories in Durham. His wife, Corky, was a dark-haired girl with a creamy skin and dark eyes which melted in quick sympathy when she greeted one. She had a wiry independence and ambitions as a writer and had sent a manuscript to Edward which won his immediate approval. *The Revolt of Youth* was a capable and convincing work. Corky went on to write many other better books under the pseudonym of Sarah Salt, but their chief merit, a Zola-like readiness to face the painful truths about human nature, prevented them from achieving the success they deserved. Corky's virtue as a writer, and part of her attraction as a character, was her love of truth.

Harold and Corky spent part of the summer living in a caravan, moving about some of the wild parts of Durham which were not too far away from Harold's work. They invited me to visit them in June and taking my light-weight tent I went up to stay with them for three weeks. I had never been north before. By a lucky chance I failed to change at Darlington and my train puffed slowly on to Kirkby Stephen before I realised that I had gone wrong. At Kirkby Stephen I had to wait for a couple of hours and set out to explore. There was a fresh taste in the air like the day when snow melts in spring. A farmer trotted down the cobbled main street on a long-tailed pony with a couple of short-haired collies grinning at its heels. Great mountains rose on one side of the town and there was a harmony between the solid stone houses and cobbled streets and their wild setting. I walked out as far as Nateby and then had to race back for my train. But that corner of the Westmorland and North Riding border had made a lasting impression on me and for the last thirty years most of my holidays have been spent in it.

The war seemed to have left no marks at Cotherstone where I found Harold and Corky encamped with a schoolmistress friend in a meadow just above the wild and rocky stream of the Tees. For a fortnight of lovely weather the strain of the war years and my worry about the future was wiped out. I seemed to have stepped back to the summer of 1914. We bathed in shallow pools, fished without success, and cooked meals. Corky lay in a hammock with a book in her hand and went to sleep. One day we saw the daughter of the farmer in whose field we were camping, slicing curd to make Cotherstone cheese. I bought one of her cheeses and sent it to Charleston. It was richer than Wensleydale and softer and more delicious than Stilton.

After a week of idleness, Harold hired a pair of horses and a boy to drive them home again and we set off, jogging slowly along the lanes for ten miles or so until we came to a lovely park-like meadow on the banks of the Tees not far from Gainford, but on the other side of the river. We lived there a week. Then Harold and Corky and the friend had to go back to work until the week-end and I stayed on alone. Soon after they had gone I saw a demobilised soldier sitting under a tree with a gun, waiting to shoot rabbits. It was Peace Day and a band was playing in the distance, at Gainford. The man's unhappy expression aroused my interest and that evening I wove a little world about him and next day wrote a story which I called *The Old Dovecote* and sent it to Duncan. By chance E. M. Forster was staying at Charleston. Duncan showed it to him without telling him the name of the author and I received a letter with Morgan's criticisms, some of which were helpful. He said, however, that in a short story one could not write from two points of view; giving first that of one character and then that of a second. I did not agree with that dictum. Later I made a few changes, and sent it to Edward and it was published in *The English Review*. Though on a tiny scale, it was the best thing I had written up to that time.

During the months which followed I lived either at Pond Place or at The Cearne, occasionally visiting Charleston and Tidmarsh. I wrote a long novel, rather in the style of Henry James, called *The Virtuous Impulse*. The hero was a young astronomer and he, and the scenes which took place in his observatory, were alive. But the heroine was a quite impossible girl. It was a moral sort of tale with the theme that the only good people are those who do disinterested work for its own sake, and that a purely personal life is wholly unsatisfactory.

I had every reason to think this as I was doing no disinterested work, and my personal life was always landing me in unforeseen difficulties. Meanwhile I was constantly looking at possible bookshops and negotiating with a firm of bankrupt booksellers who hoped to persuade me to take over their unsaleable stock at a high price.

In the autumn an awkward complication cropped up in our plans. Augustine Birrell met Maynard by chance and asked him if he thought Frankie and I had the business ability to make a success of a bookshop. Maynard, who knew well enough that we had not, had an inspiration, and suggested that we should take a Mr Bassingbourne into partnership. This was a young man of exceptional business ability who had brought himself into public notice during the war. Maynard's suggestion was in many ways an excellent one as Bassingbourne was well-fitted to direct a bookshop and make a success of it. The one drawback was that Frankie disliked him and felt that his presence would completely spoil the pleasure of the thing. On hearing from his father that he would put up capital on condition that Bassingbourne became a partner, Frankie wisely said nothing but came to me and said that I must somehow or other squash Maynard's plan, or it would not be worth continuing with it. He then had to leave for France. I realised that it would be fatal to oppose Maynard's scheme and that the only solution was to get Maynard to change his mind of his own accord and then get him to write to Mr Birrell saying that the proposal would not work. I was to meet Bassingbourne and arrange the terms on which he should participate and this was my opportunity. I had little difficulty in appearing to be a complete idiot and in leading Bassingbourne on, step by step, into making proposals quite extremely favourable to himself. He expected me to make counter-proposals, and a lot of hard bargaining to follow. Instead of which I posted off Bassingbourne's terms to Maynard with an innocent note asking if he approved of them—was this the sort of partnership he had in mind? If so, I would draw up an agreement for Frankie and me to sign. Maynard reacted as I expected and wrote to Augustine that the plan would not do.

Frankie and I were, of course, wildly unsuited to running any kind of business, and in particular a shop where close attention to detail is essential. We neither of us knew anything of book-keeping or accountancy. In most ways Frankie was less cut out for retail trade than I was. To begin with, he regarded buying an article at one price and selling it for a larger one as cheating and saw no moral difference between making a profit of thirty-three per cent when selling a new book under the net book agreement and selling a book for twenty times its real value.

"I cheated him quite successfully," he would sometimes exclaim after selling a second-hand book much below its real value but for more than we had paid for it.

He was an eager reader, but had no respect for books and instead of using a paperknife, would tear the pages open with his forefinger. Frankie's hands were always damp; they exuded sweat and our stock was always getting covered with his fingerprints.

To counterbalance these defects he had qualities which are seldom found in booksellers. While in France he had read a great deal and acquired a good knowledge of French literature. He had a quick sympathy and eager enthusiasm and was always able to help any customer in difficulties. But, most important of all, he charmed almost everyone who came into the shop so that they wanted to come again. What did it matter that his fingers made paw marks on the books? Or that he would do up his fly-buttons in the middle of a conversation about Gide, or scratch himself very thoroughly in intimate places of his anatomy, standing on one leg to do so more freely, while he recommended an unknown lady to read *La Princesse de Cleves* if she aspired to be an educated woman? It was Frankie's personality which enabled us to keep the shop going and pay ourselves a pittance of three pounds a week each.

We started the shop with a capital of nine hundred pounds and as we could not find a suitable shop at a low rent, we began by taking the ground floor of 19 Taviton Street, a stone's throw from Gordon Square. The house had been taken by Margaret Bulley, an old friend of Frankie's, to share with friends on a communal basis.

Roger Fry had just brought the Omega workshops to an end at a time when a change in public taste, which would have ensured their success, was taking place. Roger was therefore able to help me to furnish our shop with tables from the Omega for which he charged me only about a tenth of their value. Frankie brought some chairs from Elm Park Road, including an enormous Victorian armchair with deep cretonne flounces all round it. A young Quaker carpenter put up cheap deal shelves.

Our stock was small and various: two or three shelves of eighteenth-century French and English books, which we had bought at Hodgson's auction rooms in Chancery Lane, a very few modern English books, including all those written or published by our friends, those of The Hogarth Press being particularly prominent. Then we had a really good selection of the latest French books, chosen by Frankie who had arranged with *La Maison du Livre* to act as our forwarding agents. All our friends rallied round and supported us. Duncan drew a cover for our first catalogue of secondhand books which we sent to everyone we could think of. One of the first orders was from Joseph Conrad. Morgan Forster was perhaps the most useful of all our friends. He brought us not only his own custom, which was large as he had a habit of giving away books, but he also secured us orders on a large scale from two friends of his. George Antonius, who was director of education in Palestine was one; Syed Ross Masood, who bought books for Hyderabad State, the other. We soon found ourselves working extremely hard, the most exhausting part of the business being collecting books from the publishers, or from Simpkin Marshall.

We had also some good friends in the book trade. John Wilson, by far the best bookseller of new books in London and an old friend of Edward's and of David Rice's, was the most valuable. He was at that time a partner in Jones and Evans, a bookshop in Great Queen Street, Cheapside. John Wilson lent us a lot of books on sale or return and gave us a lot of advice. Once when I was in the back of his shop, he came up with his finger on his lips and whispered:

"I want you to have a good look at that man in the front, so that you would know him again. He is a book thief. I've never caught him, but I've often missed a book after he's gone."

I went to look and saw a friend of Edward's who often came

to Pond Place. I said nothing and hoped that John had made a mistake. But you never can be quite sure, and when that old friend visited our shop Frankie and I kept a very close watch on him. A very different kind of man from John Wilson also befriended me because he had some reasons for feeling gratitude to Edward. Sam, as I will call him, was a tall raw-boned fellow whose flaming cheeks gave notice of the reek of whisky which clung about him. He looked like a Bookie's Bodyguard, but was actually one of the leading figures in the ring, or knock-out, operated by all the big secondhand booksellers at sales of books in the country and often, with great effrontery, in London sale rooms. On Edward's advice I went to see Sam and he said: "You have to be as hard as nails in this game. No mercy. Now you can't get into the ring because you haven't got money enough to make yourself a nuisance and anyway you're better out of it. But if you come to a big sale when I am there, you mark your catalogue with the books you have really come for, and show it me, then I'll see our chaps don't run you up. But you mustn't start bidding for books you don't want, just because they are going cheap. Of course you can't always have what you want."

After that when I met Sam at a country house sale I would pass him my marked catalogue.

Sometimes he would laugh and say: "No. You can't have that one. There are half a dozen of us who have come just for that." But usually he would tick off my numbers in his catalogue and I would meet with very little opposition from the ring. I didn't get so many books, but they cost much less than they would otherwise have done. Frankie and I occasionally got some very good bargains at book sales. Frankie bought several hundred eighteenth-century books in very good condition at the Wrest Park sale for almost nothing. Nobody wanted them. I bought a first edition of Shelley's *Revolt Of Islam* for two pounds at Hodgson's and catalogued it at four. A young American came in and bought it and returned an hour later to offer it back to me as he had found an inscription in Shelley's handwriting to Eliz. Kent on the flyleaf. This lady was Leigh Hunt's sister-in-law. I refused to take the book back and congratulated Mr Peck on his discovery. One piece of private knowledge eventually brought us in some money. In 1892, W. H. Hudson had published a novel *Fan: The Story of a Young Girl* under the pseudonym of Henry Harford. I advertised for this almost every week in *The Clique* and eventually secured three copies for about five shillings each. We sold them after Hudson's death during the height of the boom in his first editions for high prices. *Fan* is his rarest book. I also bought the proof sheets of *Fan* at the sale of Hudson's books, after his death, for fifteen pounds and sold them immediately for fifty. It had not occurred to my competitors that the corrections in Hudson's handwriting gave them a particular value. At the same sale I bought, for myself, Hudson's own copy of *Green Mansions* and many of Constance's translations with inscriptions from her in them. Hudson wrote to me several times after I had started the bookshop, usually because he wanted to sell me two or three books. On such occasions I would go to St. Luke's Road. He would open the door, greet me with distant stateliness, and I would follow him upstairs where he would transact his business with me, regarding me with some suspicion. At the time I put this down to my having been a conscientious objector. But after the first two visits, I broke through the crust and we talked easily and warmly about books and people. He had a great liking for the poetry of the forgotten spasmodic school: Sydney Dobell, Alexander Smith and Philip James Bailey and he included Mrs Browning among them. One day I told him that I had advertised successfully for *Fan*. His eyes flared up in anger and he growled:

"What did you want that thing for?"

"Well, I read it with a good deal of interest, for one thing."

"What are you going to do with it?"

"I shan't sell it until it's acknowledged."

The fire had gone from his eye and he talked gently, but I was sorry that I had spoken of the book, as the memories it aroused seemed to be painful. It may have been because of his failure as a novelist but I think it is more likely it was because of the poverty and suffering that he and his wife underwent at the time it was written.

One day, when I returned late in the afternoon from a round of the publishers, I found 19 Taviton Street in confusion. A smell of burning fabric filled the air. The enormous cockney housekeeper, Mrs Speechley, had come up from the basement and was conducting a vigorous conversation with Ottoline who whinnied with amusement. Their subject was Frankie, who stood flustered and embarrassed and made ineffectual attempts to get Mrs Speechley to withdraw. Then I noticed that behind Mrs Speechley in the hall were the remains of the big flounced armchair, half-burned and soaking wet. Cecily Hey, one of the inmates of the communal household was standing on the half landing above, giggling with enjoyment. Her friend, Ray Marshall, peeped from above with a quiet smile. It was only after Ottoline had gone that I was able to get the full story of what had occurred. In my absence Frankie had lit his pipe and settled down with a book in the big armchair, no doubt twisting his forelock round and round as he read. Presently he dozed off, the book fell from his hand and the pipe from his mouth and its glowing dottle fell out on to the flounced upholstery. Some time later a passing couple paused to look at the books in our window and behind them, beheld flames and smoke rising round an unconscious human figure in the armchair. The young woman beat upon the front door and the young man ran to break the glass and pull the knob of a fire alarm at the corner of Endsleigh Gardens. Mrs Speechley answered the knocks and the young woman dashed into our shop where she beheld Frankie, still asleep amid the flaming flounces, like the phoenix in its nest, and equally miraculously unsinged.

The chair was dragged into the hall and had scarcely been extinguished before Ottoline and the Fire Brigade arrived simultaneously.

According to his own account, Frankie had great difficulty in preventing the firemen from deluging our bookshelves with water. Some disinterested spectators said we owed the preservation of our stock entirely to Ottoline.

Frankie's habit of falling fast asleep when tired, or bored, sometimes was socially embarrassing for him. A year or so after he had set the chair on fire he arrived one morning very much upset by what had happened the previous evening. After an afternoon spent in collecting books from a number of publishers—standing in queues at the trade counters and scrambling on and off buses, carrying a sack full of books, he had rushed home, changed, and gone off to dine with two ladies, Miss Margaret Jourdain, and Miss Ivy Compton-Burnett. Miss Margaret Jourdain had written many books on old furniture and wrote regularly on it in *Country Life*. Her young friend Miss Compton-Burnett however had not at that time published any books and her literary genius was altogether unsuspected. It was, if not Frankie's first visit to their house, the first time he had been asked to dinner. The ladies had been charmed by him at the first meeting but they were not intimate friends.

"I can quite clearly remember the soup," said Frankie, wrinkling his brows. "Then, I suppose, we must have had fish, because when I woke up there *was* a plate of fish, uneaten, in front of me. As a matter of fact my left hand was in it, covered with sauce. I was alone in the dining-room; the lights were burning, and when I looked at my watch I saw that it was past midnight. The ladies seemed to have gone to bed. Isn't it awful! Just think of me there, asleep, while they finished the other courses! But the most ghastly thing about it all was that the arm of the Louis Quinze chair in which I was sitting was smashed. I must have leaned too heavily on the damned thing while I was asleep. What on earth can I do?"

"But what did you actually do?" I asked.

"Well, I just found my hat and let myself out of the house as quietly as I could," said Frankie. "But what in God's name can I do?"

"Write and tell them that you greatly enjoyed the soup and ask them to invite you again for the courses that you missed.

And say nothing about the chair. They will think that you did not notice it."

"But they will have thought that I was drunk," said Frankie unhappily.

"Nonsense. They will feel full of solicitude because you are terribly overworked. You see: it will be all right."

I don't suppose Frankie took my advice literally, but the ladies soon sent him another invitation and their friendship with Frankie was only cemented by the disasters of that evening.

Mrs Speechley was the dominant figure of the communal household. She was an enormous woman and lived in the basement with a wizened, ailing husband. She had buried three of them already and the poor white-faced fourth did not survive many months. She had once been in the employment of Delysia and she loved to give lurid hints at the wonderful goings-on at suppers lasting until dawn given by that great revue artist. And Mrs Speechley would, what could she not have told us of jewels, lobsters, buckets of ice, magnums of champagne, female loveliness, storms of temperament and moments of passion!

Delysia was her heroine and her romance and everything was to be forgiven her—including, no doubt, having at some time sacked Mrs Speechley from her employment. Yet, on occasion, Mrs Speechley could turn into a rigid upholder of Victorian morals. One morning a policeman arrived having just caught a window-cleaner working next door whom he had seen climbing out of an upper window of number 19. He wished to ask the occupant of the room to identify articles which he had discovered in the window-cleaner's little bucket, taken while she was downstairs having breakfast.

"Yes, that's mine and those are mine, and that and that," said the young woman without a trace of embarrassment, or the faintest blush as she picked out a large variety of contraceptive devices. The girl was not one of the permanent inmates of the house but a friend of Ray Marshall's and thanks to her had been lent a room in the house for two or three days.

"Disgraceful!" said Mrs Speechley. "Only just left college too! Disgusting!" And the mountainous woman went off pursing her lips angrily with a fine scandal to embroider for the milkman's benefit. "I wouldn't stay in the 'ouse if it were one of the residents."

But for my part I felt considerable respect for the *terre à terre* common sense of the visitor, though I was puzzled by the window-cleaner's selection of valuables.

The permanent residents were more maidenly. There was Margaret Bulley, Ethel Sidgwick the novelist, a rather beautiful young American woman who was making a post-graduate study of the English Gentleman—but only, I was sorry to discover, of the English Gentleman in the sixteenth, seventeenth and eighteenth centuries, so that it was no good my trying to palm myself off on her as raw material for her thesis. Then there were Cecily Hey and Ray Marshall and my friend Robert Tatlock.

Not long after we started the bookshop in Taviton Street Duncan went to Italy with Maynard and lent me a room in 46 Gordon Square, which was occupied only by Blanche and Jessie who had entered Maynard's employment when he took over the house. Clive and Vanessa were also abroad; Charleston was empty, and Clive's flat at 50 occupied by an old cook, by Julian and Quentin and by the new housemaid, Mary. I slept in a little room on the ground floor at the end of the hall, just beyond the telephone. After I had been there some days I began to be woken up every morning by the telephone ringing and then overheard scraps of Blanche's conversation. Some disaster seemed to be occurring. "Oh. How shocking. . . . What a terrible thing. Do you want me to break it to poor Mary? . . .Oh. . . . So you really think it would be wiser not to? . . . You want me to wait until her father gets back from India. . . ."

Every morning brought new intimations of tragedy. After this had been going on for nearly a week Blanche asked to speak to me and poured out the story. I cannot swear to the exact details, but it was roughly like this: It concerned the family of the pretty housemaid, Mary.

Her brother had died of penumonia and her mother had caught it, been taken to hospital and died also.

Every morning a district nurse in Bedfordshire, who was a friend of Mary's family, had telephoned to Blanche, as the most responsible person, and given the news of the family of the pretty housemaid. The last horror was that the father, who had been on his way home from India, went mad on his arrival and had committed suicide. All Mary's family were dead and she knew nothing about it.

I told Blanche that she would have to break the news to Mary and that the poor girl had better leave Clive's flat and sleep at 46. Probably she would have to go down to Bedfordshire for a few days. If the father wasn't buried, she might like Blanche to go with her to the funeral. Soon after Blanche had finished this awful story I left the house and met Mary on the doorstep. She was an English rosebud, blooming with youth and innocence; she gave me a gay smile and ran down the area steps humming a tune.

When I went back to 46 Blanche met me with a white face. She had told Mary, who had been in floods of tears ever since, quite out of control and hysterical. Next morning I heard she was worse. The poor creature had for a long time refused to go to bed. Finally, when Blanche and Jessie had got her to bed she would not sleep and at one moment had tried to run out into the street in her nightgown. I was away for the weekend. When I returned Blanche was hollow-eyed and Jessie on the verge of a collapse. Mary had not slept at all and one or other of them had to be with her the whole time. I saw Mary then, a scarcely human figure, still sobbing and barely able to walk. I told Blanche to send for a doctor who came and ordered a powerful sedative. It had no effect whatever. Next morning Mary was taken to hospital. We were all thankful that Vanessa was returning to London and would be able to take charge of the situation. In the meantime I left the room at 46 and moved into a little room behind our shop in Taviton Street.

What I had heard and witnessed was only the beginning of the story. Mary came out of hospital and later the District Nurse wrote a letter to say she would willingly take her until she was well enough to go back to work. This seemed an excellent arrangement and Vanessa sent Blanche to accompany Mary on the journey. They had to change at Hitchin. Blanche's attention was distracted for a moment. She looked round and saw Mary running out of the station. She gave chase. When they had got out of town, Mary left the road and began to run across country, jumping ditches and climbing fences. But the indomitable Blanche kept her in sight and finally caught her. They were completely exhausted and Blanche had no idea where they were. She had little money but found a road and was given a lift to the local workhouse where Mary was taken in for the night. That evening Blanche rang up Vanessa and poured out her story, and Vanessa arranged to go down by an early train and meet the two girls next morning. But before Vanessa's arrival Mary had escaped again. Vanessa sent Blanche, who was completely done up, home by train and went on to see the District Nurse in Bedfordshire. When she reached the address from which the Nurse had written, not only was the name of the Nurse not to be found, but Mary and her family were utterly unknown to the people who lived there. Vanessa must have felt that she had been transported into the world of the Arabian Nights. At last she recollected that she had heard Mary say that a corn merchant at St Neots was a great friend of her father's. Vanessa set off to St Neots and made her strange quest known to the corn merchant—who was undoubtedly the late Mr Addington, afterwards an acquaintance of mine at partridge drives.

Mr Addington, of course, knew nothing whatever about Mary, or her family. But he made Vanessa welcome with the courtesy and sympathy habitual to him. He then had a search made of the books of Jordan and Addington and discovered that his firm had some small dealings in seed corn with Mary's father who was a small-holder in Bedfordshire whom Mr Addington had never met, or even heard of. This was a great step forward. Mr Addington, at least, lived in the real world and not in the Arabian Nights. He took Vanessa to tea, and with his help she discovered that Mary's father and mother and brother were all enjoying robust health and were astonished and dismayed by the story which she had to tell them. There had been no pneumonia, no visit to India, no suicide. . . . Vanessa did not linger once she had established the facts, beyond telling them that their daughter was at large, roaming the countryside. On her return to London she carefully examined the envelope of the letter from the District Nurse and saw that the postmark had obviously been forged—perhaps with greasy carbon from the bottom of a saucepan. All the telephone conversations when Blanche had been rung by the District Nurse must have been carried on with Mary who had rung up 46 Gordon Square from number 50. Mary's split personality enabled the innocent housemaid to remain unaware of the disasters which her romantic *alter ego* was inventing in order to make pretty Mary a tragic figure and object of compassion in the centre of the stage.

Meanwhile both Marys had vanished and though the police were notified, no sign of her was found. One morning, however, Duncan appeared outside our window making excited signs and grimaces. I rushed out and learned that Mary had been seen by the milkman and that Blanche was trying to decoy her into 46, as nobody can be certified as mad on a highway, or in the open air. I made a mental note of this fact, in case it should come in handy, as Duncan and I hung about the square, keeping out of sight as far as possible, while Blanche and Mary gossiped. Finally poor Mary was got into the house, and the door was slammed, the doctors arrived and soon afterwards she was removed in a plain van. She made a complete recovery after some months in an asylum.

One day, to my great astonishment, Boris Sokolov came into the bookshop. The figure who had predicted the European war and the Russian Revolution in 1912 had changed considerably, and it was a moment or two before I recognised him.* His cheeks which had always been lank were lined and hollow; his tow-coloured hair was growing grey and getting thin. Sokolov's real name was Volkov—which in Russian means Wolfish. He had grown to look like a wolf and a hungry one at that.

There was a wary look in his eye, but humour was never far away while he spoke. Soon I said: "Well, Boris, you were right. The European war came exactly as you predicted it would and it was the pre-requisite for the Russian Revolution that you wanted. Congratulations. I hope you are happy."

He laughed bitterly, showing his teeth.

"No. I am *not* happy. But come and lunch with me at the Holborn Restaurant. I want to talk to you." And he invited Frankie to come too.

Sokolov was passionately anti-Bolshevik. He had worked for the Revolution throughout the war, but after the Bolsheviks had come into power he had opposed them and after hairbreadth adventures had escaped from Russia and had come to England from Constantinople in order to try to bring about British intervention on a big scale.

I at once told him that I was violently opposed to British intervention in Russia and that it seemed to me he was betraying his early ideals and his life's work.

"We have exchanged one form of tyranny for another," he said.

"You won't get liberty if you conquer your own country with a British army."

"I agree. It is a choice between Caesarism from Within and Caesarism from Without. The only thing that can discredit the Bolsheviks is defeat by a foreign army. The only hope of liberty is after a rising against foreign tyranny."

"And you want us to conquer Russia so that you can organise a national movement to drive us out!" exclaimed Frankie. "Why, we haven't been able to conquer Ireland!"

Nothing daunted, Sokolov asked me to introduce him to

* See *The Golden Echo*, p. 249.

215

some Conservative M.P.s. I could not help him there. I did not know one, but Frankie promised to put him in touch with his uncle Oliver Locker-Lampson, adding that his political opinions were quite as mad as those of Sokolov and that they ought to get on together.

We parted almost angrily, but a week or so later Sokolov invited Frankie and me to his lodgings in Holloway to meet a friend of his.

"Perhaps his story will help to shake your faith in the Bolsheviks."

We accepted and found ourselves drinking Russian tea out of glasses in a miserable bed-sitting room. Sokolov was as gloomy and wolfish as ever, but his companion was a merry little man with pink cheeks, a round little nose, black hair and dancing black eyes. Unfortunately he could not speak a word of English and his French was execrable so that it was impossible to follow the promised story. However Sokolov helped him out.

He had spent the war with a dramatic company entertaining the troops at the front.

"*Je suis metteur-en-scène,*" he declared proudly. He had been caught by the revolution, had fled from the Red Army because he was wearing an officer's uniform and had then been nearly shot by Denikin's army because he had torn off his epaulettes and badges of rank. "And he had not been able to shave and as there is a streak of red in his beard he was nearly shot as a Jew," said Sokolov. Boris's story would have been far more interesting, but he was reticent. He had worked with various revolutionary groups to try and bring about the revolution and Russia's defeat in the war—then, when Lenin got into power, all was to do again.

At that time I was an ardent supporter of the Bolsheviks, not because I was a Communist, or a Marxist, but because I thought they would do for Russia what Danton and Robespierre had done for France. A lot of heads would be chopped off, but a rich happy peasantry and a diffusion of civilisation and good cooking would finally result. Moreover I was convinced that any attack from outside Russia on the Bolsheviks would only settle them more firmly in the saddle.

One thing struck me as odd. The more I attacked Sokolov for his ideas of foreign intervention, the better pleased he seemed with me personally. It crossed my mind that perhaps his beliefs were not genuine and that he was a Bolshevik agent sent over to find out how strong a movement there was in England for intervention. I came to the conclusion that this was extremely improbable. The Bolsheviks would not have sent an agent via Denikin's army and Constantinople. He could have got out far more safely via Finland. No, he was pleased with me because I reminded him of his own youth. I was voicing what he would have said himself three or four years before. He was bitterly disillusioned and thought much of what I said was comic, yet he felt a nostalgic love for my innocence and my sincerity. My idealism appealed to him more than it did to his friend, Basil Kouchitachvili, who was a Georgian. "I don't care about politics—only for the theatre," I think he would have said, had he been able to make himself understood.

He belonged to an old Georgian family who had held their castle in the Caucasus since the time of the Crusades—and the Crusaders' castle led him to tell us, in broken French, and with Boris's help, a typically Georgian anecdote about the piety of his ancestors.

The Kouchitachvilis had an ikon in the family which had worked miracles: it was their chief treasure. But the family split up and the ikon was claimed by a cadet branch which had become more powerful than the senior branch. One day the family was taking the ikon on its annual pilgrimage to a local shrine when scouts that had been sent ahead came rushing back to report that the junior branch had laid an ambush to rob them of the ikon. The head of the family reflected; then he drew his sword and thrust it through the body of his youngest child. He then hid the ikon in its belly and the party went on its way as a funeral procession, the women keening their dirges. The ruse was successful and the ikon remained in the possession

217

of the senior branch from whom Kouchita was himself descended.

Basil did not live up to these pious ancestors. He was merry, charming and incredibly helpless. Frankie and he soon became great friends. But it was obvious that there was no future in London for a *metteur-en-scène* who could speak only Russian, Georgian and schoolboy French. Paris was the place for him. He went there and soon got work with the Pitoeffs. As a result Frankie got to know Madame Pitoeff and his love for her and her art, and for her children and indeed for her husband, provided a further link between him and Basil.

Frankie saw a good deal of Basil whenever he went to Paris and once they went together for a month's holiday with Isadora Duncan, touring from one hotel to another in the South of France. I wish I had been there.

Long before this, however, Boris had grown restless and dissatisfied. All hope of successful intervention by Foreign armies in Russia had faded. Admiral Kolchak's army had fled to Vladivostok and the White Russians had percolated to Shanghai and Vancouver and were driving taxicabs in Paris. One day Boris came to the shop for the last time.

"This is goodbye," he said. "I am going back to Russia next week."

"Surely it is madness. They must know what you have been up to here and they will shoot you."

"I shall go to Finland and slip across the frontier. If I can see Gorky before they arrest me I shall be safe. Gorky will protect me. Or anyhow he will try."

"But why are you going?" I asked. "Why go back to almost certain death?"

"I cannot live in England any longer," he answered. "I cannot endure reading *Punch*. My God, what a country! There is no humour in England except family humour. I cannot stand family humour."

For a moment Volkov's lean wolfish chops were distorted by a wild laugh. His eyes were gay and merry.

"No, I can't live in England any longer. Better six months of

218

Moscow and the Artistic Theatre and then a bullet—than fifty years doddering on as a White Russian selling lacquered spoons. But it is *Punch* really." He shuddered.

I took him out to lunch and we said goodbye. He got through to Moscow. Gorky protected him and he wrote in Gorky's newspaper for a year or two. Then I heard vaguely that he had been arrested and shot.

Basil Kouchitachvili was almost penniless, though he had learned to speak good French and some English. Eventually Frankie helped him to go to New York, where he got work.

In 1950, I met someone who had visited Tiflis. Basil was then Director of the Tiflis Municipal Theatre and had become an imposing Theatrical Dictator with a background of early triumphs as *metteur-en-scène* in London, Paris and New York.

One evening when I arrived late on Friday night at The Cearne, Constance greeted me with the words: "T.T.* is here. Her mother died a week ago and she has come down here for a rest. Go very quietly to your room so as not to wake her. She is very much exhausted."

There was, however, a light under her door. Before I fell asleep my own was opened and a young voice whispered: "Is that you, Bunny? Come and talk to me."

Six years vanished in as many seconds as I held her in my arms. Constance was right. T.T. was shattered and worn-out, but she had been hoping that I would come that night. Soon she was sleeping peacefully, lying in my arms, and I lay awake looking at her till the candle guttered out, so that I should not awaken her.

Next morning I was woken by hearing Constance padding down the passage to my room. Then I heard a little sound of surprise as she saw that my bed was empty. A moment afterwards she had gone downstairs. I at once slipped out of T.T.'s room and stole silently up the ladder into the attic. A minute or two later Constance was back, looking for me, irresolutely.

* See *The Golden Echo*, p. 261.

I picked up a copy of the Bohn Library: Caesar's *Gallic Wars*, and came down the attic steps.

"What have you been doing in the attic? I wondered where you could have got to!"

"I want to see if Caesar said anything about Stonehenge," I answered.

That night T.T. and I chased each other in the moonlight and lay together under the tall pine trees and she took my love and gave me hers. But it was a child's love—a child intoxicated by moonlight, by woodland autumn scents, by the prickling pine needles, by wild happiness after sorrow.

And because of that an evil spell entered into our embraces: I became angry that the child was not a woman. So in the first flush of passionate love, we quarrelled.

After I had gone back to London she wrote to me:

> You know you looked far more beautiful than you have ever done, or ever will do, sitting at this table with your pipe; your mouth and your whole body in a passion of disgust. Perhaps it's a bit callous to mention it. It's a great pity you don't always look like that and that I am always in a state of bodily exhaustion.

After that we saw each other often. T.T. would come unexpectedly into the shop, about closing time, after Frankie had left, and say: "I've got a couple of tickets for the Queen's Hall to-night." We would wander away together, eat an eighteen-penny supper at The Swiss in Fitzroy Street, where the waiter was a friend, and then walking on towards the Queen's Hall I would look at the little sensitive face with an unspoken question. So, often, we missed the concert. But she could not be held. If I were expecting her, a postcard or a letter would fall through the box. She was having to deal with tiresome people. . . . She thought I had said Monday, not Tuesday and the shop had been locked up. Or she wrote, "I don't want to see you for awhile. You will not want explanations."

She never felt jealousy, or shame, and when I suggested that I might have offended her in either way would laugh and complain: "Why, do you take me for a fool?"

She was poor, but now and then a Rolls Royce would drive

up and she would vanish with some rich relative to Florence, or to Paris, or to Ireland, or would spend a few weeks living in great houses from where she would write:

"*Je t'embrasse tendrement mon amant, mon amant, si bon, si bon.*"

A week later she would steal unseen into the shop as I was entering up the evening's takings.

"Shall we go and hear Jelly playing some Bach?"

Or a letter would come:

"*Je n'ai pas de place pour toi, à présent, dans mon coeur. Je ne sais pas exactement pourquoi.*"

But I knew and did not require further enlightenment.

> I met a lady in the meads,
> Full beautiful—a faery's child,
> Her hair was long, her foot was light,
> And her eyes were wild.

T.T. was not *sans merci*; she was neither without pity, nor heartless, nor without gratitude. Yet, even while I was with her, I always knew that I should wake alone upon the cold hill's side—and that in all probability she would also—but upon the other side of the hill, alas.

She sent me, on separate occasions, two explanations of why this was inevitable. In one of them, sent to me four or five years later, she had copied out that poem of Blake's from the Rossetti M.S.S. which begins:

> I dreamt a dream! What can it mean?

And which contains the verses which she felt were the crux of our relationship:

> And I wept both night and day,
> And he wiped my tears away,
> And I wept both day and night,
> And hid from him my heart's delight.
>
> So he took his wings and fled;
> Then the morn blush'd rosy red;
> I dried my tears and arm'd my fears
> With ten thousand shields and spears.

Soon my angel came again.
I was arm'd, he came in vain,
For the time of youth was fled,
And grey hairs were on my head.

C'est la vie, Eh?

At another time she wrote:

It is funny that we are so intimate and yet I still feel curiously out of touch with your mind. I don't really know how or what you feel and think. In fact I have never been so out of touch with any intimate friend's mind. Why? You don't take me seriously at all, do you? You don't depend on me?"

But how could I depend on someone who left me always on the cold hill's side, even though I knew I could be certain of her coming back? And how could she depend on me? We were too much alike. We would never make a sacrifice for each other—and we didn't want, or expect, sacrifices.

When I had published my third, or fourth book, T.T. wrote to me:

I think you are more ambitious, more adventurous than any writer I know of in England today, and that because you always attempt something greater. You look forward, no, not forward, outward, to create something of your own imagination. Whereas H**** *et tous les autres* look at what is all around them and reproduce it in the light of their own eyes. To me theirs is an infinitely less valuable contribution and an infinitely less difficult task. In the long run, except for historical interest, their work simply won't count. Yours will either last forever, or not at all. Eh?

In her last letter to me she wrote:

I must talk to you and see you and tell you about myself. And, my dear, I have a fear of having behaved strangely once too often—but I must know and I believe you can trust me not to run away and hide again.

Soon after that she ran away and hid in a place from which there is no return. I have written these few pages about her because she is the ghost whom I most often hear: "With naked foot stalking within my chamber."

During the four years that I was a bookseller, I used to see Betty May occasionally. She had reappeared, after an absence, in London, having by some means or other completely cured herself of the drug habit. She was still strikingly handsome, but the intense feelings which she had aroused in me, when I thought her a childlike creature doomed to destruction by a terrible vice, had long since passed away. I knew that she was well able to take care of herself and I was amused to hear her latest tales. She was still as capricious and as indifferent to her own material advantage.

Nevertheless I fairly frequently had to raid the till when she appealed to me desperately for help. On the last of these occasions she sent me a note by the hand of an unlovely little man. Betty wrote that she was ill and starving and that her landlady had seized her clothes in lieu of rent. I sent her three pounds and happened to go into the Café Royal late that night with Ray. There sat Betty—the life and soul of the party grouped around her. Rather unkindly I went up to her and said: "I am glad you have made such a rapid recovery."

Betty had the grace to look rather embarrassed, and I did not send her money by messengers after that. Our friendship was, however, too genuine to be damaged by such trifles and, on one occasion, when she said she was hungry, I took her home, after my marriage, to have supper with Ray at 27 Brunswick Square.

It was shortly after my bookshop days that Betty embarked on the most extraordinary incident of her career. She had visited Oxford, like Zuleika Dobson, and had got to know a young man called Raoul Loveday, a poet whose head was full of romantic and occult ideas. They fell in love and she married him. The extraordinary story which followed after he became a disciple of Alastair Crowley's is told in her autobiography *Tiger Woman: My Story*, by Betty May, published by Duckworth in 1929.

A fascinating interpretation of what really occurred at Crowley's Abbey in Sicily is to be found in Arthur Calder Marshall's book: *The Magic of My Youth*. As Calder Marshall says, Betty was a romantic and intuitive character whereas Loveday was a romantic intellectual. I, whatever my natural inclinations, was not a romantic. Indeed I had learned from my friends in Bloomsbury to use the word contemptuously. Romanticism, I would have said, defiled the pure stream of art with irrelevant associations. It was I, by the way, who put it into Betty's head to write a book and she once gave me a large wad of manuscript. I don't know who it was who helped her to produce *Tiger Woman*, but anyone who reads it can acquit me of being her ghost. Incidentally, the Bunny who figures in the early pages was not me but her first husband, a young doctor killed about 1915. One of the last stories I heard about Betty particularly delighted me. In the nineteen-thirties she appeared in Court on a charge of insulting behaviour. A very good-looking young policeman went into the box and gave evidence. He had been on point duty at the junction of Goodge Street and the Tottenham Court Road and Betty had interfered with him in the execution of his duty.

"What did I do?" asked Betty.

"The accused put her arms round my neck and I was forced to arrest her," replied the constable, turning rather red.

"What else did I do?" asked Betty shamelessly.

"The accused insisted on kissing me repeatedly."

"What have you to say in your defence?" the Magistrate asked her.

"Well your Worship. Just look at him . . . he's so handsome. . . . I could not help it," said Betty in her demurest tones. She was bound over not to kiss any more policemen when they were on duty and discharged.

Betty is a darling. And had any writer with the discernment of the Abbe Prévost been around, she would have been immortalised as a Manon L'Escaut of the twenties.

Fortunately the shop began to show signs of prospering. We were beginning to have a stream of the right sort of customers. One of those who came was Lady Rothermere, a beautiful but unhappy woman, who sought for consolations by dabbling in literature and mysticism. I sold her about twenty pounds' worth of books—chiefly first editions of modern French poets—on her first visit and she invited me to dinner.

It was one of my first experiences of the very rich, and I spent an interesting evening. The first thing to strike my eye was the profusion of gold nicknacks. The matchboxes were of solid gold with embossed coronets on top and frightfully heavy. We ate our dessert with gold knives and forks off what looked like solid gold plates and the coffee spoons were solid gold and the coffee cups of gold lustre ware. My fellow guests were T. S. Eliot—Lady Rothermere was about to finance the *Criterion* under his editorship—and Mr Ouspensky the famous mystic who was unriddling the universe for her. Then there were Mr and Mrs Sydney Schiff. Schiff was a rich man, who wrote novels under the pen name of Stephen Hudson. He had the manners and appearance of an old-fashioned British colonel on the stage which prejudiced me against him, probably unfairly.

The dinner was the first occasion on which Eliot and Ouspensky had met and they eyed each other with cautious curiosity. Lady Rothermere had, I suspect, rather exaggerated notions of their knowledge of Sanscrit and early on remarked that they both knew it. But though she tried hard to get them to converse in it, neither of them could be induced to show off, and I thought they seemed slightly relieved when Mr Schiff turned the conversation to the great work which his great friend Marcel Proust was engaged in writing. As I had just sold expensive special copies of *A l'Ombre des Jeunes Filles en Fleurs* and *Du Côté de Chez Swann* to her Ladyship rather against her will (*exemplaires en 16 Jésus sur papier vélin pur fil Lafuma-Navarre*) I was extremely grateful to him.

After dinner Wyndham Lewis joined us, for Lady Rothermere was interested in modern painting and it was as a painter that Lewis was then best known. I was amused to hear Schiff draw him into a corner and hold forth upon the iniquities of the income tax, which had reduced him to being a very poor man. It was the kind of subject which Schiff liked talking about to impoverished artists.

It so happened that Ouspensky was staying at a hotel in Bloomsbury close to Taviton Street, so we shared a taxi on the way back. I found nothing to say to him and as he was probably wondering what came next after OM PADME MANI HUM he said nothing to me. He was a tall man who was strikingly like the photographs of President Wilson at the time of the Peace Conference. There was the same lavish display of false teeth, the same baffled, unseeing eye, the same spiritual aura of high thinking and patent medicines. But the Russian sage had led a less sheltered life than the President, and it was obvious that he had not always eaten hothouse grapes off gold plate in his progress through this vale of illusion.

One day Venetia Montagu, the wife of Edwin Montagu, then Secretary of State for India, walked into the shop with Lady Diana Manners and a Bedlington terrier which was as much of an aristocrat as the ladies he escorted. Lady Diana was the most famous beauty of her generation; Venetia was a strikingly handsome and impressive figure. Both ladies loudly demanded Frankie, who happened to be going the rounds of the publishers, and both loudly lamented their misfortune in missing him—nor would they be consoled by my showing them books.

"That would be *no good at all*. That would *not be the same thing*. Frankie is *so adorable*. And it was *so clever of us* to find the shop." I could but agree and, having failed to interest them in any books, or to detain them, I was forced to watch both ladies wander out inconsolably into Taviton Street accompanied by their well-bred companion. Just as they were leaving, however, Venetia gave me a very mischievous look. This baffled me: as up till that moment both ladies had apparently been equally unaware that I was a sentient being. Some years after I had learned to fly, I made friends with Venetia Montagu and came to feel a great affection and admiration for her.

One of the people I met as a result of the bookshop was E. S. P. Haynes. Like many of our author customers he liked us to stock his books and was delighted if we displayed one of them in the window. We discovered that though our friends' works were not normally very saleable, it paid us well to display them. For the authors liked to bring a friend along, ask if we had the book, and then write an inscription and give it away. Morgan Forster was most generous in this way.

Ted Haynes was one of the most original characters I have ever known. He was a solicitor, with chambers in New Square, Lincoln's Inn, where it was rumoured that he had not spoken to his partner, Hunter, for many years. Ted was a very large man with a big fleshy face and neck, greenish grey in complexion, with a lock of hair rising like a crest over his big forehead. He was careless in his clothes, wearing flannel shirts and loosely made, ill-fitting suits. He went without a hat, but usually carried an umbrella. He was the kind of man who never folds up his copy of *The Times* even on the windiest day, but walks along the street holding it in one hand by the scruff of the neck, letting it flap its wings like a captive goose.

Ted was a strong rationalist with many Roman Catholic friends—Belloc, G. K. Chesterton and Lord Alfred Douglas were among them. He was a passionate believer in individual liberty, sexual equality and sexual freedom. I share his views on all such matters. He was a lifelong worker for divorce law reform.

He disliked eating alone and was also extremely hospitable and often invited Frankie or me to have lunch with him. We soon learned that this meant no more work for that day. Lunch was at White's oyster shop at the top of Chancery Lane. In those days it was kept by an old man called George who did his best to stop strangers from using the little back room after half past one. Ted did not like listeners at the other table.

"You a friend of Mister 'Aynes?" he would ask suspiciously as one pushed past him about two o'clock in the afternoon. At a quarter past two Ted would come in puffing, having finished his day's work and dictated all his letters.

Lunch consisted of oysters when in season, lobster or crab when they were not, brown bread and butter and a bottle and a half of hock, between two. After that one was allowed a bit of Cheddar cheese and a bottle of port was opened and finished. Favoured guests, of whom I was one, were given a cigar, which Ted went out to purchase next door. At intervals he would put his hand in his waistcoat pocket and draw out a clove of garlic and chew it up and swallow it. The reason for this unsocial habit was that he believed he would die of cancer and that garlic was a specific against it.

At four o'clock the guest staggered out into Holborn and returned to the bookshop to sleep off the effects of the port and Ted went back to New Square to sign his letters in a shaky hand before returning to St John's Wood.

On the other hand if you accepted an invitation to an evening at the Oxford and Cambridge Musical Club in Bedford Square, you were only allowed a glass of ginger ale. Once I bravely said that I should prefer a glass of bitter.

"Any alcoholic drink impairs the appreciation of music," remarked Ted frostily.

Ted was a cousin of Sir Frederick Pollock and, as a young man, had been one of the most regular of Leslie Stephen's Sunday Tramps. Stephen was one of his great men—and he worshipped the Stephen family. Adrian, Virginia and Vanessa all, however, fled at the sight of him—because he would never talk to them about anything except Sir Leslie!

I could, as they say, fill a volume with anecdotes about Ted Haynes. But as he wrote several such himself I will confine myself to one remark of his worthy of Voltaire. Ted once dined at a regimental mess as the guest of a young officer. Casting about for a topic of universal interest, he began discussing venereal disease and its prevention.

The colonel, who disliked the choice of subject, said to Ted severely: "The disease that you refer to is a Divine Punishment for breaking God's Commandments. If a young feller confesses to me that he has got syphilis I tell him it is the Finger of God."

"If syphilis is His Finger, I wonder what the rest of Him is like?" remarked Ted meditatively.

XI

WHILE I was living at Taviton Street I saw a good deal of Robert Tatlock, Ray Marshall and Cecily Hey. Thanks to the influence of Roger Fry, Tatlock had just become the editor of *The Burlington Magazine of Fine Art* and was studying the history of Art with Scottish thoroughness and determination. Soon after he got the job, he took on Ray Marshall as his assistant. I was becoming a good deal attracted by her strong and gentle character and was for a time afraid that she might fall in love with him.

However, an incident occurred which made me think it unlikely that she would.

One evening the four of us were sitting in the shop after dinner and the conversation turned on reading aloud and the two girls asked us each to read something aloud in turn. Without a thought of malice I took down a copy of Lear's *Nonsense Verses* and, opening it at *Calico Pie*, suggested that Tattie should read it aloud.

He did as I asked, but by the time he reached the second verse:

> Calico Jam
> The little fish swam,
> Over the syllabub sea,
> He took off his hat,
> To the sole and the sprat
> And the Willeby-Wat
> But he never came back to me!

his voice was rasping with anger and he shut the book.

"It's joost puir nonsense! I'll read no mair of it!" he exclaimed with his Glasgow accent becoming more pronounced.

Cecily, who laughed at everything, shrieked with laughter, but Ray could see that he was really angry and that he fiercely resented our enjoyment of meaningless rubbish. I felt sure that Ray would not fall in love with a man with that particular deficiency.

Ray was dark, with brown eyes set very wide apart, a large round head with dark brown straight hair, bobbed and cut in a fringe. She had a rather brown skin with a touch of colour in the cheeks, high cheek-bones, an odd-shaped clumsy mouth and she was neither tall nor short, and had square shoulders. Her clothes were usually a cross between those of the sensible country girl and the art student, and she would not have looked out of place at a point-to-point meeting. She was extremely shy but her shyness was not always painful: it was usually like the natural shyness of a wild animal, or bird.

About once a week she would come into the shop when I was alone to collect the money that I owed for my breakfasts, or to pay me what the other inmates owed for the use of our telephone and I seized these opportunities to try to hold her in talk.

She had been a student at the Central School of Arts and Crafts, had paid a visit to Russia in the early summer of 1914, had travelled through the Caucasus and had ridden, with a Russian girl as her only companion, on an adventurous expedition through the mountains almost to the border of Persia. From this expedition she had just got back to England before the war. Then she had worked on a farm near Salisbury. One of her cousins was my old friend Dominic Spring-Rice and her elder sister was married to Dick Rendel, a grandson of Lady Strachey's. We had thus had comparable experiences and many of her friends were friends of my friends. The Marshalls came indeed from the same world as the Stephens. Mr Marshall had been one of Leslie Stephen's Sunday Tramps and Ray and her sisters used to call at 46 Gordon Square, when they were little girls, to take the Stephen sheepdog, Gurth, out for walks.

Ray was the most silent woman I have ever known. Sometimes her silence was painful when it was an inability to break through her shyness. Sometimes it was an accusation when I knew that she felt what I was saying was shallow, or insincere. But usually her silence was delightful and she would caress me with her eyes when she felt perfectly happy and say nothing.

Owing to her shyness, it took me a long time to win her confidence, and often I felt more like a bird-watcher coaxing a rare moorland bird to accept his presence than a young man trying to win a girl's heart. Wyatt felt like that:

> but sometyme they put theirselves in daunger
> to take bred at my hand.

One day she said that we ought to have a gramophone: she wanted to buy one, but they were expensive. I suggested that we should share the expense and that the gramophone should be our joint property. We accordingly went off and bought a large H.M.V. machine. One day we passed each other on the stairs. I put my hand lightly on the banister, thought of speaking, but hearing footsteps coming down the flight above, turned to go on. Ray had stopped also. Suddenly she stroked the palm of my open hand with her finger and went upstairs. I walked slowly down into the the bookshop and realised that I was seriously in love with her and she with me. I was disturbed by this, for I thought that, with my character, I was bound to make her unhappy. Also I did not see how she would fit in with my friends.

I went down two or three times to her home. Her father, William Cecil Marshall, was an old man, paralysed and very near death. I never saw him. He had been a successful architect who had lived and had his office at 28 Bedford Square, but had built his family a home for the holidays at Hindhead. This had been added to and enlarged several times; it was a large house, on different levels, with an unused ballroom that nobody went into. Scots pines grew all about, overshadowing the lawns and terraces. The vast, typically Edwardian, Surrey house stood in a triangular piece of ground between the main road from Hindhead to Haslemere and a lane leading to Shotter-mill, and for that reason had been given the horrible name of Tweenways. The more I learned about Ray's father the more inscrutably removed he seemed from me by time and taste. And yet for many things I should have admired this strange dominating man.

Mrs Marshall was a dark, very brown-skinned Irish woman whose mother had come from Galway and whose father had been a missionary among the Maoris in New Zealand.

Mr Marshall had died before my later visits to Tweenways. On the last of them Dick Rendel was there, an elegant young colonel, a regular soldier with an eyeglass which appeared permanently fixed in his right eye. He had to the full the Strachey intellectuality and intelligence and violence of expression in putting forward his opinions. But he had also a never-resting sense of humour, a love of leg-pulling and of aping the brainless idiot, which was irresistible. His presence, I discovered, had a wonderfully stimulating effect on the Marshalls whose fault, as a family, was a tendency to what they very rightly called *mouldiness*. Ray had two brothers and three sisters. Horace, an engineer, was a big man, who blew his nose like a trumpet when he first saw me and said nothing. Her other brother, Tom, had been interned throughout the war at Ruhle-ben and seemed to be extremely like Ray. Judy, Dick Rendel's wife, was puzzled by me until the following summer when I ducked her while we were bathing. After that she accepted me as one of the family. Eleanor was a dark immature creature who wanted to be a singer. Frances was the beauty: she had been to Bedales and was at Newnham. They were not an effusive family, and I was grateful to Dick Rendel who woke them up.

In March 1921, Ray and I were married at St Pancras Register Office. We went there with Cecily Hey and Tattie, by tram. In the waiting-room was a notice:

Under the Defence of the Realm Act
It is forbidden to throw confetti in this building.

None of us had any confetti, so it was all right.

Ray and I took two small rooms in Wells Street off the Gray's Inn Road and installed the furniture from Ray's room in

Taviton Street, and a huge double bed in which all the Marshalls had been born. We had little money. I drew three pounds a week from the shop and earned a few pounds a month by reviewing books. Ray earned a little from *The Burlington Magazine* and had a hundred pounds a year of her own. Nobody was at all enthusiastic about our marriage. Duncan, however, promised to give me a portrait of Ray which delighted me not only because of the picture, but because they would get to know each other while it was being painted.

"She sits like a cream cheese on a plate," was his only comment, but I got the impression that he liked her for other reasons also.

Edward was, I think, the only person who welcomed my marriage whole-heartedly, and realised almost from the first that I had made a wise choice and been very lucky. Ray had undergone some unfortunate experiences in her childhood which had left her scarred and vulnerable. A governess with a love of power who had won her passionate adoration as a child was suddenly discovered to be a thief and turned out of the house. Ray had felt the greatest horror at the scene in which the woman was dismissed. Her emotions were violently divided and she felt guilty for loving a thief more than her parents.

Tom and she were the most intelligent of the children and Ray was her father's favourite. He used to take her into his office and discuss his plans for buildings with her, completely forgetting that she was a child. He would ask her to make plans and when, as was inevitable, she made some elementary mistake, such as making the inclination of the staircase much too steep, he would explode with wrath and terrify her. Thus the intimate relationship with him that she longed for was poisoned by fear.

Edward was intuitively aware that Ray could not stand up for herself and he never teased her. She, on her side, became devoted to him.

Constance had greeted the news of my marriage with the

233

words: "A daughter's a daughter all your life. A son is a son till he gets him a wife."

However, Ray very soon won Constance's regard, then her affection and then her love. Constance was surprised to find that she asked nothing, and accepted the way of life that she found. I think Constance would have been happier if I had married someone whom she knew and loved: T.T. would perhaps have been her choice. It took Constance long to become used to a stranger.

I have always tended to be attracted to the people who have made a success of life and who have left their mark in the world. Ray, on the other hand, was often attracted by "the despised and rejected," and by the weak. My uncle Charles had made a failure of his life. By 1922, he was a red-faced old man with a fringe of grey hair round his bald head, a watery, bloodshot blue eye and a shaky hand, timid and unsure of himself.

Fortunately Charles was able to come down to Gracie's cottage and was very happy there, pottering about and making improvements. Ray saw, immediately, what no one else had bothered to appreciate: the modest unselfishness, sweetness and goodness of Charles's character. She liked him very much indeed, and would spend an hour chatting with him in his little shed where he kept his carpentry tools, and her regard for him added greatly to his happiness and self-esteem.

Ray was a woodland creature. She wanted the protection and shelter that woods gave, and among the beeches and the pines I saw her as I could never see her in London. For that reason it was at The Cearne and in the High Chart that we became aware how passionately we were in love.

Less than a year after our marriage, Ray and I went to live with her mother whom we called Mam, after her initials: M.A.M.

Tweenways had been sold and Mam took 27 Brunswick Square. Ray's sisters Eleanor and Frances were to live with her also. Ray and I had the big dining-room on the ground floor and a bedroom on the second floor. Mam had the rest of the house. Our big room had a round end and was almost a replica of the room which Duncan and Etchells had decorated in Adrian's house on the north side of the Square.

We were thus able to give little parties and the immediate result of our move was the revival of the Caroline Club. Once more we had our weekly play-readings. At these the chief figures were Frankie, Arthur Waley, Stephen Gooden, Bob Trevelyan, G. H. Luce (while on leave from Burma) and his sister. We were not so well off for women, as formerly. Noel and Daphne Olivier came once or twice, Frances Marshall could be relied on to do well. Ray would not read but liked to listen. Bob Trevelyan had idiosyncratic ideas of half-chanting blank verse which were utterly destructive of its dramatic content. Altogether the level was not so high as it had been in 1914. But again Frankie was the mainstay of the club.

Ray and I gave them cocoa. We were still extremely impoverished; our marriage was regarded dubiously by our friends and relations, but we loved each other deeply and were happy.

Early in 1922, Frankie and I made friends with Ralph Wright who was employed at that time in the Central Library for Students. He was a rather short man, whose head of glossy black hair, brushed straight back, made me think of a seal's, as it emerges from the water—and Ralph had one seal-like characteristic—he was fond of tossing balls into the air and catching them—not upon his nose, it is true, but behind his back. When he was worried, or unhappy, it was the only thing which seemed to give him relief. Ralph's eyes were very lively; he was responsive, sympathetic and intelligent. He was a good conversationalist and he had a wide knowledge of French and English literature and was very fond of reading.

After we had known him for a few months, he proposed that he should become a partner in our firm and invest a reasonable sum of money in it.

"We have found the business man we have always needed."

235

Frankie and I exclaimed to each other when he left us, after making his proposal. It seemed too good to be true—and it wasn't. However, Ralph's money enabled us to move the shop to 30 Gerrard Street, to equip it with beautiful and practical bookshelves designed by Ralph's architect brother Kester, and greatly to increase our stock. Neither Frankie nor I ever regretted taking Ralph into partnership, and we became very fond of him indeed. His faults were that he was no more of a business man than Frankie, or I, and that he was not a very hard worker. We came to the conclusion, later, that his lack of energy was due to a great extent to his war experience. He had fought hard in Gallipoli, where one of his brothers had been killed beside him; he had done a lot of fighting in France and his supply of energy had been used up. Once Ralph was deep in a book on a bus as it was passing the Cenotaph and an old gentleman tapped him angrily on the shoulder.

"Take your hat off, young man. Why don't you pay some respect to our glorious dead?"

"I am one of our glorious dead," replied Ralph in a mild voice. Mark Twain would have called this a gross exaggeration but there was a truth in it which applied to thousands of survivors of the war. It was not only the body and the brain that could be killed or wounded, but the spirit.

After the move to Gerrard Street we took on my sister-in-law, Frances Marshall, as an assistant. She had left Newnham that summer, was fond of books, extremely intelligent and a conscientious worker. Not only was she an ideal assistant, but she was one of the most adorable and beautiful young women I have known. I was, at first, a little in awe of her.

The move to the new shop was followed by a spell of real wintry weather. One night, as Ray and I were walking home from the theatre I complained, perhaps excessively, of the bitter blast which seemed to be going to freeze my nose and cut off my ears.

"You really ought to wear a nose muff like Frances and her friend Dot Mackay," said Ray.

"What on earth do you mean?" I asked.

"A nose muff," repeated Ray.

"I've never heard of such a thing."

"Don't you know that Frances and Dot always wear nose muffs when they go out to a dance in winter so that they should not arrive in the ballroom with red noses? Lots of the smartest debutantes are taking to them. It's the latest thing."

Next morning the blast was even more icy and as Frances and I struggled against it, on our way to Gerrard Street, I said to her:

"Why don't you wear your nose muff?"

"My what?" asked Frances.

"I suppose you are shy of being seen wearing it in the day-time. But Ray says all you smart girls wear nose muffs in the evening when you go to balls, or to the theatre."

Ray had taken me in so successfully that I could scarcely believe it when Frances went into fits of laughter and said she had never met anyone as simple as I was to swallow any tale that Ray told me. I was a good deal disappointed also as I had rather fallen in love with the idea of these elegant little fur-lined aids to female beauty; and was beginning to speculate on whether the fashion would lead to a revival of ladies wearing masks in the evening, like the Venetians.

Gerrard Street was conveniently situated in the centre of London with the result that our friends were continually drop-ping in at the shop and there were usually two or three people sitting on the green sofa. Frankie and Ralph were great talkers —some people came to listen, others who had come to buy a book found it impossible to drag themselves away. The shop was, in consequence, often as full as a public house at closing time. The drawback to this was that it made it difficult to work at jobs such as cataloguing books during the day and that a strange would-be purchaser hurriedly retreated without buying anything, feeling that he was interrupting a private party.

On a typical day, just before or after lunch, Frankie would be standing in the middle of the front room beaming with sociability and happiness and holding forth on any subject on earth, from the Reform of the Prayerbook to Corbusier's theories of architecture, to three or four people, three of whom would have become fixtures on the sofa. Ralph, who had begun the day full of good resolutions, would come out from the inner room with a calf volume in his hand which he was polishing, after applying our special patent preparation of paraffin wax and castor oil, which preserved the hinges from cracking but was apt, in excess, to show a greasy mark round the edge of the pasted back leaf and on the first fly-leaf. By giving this volume an occasional rub, Ralph was able to persuade himself that he really was doing some work.

"But don't you really think . . ." he would begin, only for his opinion to be squashed by Frankie and to pop up again next moment like a dabchick, in an unexpected position. So it would go on until the arrival of—let us say—Harold Las!.i, who looked like a mixture of an impudent Charlie Chaplin and an abnormally intelligent foetus, in spectacles. Harold could out-talk either of them, and he would begin telling highly improbable anecdotes on most secret political matters.

On his last visit to America the President had sent for him to the White House and received him in his bath—the only place where he could talk absolutely freely without fear of being disturbed. We should soon see that things were going to be very different as the result of Harold's advice.

Or the conversation would be brought to an end by the arrival of Robert Trevelyan, the poet—the Mandril—as he was rudely nicknamed by Virginia and Vanessa. There was, indeed, a faint likeness between his benign, intellectual face, spiritually rather akin to Roger Fry's—and that most repulsive of the apes—something in the angle and length of nose and jaw, perhaps. Bob Trevy was tall, with grizzled hair, lively intelligent grey eyes behind glasses, with a pale terracotta complexion. He wore greenish tweeds, a wide-brimmed felt hat and an unbuttoned overcoat and he often entered the shop with his arms full of parcels.

"I'm so sorry I'm rather late," he would ejaculate, though none of us expected him to come in that day. "Bessie asked me to get some things for Julian . . . I'm not sure that I've got them all . . . I must look at the list . . ." At that moment a parcel would crash to the floor and Bob would begin his act of dropping one parcel while he retrieved another. This would be brought to an end by Frances taking them out of his arms and offering to do them up in one or two more manageable parcels.

Then the talk would start again, though Bob was constitutionally unable to talk about one subject at a time. Though nobody except Desmond MacCarthy seemed ever to realise the fact, Bob was a very fine poet, I should put him among the first dozen poets writing in English in the twentieth century.

I have the greatest admiration for the plays of Thomas Heywood and wish I could see a revival of *The Fair Maid of the West*, but I had not realised that the fine dramatist was also a literary hack until I had bought copies of his *Historie of Women* and his *Hierarchie of Angels*. I was therefore very pleased when a customer came in and asked to see the latter book. He was at first sight not a very attractive individual. He was a small man whose dirty-looking unhealthy face was fringed with a little moth-eaten black beard in the style of Toulouse-Lautrec, which failed to conceal a circular scar which appeared to run right round his neck. He was subject to nervous spasms and twitches which gave me the impression that he was probably an epileptic. He walked with an unnaturally high springy step. His clothes were seedy and, like Conrad's Secret Agent, Mr Verloc, "he had an air of having wallowed, fully dressed, all day upon an unmade bed".

But he liked the copy of *The Hierarchie of Angels*, an exceptionally fine one, and said he would like to buy it, but that it would be easier if we would take some books in exchange. Would I go and look at his library? I was not very keen; however, as it turned out that he lived only a few yards from Brunswick Square in Hunter Street, I made an appointment to go first thing next morning. I have seldom seen a more unattractive old witch than the woman who opened the door. She had a long, expressionless face with a large hairy wart on the extreme point of her chin and sparse grey locks hanging

239

about her face. She was dressed in a dirty flannel dressing-gown.

"I'll call my husband," and she left me standing in the hall for some time during which one or two furtive young Hindus slipped out of the house. Mrs Peters kept lodgings, leaving her husband free to pursue his extraordinary activities. At last he came down and, after unlocking the door, ushered me into the front room on the ground floor. The first things which I noticed were two large photographs of Tsar Alexander III and Tsar Nicholas II. Alexander III was such a surprise that I went up and examined it and saw that it appeared to be signed and inscribed to Mr Peters. My host, however, brushed aside my remark upon it and we got down to business. "I thought this might appeal to you," he said, handing me a small nearly quarto volume in perfect contemporary seventeenth-century calf. It was the first edition of Donne's Poems, 1633—as perfect a copy as anybody could ever hope to see with *The Paradoxes and Problems* bound up with it. "I could let you have it for twenty pounds," said Mr Peters. I put it immediately into my pocket. His collection of seventeenth- and eighteenth-century occult books was magnificent: but I had no customers for such books, and he did not particularly wish to sell them. He had, however, the *Poems of Bishop Henry King*, but his price was high. We went back together to Gerrard Street and I handed over *The Hierarchie of Angels*.

On the way he told me that book-collecting was a passion which he could ill afford. He was able to do very little work, and he went on to explain that he was a professional medium. But the work was a strain and he was not always up to it.

"Was that Landru?" asked Ralph after Mr Peters left the shop. "He must have had his head sewn on again after he was guillotined." This grisly image was so perfect a description that Mr Peters was "Landru" from that day on—for we saw a lot of him. It soon became apparent that the ethos of our bookshop appealed to him and he became almost one of the habitués, sitting down on the sofa and listening to Frankie. At first I thought this was a purely intellectual interest—for Landru was an intellectual. He was not very well educated but he was interested in ideas; he was half-baked, perhaps, but a real original. But one day we all realised that he was making Frankie into a hero on whom he wished to model himself.

Frankie had got his tailor to make him a complete country suit of thick brown corduroy which he wore when he was going away for a week-end in the country. Landru saw it and about three weeks later he came into the shop almost dancing with delight wearing an exactly similar suit. It was a touching proof of his admiration and I am glad to say that Frances played up nobly, telling him that it suited him perfectly and that he looked really well in it. I don't think Frankie was altogether pleased and I was oafishly amused. After a time we rather discouraged his constant visits and I wish I had found out more about him. I asked again about the portraits of the Tsars and he murmured something about "been of service . . . an historical connection," which meant nothing.

I was more successful in getting him to talk about spiritualism. Once, when he hesitated over buying a book lacking the engraved title, I remarked: "That can't matter to you, Mr Peters. You can ask the spirits to materialise one and paste it in."

He giggled with delight and presently said: "We could make a lot of money between us, couldn't we? I could get the spirits to supply the pages missing in all your defective copies. Ha! Ha! Ha!"

He was entirely cynical about the spirits. Yet he did believe in something. I told him I was a rationalist and thought that spiritualism was invented to occupy the weak-minded. He laughed and said:

"It would not do for me to agree with that, would it? Oh, no. It wouldn't do at all."

I came to the conclusion that the something which Mr Peters believed in was himself. He believed that he had supernatural powers. He did not believe in a supernatural world, or in spirits.

He told me that he gave lectures and organised séances, but

241

the work of which he was proudest was having supplied some of the evidence included by Sir Oliver Lodge in *Raymond*, a work in which the aged scientist described how he had got in touch with the spirit of his dead son.

One day, many years after I had given up being a bookseller, happening to go into the Reading Room of the British Museum, I was astonished to see a printed announcement of recent acquisitions to the Library. It was headed: *The Alfred Vout Peters Bequest*. I like to think that the hours he spent listening to Frankie may have put this public-spirited idea into his head.

During a visit to Tidmarsh Carrington had told me she had been seeing a friend of her brother's at Oxford called Major Partridge and his close friend Gerald Brenan. She described them with lively interest and Lytton showed some amusement. Both friends, I gathered, appeared to be in love with Carrington and she had not discouraged them. On my next visit, a few months later, Lytton and Carrington spoke of them in very different terms. Captain Brenan was said to be altogether too romantic a figure—a modern version of Trelawny's self-portrait in *The Adventures of a Younger Son*, but it was clear that Carrington had lost her heart to Major Partridge and that Lytton liked him very much. I soon got to know Ralph and became very fond of him. He is a large magnificently built man with light blue eyes and a ruddy complexion. He had left Oxford early to go into the army, had distinguished himself on the Western Front during the war and risen to the rank of Major, commanding a battalion at the age of 23.

Carrington and Ralph Partridge were married not long after Ray and me, and he joined the household at Tidmarsh, though for a time he worked in London during the week with Leonard and Virginia in The Hogarth Press. Later he learned bookbinding. Ralph had a great interest in psychology and his ruthlessness and dogmatism in analysing the characters and secret motives of his friends have always rather appalled me. I have an unfortunate tendency to see my friends through a rose-coloured mist and to turn a blind eye to their more unpleasant qualities. I am well aware of this fault and have tried to reform, but sometimes listening to Ralph at the breakfast or dinner table I have asked myself whether loopholes could be left open for the possibility of noble or mistaken impulses, for accident or aberration? Must we all be knocked flat and then strung up? For Ralph combines being a hanging judge at the dinner table with a large geniality, and a passion for dispensing lavish hospitality. I have always been puzzled by Ralph's affection for all his friends considering that he believes that all of us are animated by criminal motives.

The success of *Eminent Victorians* had been followed by the even greater success of *Queen Victoria* and success sat very well on Lytton. He became even kinder and gentler without losing the sharp edge of his critical faculty or his intellectual extremism. Nor did he assume the airs of a great and famous man, although Carrington's almost idolatrous care might have led anyone else to adopt them.

In the spring of 1922, a year after our marriage, Ray and I went down to The Cearne together for a holiday. There seemed no prospect of my making more money than I could draw from the shop, we could only barely exist upon the pittance that we earned between us, but we decided to have a child. The weather was perfect and Ray and I spent almost all the daylight hours in the woods. When we returned to London she was pregnant. Two months later we took another holiday at The Cearne and one afternoon I took Ray to the northern border of the High Chart where the first field looking towards Westerham made a corner bounded by a larch wood on one side and by the High Chart on the other. The spot had always seemed to me exciting and propitious. It was there that Colonel Warde's young keeper Stan Ruffett had shot a hen sparrow-hawk on the nest and had then swarmed up the tree to get me the eggs. For some reason I was convinced that there were fox cubs about and Ray and I sat motionless for about half an hour in the hope of seeing one. But I realised that there was no reason why we should and eventually I said to Ray: "There's no hope of seeing a fox—unless you were suddenly to turn into one. You might. I should not really be much surprised if you did."

"What would you do with me?" asked Ray.

She had no opportunity to speak again, even if she wanted to, until we were back at The Cearne. Then she said: "You must write that as a story."

I was a little surprised, as I had not been thinking of a story but had only been occupied in teasing and making love to her by telling her how like she was to a wild animal, and how easily my intense love for her would overcome the trifling difficulties that would arise if she actually were transformed into one. I thought about the idea of a story all through tea and then wrote a synopsis based upon what I had been telling Ray, giving it the title of: *The Metamorphosis of Mrs Tebrick*.

I read my synopsis aloud to Ray and she was fascinated and absorbed and we went down together to the summer house at the bottom of the garden to discuss it further.

Next morning I went down alone to the summer house and began to write, and for the remaining two or three days we were able to stay at The Cearne I wrote every day, slowly, and turning every sentence over in my mouth before I wrote it down. There was no table and I wrote on a small slab of wood sawn from the outside of a Scots pine. When we went back to London I took the slab of pinewood with me and continued to write on it instead of on a table. I had become fond of it and the tiny details of habit are important. For some reason Ray was annoyed by my affection for this piece of wood, and when *Lady Into Fox* was finished she threw it away, or burnt it, without telling me. I wish the talisman had been preserved.

After returning to London, I had to work all day in the shop and could only write in the evening after my return to Brunswick Square. Each day was filled with terror lest by evening I should have lost my continuity. Indeed I felt slightly sick all day, because I was so obsessed by my story. For by that time I knew that I was creating a work of art as good in its way as I could hope for. Moreover I was beginning to feel the strain

244

of it. After about a week or ten days I felt that I must escape. I turned for help to Duncan and asked if Ray and I could go down to Charleston for a week. For some reason this was impossible, and Duncan arranged with Maynard who had recently leased Tilton that I should be lent a cottage there which was furnished but standing empty. Ray and I went down and I wrote all day for three or four days. This gives a wrong idea of speed for I wrote very slowly, always turning every sentence round and round and tasting it before I finally wrote it down.

It was, for me, an entirely new way of writing. I was very conscious of what I was doing, and never let a phrase or sentence pass with the promise of cleaning it up later. I wrote about five hundred words in a full morning's work.

I should never have written the story without Ray's encouragement and approbation. When I had finished the pages I had set myself for the day I always read them aloud to her. Very early on, we had decided that she should illustrate the book with woodcuts and she began work on them long before I had finished. We found the title early, standing in the porch at The Cearne. *The Metamorphosis of Mrs Tebrick* did not satisfy either of us and Ray reminded me of the little book of *Ovid's Metamorphoses* with Geoffrey Tory's woodcuts and borders (printed by Bernard Solomon about 1530) which I had picked up for half a crown in old Mr Jarvis's shop in Newbury. It is imperfect, but one of the treasures of my library.

"Don't you remember *Daphne mouée en laurier?* What a pity there is no English word for the old French word *mouée*," she said.

"Of course you could say turned into, or transformed into but one wants one word," she added.

"Why not just *into?*—*Lady Into Fox*. The meaning is clear enough," I said.

Ray thought it impossible, but I stood my ground and each time that I repeated *Lady Into Fox* I felt more certain that I had found the right title. It was not till a much later stage that we dropped the subtitle of *The Metamorphosis of Mrs Tebrick*.

There can be very little doubt that the oddity of the title had a good deal to do with the immense success of the book.

The scenes when Silvia tries to escape from the walled garden were written at Tilton and visualised as taking place in the garden at Charleston. Indeed I examined an apple-tree there to see whether a vixen could possibly climb it. The end of the story was written after we had got back to Brunswick Square. Finally, when it was done, I realised that the original opening was hopelessly weak and that it was essential to start off with a bang of the drum in the first paragraph. The first two pages of the book were therefore the last to be written and perfectly achieved my purpose.

Not until the story was finished and typewritten did I show it to Frankie. I gave it to him before going out on a round of collecting books at publishers. When I came back he had finished reading it and got up to greet me, twisting the hair of his forelock into strings. He thought it good, but was considerably puzzled. I could see he wanted more time to think the thing over and to become used to it. It was one of the rare occasions when I saw him rather at a loss. I could scarcely avoid laughing at his predicament. For I knew my story was good and needed no praise or confirmation. That evening I posted it to Edward, whose verdict I awaited with curiosity.

He led off by telling me that I had written a little masterpiece and that not a word needed changing—and that he would not be competent to advise me on style—yet was a little doubtful of some archaisms. He then said that he thought it would meet with a certain success among the highbrows but would puzzle the ordinary reader. He suggested that he should recommend Cape to publish it as a limited edition for half a guinea.

This was nonsense. Whatever *Lady Into Fox*'s chances of success might be, I knew it would be damned forever by being issued as a *jeu d'esprit* for the intellectual public. I had lunch with Edward next day and told him he was wrong and that I would rather be published by Chatto and Windus as their list included Lytton and Aldous Huxley. It might be awkward being published by Cape if they didn't want my next book. Edward was interested in my summary rejection of his advice and rather encouraged me to go ahead. If Chatto rejected the book I could come back. There was no time to be lost as I wanted the book out in plenty of time for Christmas. So I sent the typescript to Chatto asking for an immediate decision.

To my intense astonishment I received a reply within twenty-four hours to the effect that they would like to publish the book but would prefer, as it was so short, to make it one of a volume. Had I written anything to go with it? Or was I willing to wait until I had done so? The letter was signed C. H. C. Prentice. I went to see Mr Prentice at once and our interview was fateful. He urged his view. My story was charming. He was most anxious to publish it, but a single short story was not a practical proposition.

The moral courage which I never expect to find, but which rarely deserts me at the crucial moments in my life, led me to say: "How many copies did you sell of *The Young Visiters*? I believe *Lady Into Fox* may do as well."

Prentice was staggered by my confidence—for *The Young Visiters* had sold about 100,000 copies. Since then the world sales of *Lady Into Fox* have been, at a rough guess, about five times as much. However, he was too polite to tell me I was crazy, though if he had done so I should not have been offended. But my blunt refusal to include another story or to postpone publication, and my confidence, influenced him and he agreed to publish it, well in time for Christmas, with Ray's woodcuts, not all of which had been completed.

The move to Gerrard Street followed the acceptance of my book by Chatto and Windus and I had so much to do that I did not worry about it. I was delighted with Ray's woodcuts and with its appearance in proof. Finally, when the day of publication came and our order was delivered at the shop, I had a moment of embarrassment as I asked myself: "Shall I put it in the window?"

Then I said to myself: "What nonsense. I am a bookseller and my job is to sell all the copies I can of it." So without more ado, I filled the whole of one window shelf with it. When the first customer came in I sold him a copy and hardly allowed anyone to leave without having bought it.

Augustine Birrell was delighted with it and as he dined out a great deal, and was the literary mentor of a good many fashionable ladies, it was immediately read and talked about by the fashionable world and its fame spread in that way. All my friends in Bloomsbury read it. I had shown it to Duncan in manuscript and he was delighted with it, though I do not think he was as surprised as other friends. Virginia wrote me a letter full of praise in which she said: "the most interesting thing, I think, is your capacity for incident. Something is always happening and it is apparently effortless and alive." When the book was given a prize the following summer, she wrote again: "At last, at last, the Hawthornden has chosen the right book. A thousand congratulations and please spend the £100 in writing another." Both Maynard and Lytton liked the book and no doubt helped its sales by talking about it.

A review by H. G. Wells came out several months after publication, in the *Adelphi*. He wrote:

I have nothing to say about how it is done, because I think it is perfectly done and could not have been done in any other way. It is as astonishing and it is as entirely right and consistent as a new creation, a new sort of animal, let us say, suddenly running about in the world. It is like a small, queer furry animal, I admit, but as alive, as whimsically inevitable as a very healthy kitten. It shows up most other stories for the clockwork beasts they are.

I had not seen H.G. for many years and it gave me immense pleasure to be so warmly recognised by him. Far more important to me than most reviews were the letters from people whose opinion I respected. Conrad wrote to Edward:

Many thanks for D's little tale. It is the most successful thing of the kind I have ever seen. . . . The whole psychology of man and beast is, I should say, flawless, in essence and exposition. Altogether an accomplished piece of work, touchingly amusing and without a single mistake (that I can see) in style, tone or conception. My most friendly congratulations to David on this little piece so thoroughly done. Nothing of the amateur there.

Edward had told W. H. Hudson about my story and I had received two letters from him in which he mentioned it just after I had written it.

I shall look out for the Fox-Woman and order it and ask those I know to get it for themselves. It is a fascinating idea but one must read the book to see what you have made of it. E.G. thinks highly of it but he is not to be trusted in this case. You will be judged by those who are not your father.

I knew that Hudson would like my story better than any of my friends, but he died, alas, before the book was printed and mixed with my sorrow at his death was the regret that I had not shown him the manuscript.

One of the most charming letters was from my Aunt Clementina Black. She congratulated me on:

that excellent, plain classic English which nobody, nobody writes nowadays, and which I have never succeeded in writing myself. You make me think of Defoe and Swift and Goldsmith. In short I perceive the first work of a writer who is going to suit my own particular taste exactly and I feel really annoyed to think that I shall never read his complete works.

I had always enjoyed Clementina's novels, though they are constructed upon the traditional pattern of the tom-boy damsel in distress and travellers upon the Dover Road. But one early memory of the little bent, bespectacled old lady is more precious than her stories, or her praise of mine.

She had come to see Constance on a blustery March morning when one felt it was unsafe for such a frail figure to be out of doors.

"I have just written this on the top of the motor omnibus as I was coming here," and she read us the following poem which she had scribbled upon the back of an envelope.

The West wind from the ocean
Is blowing clean and strong,
The trees are in commotion,
The throstle cock's in song,
And men who live in houses
Dream from behind their bars
Of battles and carouses
And nights beneath the stars.

It seemed to me a most delightful poem to have been written by a maiden lady in her sixties.

I was pleased by a letter from the brilliant young novelist Romer Wilson who came into the shop and introduced herself shortly afterwards. I had greatly admired her novel: *The Death of Society*. She was fair with a mass of blonde hair brushed back off a fine forehead and with eager and alert features. She was a real artist and her death a few years later from tuberculosis was a great loss.

But though I had hardened myself to selling the book, and indeed rather enjoyed pressing it upon unwilling buyers, many of the letters I received about it rather embarrassed me. I was delighted that those who wrote should have liked the book but I did not at all look forward to being asked out to lunches or dinners as the latest literary curiosity. When I felt that a letter was inspired by a desire "to take me up" I replied very briefly and in some cases, I am afraid, I did not reply at all.

This was no doubt put down to shyness, or to rank boorish bad manners, but it was actually due to a streak of puritanism in my character and upbringing. The notoriety and self-advertisement of successful authors is repulsive to me. Books are written to be read and enjoyed like other works of art—but it can make little difference to the reader to know whether an author is tall or short, dark or fair. Such a puritanical mood came over me when I became a much-talked-of author in the year following the publication of *Lady Into Fox*. Perhaps I was unconsciously afraid that social success might turn my head, or interfere with my development as a writer.

Hope Johnstone came into the shop early one morning just after I had opened it. I had first met him at Dolly Radford's

RAY GARNETT WITH RICHARD

when I was a boy of sixteen and he had been one of the earliest of our customers at Taviton Street. He had been tutor to Augustus John's sons, had a brilliant intelligence with a passion for out of the way bits of learning, and I never knew whether I should meet him arrayed in a morning coat with a gardenia in his button-hole, or in the shabbiest of clothes. He had a room in Frith Street and that morning was unshaved, in his shirt-sleeves and carried a milk bottle in his hand.

Suddenly he said: "You've had a great success and all the Mayfair hostesses will be sending you invitations—so I thought I would come in and give you a tip. *J'ai passé par là, mon vieux.* Never accept a first invitation to luncheon. If you do, you'll never get an invitation to dinner at that house. When you've stood out and the woman knows she can only get you by asking you to dinner, you can relax and go to luncheon occasionally. But never accept an invitation to luncheon the first time. You've no idea of the meanness of those women. Some of them will even ask you to tea and try to get you to entertain a room full of people for a couple of hours in exchange for a cup of tea and a bun!"

I kept a very straight face and thanked Hope for his advice which was no doubt excellent. But the incident seemed to me to come straight out of Balzac's *La Comédie Humaine.* More important than possible social success, to my mind, were the book's sales, which went on steadily. By the time our child was born, Ray and I would no longer have to count every shilling. The writing of *Lady Into Fox* had made Ray extraordinarily happy and its success came just at the time when she needed to have no worries and to have confidence in the future.

Ray lay in at 27 Brunswick Square and the baby was born in the big Marshall bed, in which Ray had been born herself. Her pains came on about five o'clock one morning and I chased round London in the dark before I ran the nurse to earth somewhere beyond Earl's Court. I spent most of the day with Ray. She was perfectly calm and seemed much less agitated than I. When I was finally turned out of the bedroom, I sat on the stairs just outside and read *Tristram Shandy,* the only book that

251

I found readable at that moment. All went well. I could hear Ray giving little grunts of pain and then suddenly there was a little wail and, without waiting to be summoned, I went in. It was a boy, still streaked with blood. I had a son. Ray looked at me happily.

We called him Richard, after the author of *The Twilight of The Gods* and a long line of Richards, and, as a second name, Duncan. When he was born, and for a few weeks afterwards, Richard was distinctly like Ray's mother. But except for his dark eyes he grew up looking more like one of the Garnetts than I do.

END OF VOLUME TWO